Echoes of the Ancient World
Series editor Werner Forman

THE INDIANS
OF THE GREAT PLAINS

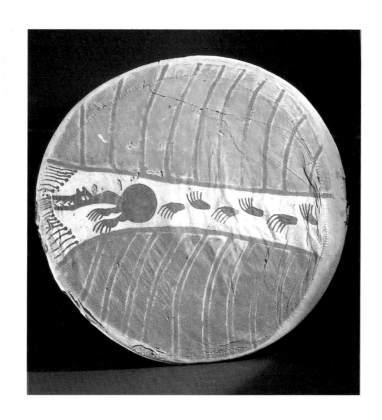

THE INDIANS
OF THE GREAT PLAINS

Text by Norman Bancroft-Hunt
Photographs by Werner Forman

LITTLE, BROWN AND COMPANY

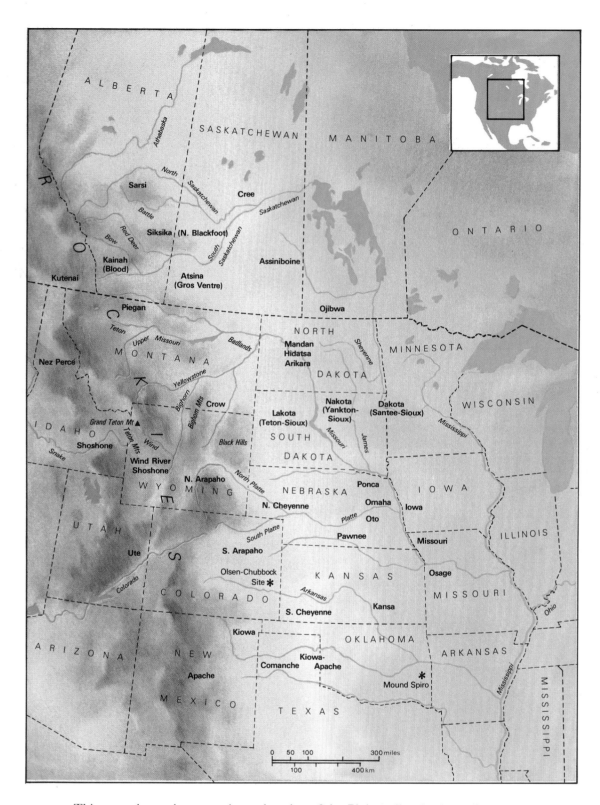

This map shows the approximate location of the Plains tribes in the early 1800s.

CONTENTS

Page one: A painted shield, whose symbols gave its owner spiritual protection.
Title page: Chief Mountain, northern Montana, sacred to the Blackfoot
who would visit the area for meditation and to gain spiritual power.

THE MIGRATIONS

In the beginning, Napi (Old Man) created everything: the earth, moon, animals and people. From the east he journeyed towards the west, spreading mud before him to form the earth and making this large so that there should be plenty of room. He went to the south and, travelling northwards, made the birds and animals, all of which could understand him; he also made the prairies, mountains, rivers and valleys, and put trees into the ground. So that the animals should have something to eat he covered the prairies with grass; then he marked off a section in which he caused the various roots and berries to grow: the camass, bitter-root, sweet-root, sarvis berry, and so on. In certain places he put red paint in the ground.[1]

With these words the Blackfoot Indians tell of the world's creation. The lands referred to are the Great Plains of North America which lie approximately between the Mississippi River and the Rocky Mountains, and stretch from Texas into the Prairie Provinces of Canada. Covering about a million square miles, it is a country of bluffs and crags, of flat-topped mesas several hundred feet high, richly wooded valleys and picturesque streams. It contains rugged terrain in stepped terraces as well as cliffs and chasms with spectacular colours, forms and shapes; but mostly it is grassland.

The true plains in the semi-arid western half of the region are dominated by short, hardy grasses: the so-called 'buffalo grass' that cures naturally into a nutritious winter forage on which the vast buffalo herds that roamed here subsisted. These give way in the more humid eastern river bottomlands to 'deep clad prairies'[2] that reach depths of eight feet and form perfectly level meadows extending 'as far as the eye can see and thought can travel'.[3]

Their immense size, emphasized by low relief and a virtual absence of natural barriers, creates an awesome effect; immeasurable, almost inconceivable space seems to reach in all directions. Persistent winds sweeping through this meet little resistance. Grasses sway before them and the passage of wind-blown clouds is repeated by fragmented reflected images in the swiftly flowing shallow rivers; earth, air and water combine to convey an impression of continual motion. This was formalized by the Plains Indians who lived here into a belief that every element of the environment was vital and dynamic but that no part could be considered as separate, or separable, from any other: everything existed, interrelated and harmonized, within a continuous expanse where movement on a massive scale was able to occur.

The source of motion, harmony and unity lay with the Sacred Powers, and the landscape therefore had both physical and metaphysical meaning: man moved, theoretically, from one spiritual state to another in much the same way as he moved physically. Although Plains Indian nomadism, the recur-

Left: Two-Ocean Pass in northern Wyoming, called Mountain Sheep Pass by the Indians, crosses the dividing line of the Rocky Mountains. The pronghorn antelopes just visible in the photograph are perfectly adapted to the Great Plains environment and were formerly a common sight in the area.

ring cycle of the seasons, and the migratory habits of game were obvious and direct expressions of movement that tended to reinforce this belief, it was established by the nature of the environment.

Motion is epitomized by the greatest of Plains rivers, the Missouri, as it races, swirls and whirlpools its way across the northern grasslands to its confluence with the Mississippi, where it continues on the four thousand mile journey from its headwaters in north-western Montana to the Gulf of Mexico. Nicknamed 'Big Muddy' because of the opaque colour of its waters – caused by the falling in of earth from its banks – the Missouri passes through country that demonstrates the extremes of Plains landscapes: from rugged mountains to flat bottomlands, and from lush grasslands to semi-deserts. In places there are desolate, bleak wastes of barren rock where an uncanny silence prevails; but there are other areas where trees grow thickly along its banks and on its countless islands, and here the air is filled with a medley of bird song and sometimes the whistling of elks and howls of wolves.

For part of its course it flows between wind-eroded sandstone formations that have received evocative names such as Citadel Rock and The Stone Walls, or it twists a tortuous path about rounded hills that reach down to the water's edge. Isolated bands of coloured clays or white limestone, left where surface waters and sudden storms have stripped the turf from exposed hillsides, stand out in sharp relief against the deep greens of the valleys that surround them, stark reminders to man of the strength of the natural forces.

Yet the environment is not always so startling; it contains elements of exquisite subtlety, such as the delicacy of grassland flora or the beauty of colour and pattern in a dragonfly's wings. This was recognized and given an important place in the lives of the Plains Indians who held that 'every little thing is sent for something, and in that thing there should be happiness and the power to make happy'.[4]

Within the wide, sweeping expanses of the low-lying valleys in the western buffalo ranges another subtle contrast was given symbolic meaning. Small circular depressions of only a few feet across were marked out here by a slightly darker colouration. Such 'fairy rings', often in great numbers together, were formed wherever buffalo had dug into boggy areas to create wallows; as they filled with seepage they accumulated rich, damp soils that supported extensive growths of puffballs: round fungi which emit puffs of brown dust when pressed, and which the Blackfoot called 'Dusty Stars'.

Dusty Star was also the name for a meteor, said to be 'a star changing its place in the sky',[5] and those around the wallows were 'meteors that had fallen from the night sky'.[6] The relationship between sacred and secular elements of the environment, between sky and earth, and the belief that the world was a harmonious whole, were succinctly expressed on the Blackfoot painted tipi, or conical skin tent, which had a broad band of dark colour painted around its base to represent the earth and on this was a series of circles, or Dusty Stars.

The wallows also had practical importance since they indicated valleys that were regularly frequented by buffalo. It was on this animal that the entire nomadic economy centred: they provided man with food, clothing and shelter and were indispensable to his existence. Only their presence in large numbers – it has been estimated that the mid-west and western herds totalled sixty million as late as 1860 – permitted the Plains cultures to

Right: The buffalo was of paramount importance to the Plains Indians, since the products of the hunt provided food, clothing and shelter. One ancient method of hunting was the piskun or buffalo-jump, a high cliff edge over which a herd could be stampeded by pedestrian hunters. This is the Ulm Piskun, which is well documented by associated artefacts and arrowheads from AD 600.

survive, flourish and expand; and, as buffalo are gregarious, their gathering places were an important focus for Indian hunters.

Herds of considerable size could often be found at salt licks, the dazzling white lakes left by the evaporation of salt-river flood waters which covered acres of grassland with their saline deposits. But it was during the autumn rut that the greatest numbers came together and then, as George Catlin observed in the 1830s, they:

> congregate into such masses in some places, as literally to blacken the prairies for miles together. It is no uncommon thing at this season, at these gatherings, to see several thousands in a mass, eddying and wheeling about under a cloud of dust, which is raised by the bulls as they are pawing in the dirt, or engaged in desperate combats, as they constantly are, plunging and butting at each other in the most furious manner.
>
> In these scenes, the males are continually following the females, and the whole mass are in constant motion; and all bellowing (or 'roaring') in deep and hollow sounds; which, mingled altogether, appear, at the distance of a mile or two, like the sound of distant thunder.[7]

A buffalo bull, which can weigh as much as two thousand pounds, is a huge, shaggy beast with deep-set, tiny eyes that glint beneath a profuse mane. Although notoriously short-sighted, it compensates for this with a keen sense of smell and a ferocious, bad-tempered disposition when cornered or aroused. It is also characteristically stubborn. Even an old bull, too weak to keep pace with the herd and, straggling behind, finding himself surrounded by a pack of wolves, will put up a formidable resistance for hours.

With the exception of man, no creature challenged the might of a young, healthy bull.

Plains Indian hunters, using only a short bow and arrows or a thrusting lance, killed them with practised skill and efficiency and utilized virtually every part of the animal to supply all the basic necessities of life. Although other large game animals were regularly hunted, especially elk, deer and antelope, none of these had the importance of the buffalo and when the herds were decimated by indiscriminate slaughter following the advent of the fur trade and through the 'sport' of shooting them from train windows once railways began crossing the grasslands, the livelihood of the nomads was taken away.

The importance of the buffalo is reflected in the special place they occupy in myth and ceremony, with much of Plains ritualism indirectly related to ensuring success in the hunt, and in the tremendous influence that the animals' migratory habits had on the movements of the tribes. People crossed the long grass prairies by following the zig-zag paths beaten flat by the herds, so avoiding the tangled undergrowth and the Ghost's Lariat, a vine with a light blue bloom that wound its way around and through the grass stems, catching people by the ankles and tripping them unexpectedly; or they stayed close to the streams and creeks where buffalo might be found.

Whereas winters were spent camping in relatively small hunting bands, or tribal divisions, near the valleys in which the scattered herds took shelter, spring and summer saw the Plains Indians at their most nomadic, for they followed the rapidly moving herds that travelled to specific areas for the rutting season. When the herds came together in midsummer in preparation for the rut, so the bands gathered as tribes to hold major ceremonies and a tribal hunt.

Larger rivers marked the boundaries of certain tracts within the buffalo ranges that were considered the exclusive hunting grounds of a particular tribe. Within these boundaries individual bands had favourite localities;

Left: The buffalo was looked upon as sacred, and was honoured in rituals and ceremonies. An effigy, such as this green quartzite carving, gave humans a measure of control over the herds by capturing an image of the animal for ritual purposes.

Below, right: The successful hunter, respected because he procured meat and hides from which several families benefited, recorded his hunting skill in pictographic drawing on his buffalo robe. This Shoshoni robe depicts a chase on horseback, the most popular method of hunting after the introduction of the horse to the tribes in the seventeenth century.

based on particular river reaches, these were so fixed that a hunting or war party which had been away, perhaps for several months, could always locate the camp by going back to the area they traditionally occupied at that time of year. But in addition to the attraction they held for buffalo, river valleys supplied the elemental needs of wood and water, both of which were relatively localized. They also supported a rich variety of game and were the principal source of plant foods.

Many valleys in the south were filled with extensive, sometimes impenetrable thickets of plum trees which bore astounding quantities of fruit – so much that at times their heavily laden branches broke under the weight – and almost smothering the ground among them were wild currants, gooseberries and prickly pears. In the cooler north, where the plums grew in clusters rather than masses, there were stands of sarvis and buffalo berry bushes 'forming almost impassable hedges'.[8]

Such bounteousness was used to full advantage. Wild turnips, plantain, milkweed and sunflowers, together with a variety of other fruits, plants, herbs and roots, were gathered in quantity in those areas where they were common. Even the caches of ground beans stored by voles were raided, although only half the cache was ever taken since the vole too had to live. Such concern was typical; most resources were believed to benefit man only when he respected them and did not take them for granted.

Left and right: Rock carvings and paintings have been used since prehistoric times at sacred cultic places, and are frequently associated with flint quarries, where arrow- and spearheads were chipped from the rock, or with ocreous clay deposits that were sources of paint pigment. By making a mark on stone, which is itself a symbol of permanence, human beings associated themselves with the Sacred Powers of the environment and indicated their willingness to live according to the dictates of those Powers. The rock engravings at Wind River Basin, Wyoming (left) are in a landscape setting typical of stone quarries; and the carvings at the Bighorn Basin, which include this warrior with a feathered headdress (right), have estimated ages of between 250 and 3500 years.

Dense groves of cottonwoods, known to the Indians as the 'rustling tree' from the characteristic sound its leaves made in the wind, not only provided refuge in the valleys from the constant winds and weather extremes of the open grasslands, but, during the bitter winter months, their bark could be stripped as a supplemental feed for Indian ponies when snow lay thickly.

Trees grew on the rich alluvial deposits of the river banks though never widely enough to be classed as forests, but woodland animals followed these ribbons of vegetation on to the Great Plains in considerable number and variety: among them white-tailed deer, elk, cougar and wild cat, the black bear and smaller fur-bearers such as the mink, otter and raccoon. The whimpering chatter of their young might disclose the presence of a family of porcupines, while the beaver was apparent everywhere from the dams which blocked smaller streams at regular intervals. Along these tributaries, and on the sandbars and islands, white whooping cranes in flocks of thousands added their distinctive call to those of the kingfishers, jays, woodpeckers, magpies, and hundreds of other bird species that were attracted by the tree cover.

As well as its woodland creatures the Plains supported many ranging and prairie animals which made it one of the world's greatest natural game areas. Pronghorn antelope with their keen sight, fleetness and nervous curiosity were well adapted to its wide spaces. Kit foxes and coyotes roamed here, and large packs of grey wolves followed the buffalo herds which shared their grassland habitat with a type of grouse known as the prairie chicken and the ubiquitous, squirrel-like prairie dog.

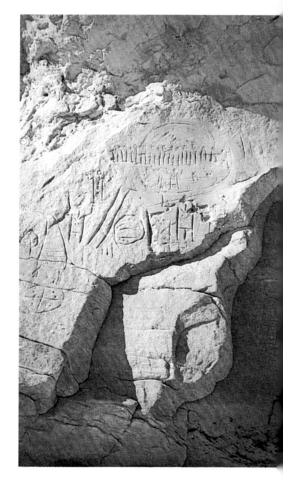

Metaphysical powers were believed to manifest themselves through these animal intermediaries. The grizzly bear was respected as much for the spiritual influence he was thought to wield as for his enormous physical strength; as 'Caleb'[9] he was legendary in tales of both Indians and fur trappers who were equally fond of anecdotes about narrow escapes that they or their acquaintances had experienced from either the ordinary or the supernatural grizzly. Similarly, the eagle was sacred to Plains tribes as the symbol of complete independence in the physical and metaphysical senses, since he could reach the sky yet had chosen to live on earth. A measure of the eagle's sacredness is the fact that although its feathers were eagerly sought for use on headdresses, shields and ritual paraphernalia, the practice of eagle catching was restricted to men who had received supernatural sanction in dreams or visions.

It would, nevertheless, be a mistake to give too glowing an impression of the Great Plains environment, astonishing though its abundance may have been, for it is also subject to extremes of climate that can be terrifying and to sudden, unpredictable changes. There are pronounced daily and seasonal temperature variations; and periods of drought, which can sometimes be measured in years rather than weeks or months, might end with short, violent thunderstorms, destructive winds and extensive floods.

The magnitude of Plains storms is impressive. Vivid forks of lightning seem to fill the sky and the roar of thunder appears to come from somewhere deep in the earth, slowly rising, increasing in intensity, until finally it crashes overhead and echoes through the vast spaces of the sky. Storms can rage for hours, even days, before the first heavy drops of rain fall; or skies might suddenly blacken without warning and blinding rain crash down in sheets that obscure everything, lasting only a few moments but flooding hundreds of acres, then clearing to be replaced by a hot sun which turns the landscape into a world of steam as if so many geysers were boiling beneath its surface.

Dry thunderstorms, accompanied by heavy, oppressive air, may follow hot winds that raise shade temperatures to above 100° Fahrenheit (40° Centigrade), turning the grasses brown and tinder dry. Lightning flashing over this can be a fearful prospect, presaging the terror of a prairie fire.

A distant wisp of smoke prefaces the dreadful smell of burning and the roaring of a sea of flames which, beneath billowing black clouds, can sweep unopposed across the level lands; the 'Spirit of Fire' relentlessly pursues any that attempt to outpace it.

But in winter the pursuer is the North Wind which was said to bring cold weather, storms, disease and death, and against which the people stood with the strength and endurance of the buffalo. Bitterly cold blasts drive the snow in dense clouds at eye level; and sometimes are of such velocity that it is impossible to walk against them. Maximilian, Prince zu Wied, exploring the Upper Missouri in 1834, noted in his diary that 'the mercury of Fahrenheit's thermometer had been for a whole fortnight at 45° below zero (77° below freezing point)'.[10]

It is a testimonial to the fortitude and hardiness of the Plains Indians that, while Maximilian spent the winter indoors, they were out hunting and supplying him with fresh meat. He mentions that some of these hunters wore only a buffalo robe on the upper part of their bodies, and that the Indian women regularly broke the river ice so that they were able to fetch water and bathe.

Coping with the extremes of the environment was a skill that the Plains Indian perfected and it was only during unusually bitter winters, or when an accident of fate created a dangerous situation, that there was any real privation or threat to the survival of the nomadic communities. Any suffering was more frequently caused by lack of mobility, for example when blizzards made hunting impossible, than by lack of resources. He considered the forces of nature as allies which offered protection and assistance rather than as something negative against which he had to pit his strength. Indeed, against the natural powers those of man were insignificant; but, by relying on the intercession of spiritual forces, he could establish a rapport with the world about him.

The close relationship that man felt with his environment was summed up by Chief Joseph when he said: 'The earth and myself are of one mind. The measure of the land and the measure of our bodies are the same'.[11] This was an ancient attitude and is an example of the remarkable consistency shown between Plains history and prehistory as it is recorded in myths and supported by archaeology.

The character of the Plains environment was established in the Pleistocene Ice Age, as evidenced by an animal population adapted to grassland, and it is clear that man was in the area at this time. While it is impossible to hazard a guess as to what his attitudes may have been or whether he was related to the historic tribes that occupied the region, we know that prehistoric man hunted the mammoth here and his antiquity is indicated by a child's skeleton found near Taber, in southern Alberta, which is estimated as between 25,000 and 60,000 years old.[12] The date remains to be proven, but it could well be that this is the oldest direct archaeological evidence of people anywhere in the Americas.

With the extinction of the mammoth herds some 10,000 or so years ago as a consequence of climatic changes, when increasing temperature and decreasing rainfall altered the vegetation slightly and caused critical problems of adjustment for the Ice Age mammals, buffalo became the principal game animal. By this time man was already using hunting techniques which were so efficient that they remained basically unchanged until horses were introduced by the Spanish in the seventeenth century. At Olsen-Chubbock in south-eastern Colorado were found the remains of a small buffalo herd that had been stampeded over the edge of an arroyo so that the animals were killed in the fall. It is obvious that their hides were removed for clothing since the tail bones are missing, which is a necessary result of the skinning process, and hide working tools were also found which confirm this. These

Left: Castle Garden in Wyoming is a prehistoric sacred site containing a great variety and number of carved images on rocks, among them a circle containing a cross, which symbolizes the Sacred Circle enclosing the Four Directions, Four Winds, or Four Powers of Creation.

Above: This man lived 1300 years ago in the Rocky Mountains, between present-day Cody in Wyoming and Yellowstone National Park. His body had been deposited in a cave in the foetal position typical of early Plains 'burials' and symbolic of rebirth. The use of red ochre, traces of which still adhere to his sheepskin garment, symbolized the return of his body to the earth, while his spirit was thought to return to this world in human or animal form, or to travel to the 'Other World' from where it originated.

tools, even though they are 8,500 years old, bear a marked similarity to those used during the historic period.[13]

Also associated with this type of buffalo kill site are a number of implements with graver points for marking wood, bone and other surfaces; small tablets used for crushing and mixing paints, together with traces of red and yellow ochre pigments; and awls, needles, beads and incised gambling sticks made from bone, all of which indicate the awareness of the people and their conscious demonstration of their individual identities.

But the archaeological record is scanty – coming almost exclusively from sites like Olsen-Chubbock – and although it is clear that the early occupants of the Plains had fire, made shelters, manufactured clothing and lived in fairly large communities that must have been socially well organized, there is no evidence of permanent camp sites or villages. Some of the sites had obviously seen repeated occupations and it is therefore likely that they were used as transient camps by roving bands of nomadic hunters.

Part of these hunters' culture is available to us through the rock carvings and paintings they made. There are sacred images that relate to the myste-

rious forces of the metaphysical world, and among them is the Sacred Circle, the symbol of harmony and unity. Belief in the Sacred Circle was widespread. Scattered over the grasslands, singly or in groups of up to two hundred, are an estimated five million circles of small boulders, generally referred to as 'tipi rings'. Undoubtedly many of the rings were used relatively recently as weights to hold down the edges of tipis during temporary camps; but others give an impression of considerable age and are in very exposed areas that lack wood and water, rendering them unsuitable for camp sites and unlikely to have been used in this manner. Some of them overlap and form complex geometric patterns of intersecting lines and shapes.

What purpose they served is unknown; however, their analogy with the painted Sacred Circle suggests that they may have been connected with spiritual symbolism. Maybe they were only reflections, in the words of an aged Dakota Indian named Black Elk, of 'the real world that is behind this one, and everything we see here is something like a shadow from that world'.[14]

Shadows from the ancient world and Sacred Circles are combined in the 'Medicine Wheels' found on scattered, remote hill-tops from north-western Wyoming into southern Alberta. The best known and most spectacular of these is the Great Medicine Wheel in the Bighorn Mountains near present-day Lovell, Wyoming. Here a small central circle of piled stones is surrounded by boulders that form twenty-eight radiating spokes that connect with an encompassing circle eighty feet in diameter.

On approaching these silent monuments their spiritual presence is immediately felt, for the lonely hills have an air of isolation from the activities of the human world and a brooding quietude where only the natural forces are in evidence. Their piled stones express man's relationship with these forces, connecting the physical world with the metaphysical and the past with the present. The Great Medicine Wheel, as first described by Europeans, had a bleached buffalo skull resting on a platform in the centre of the structure and facing the rising sun, which is the symbol of life and has the power of renewal. The benefits derived from the sun could be conveyed along the radiating spokes to the outer circle, thus linking the gift of renewal with the circle of harmony and unity.[15]

Smaller circles are frequently located on the tops of prominent nearby hills, and the presence of these has given rise to a considerable quantity of fanciful speculation. Perhaps, as is commonly suggested, they indicated the positions of the larger structures to migrating bands of nomadic hunters some five thousand years ago: the earliest date we have for a central cairn. But the major wheels were of such significance and the nomads so well adjusted to their environment that this form of locator would probably have been superfluous, and such excess is not in the nature of the Plains Indian.

It seems more feasible that the spokes of the small wheels, which may point to each other as well as the medicine wheel or else indicate the four cardinal directions (the essential divisions of the Sacred Circle), symbolized lines of spiritual force, connectors through which sun-power was transferred and dispersed to bring renewal and harmony into the physical world. But the significance of Medicine Wheels may well go further than this since the spokes that extend beyond their outer circles sometimes align a central cairn or post-hole with the summer solstice and the morning-star, suggesting that early Plains culture might have been based on and adapted to astronomy.[16] This theory gains credibility when compared to the traditions of the historic Indians which fixed the limits of the world by the circular path of the sun.

The circle, therefore, was an ever-present force in the lives of the Plains Indians. It imposed boundaries within which men, animals, and the natural and supernatural powers moved and co-existed, and it could be seen repeated in the skies by the similar motion of the celestial bodies. This concept of continual movement within a continuous space, since the circle has neither beginning nor end, pervaded all aspects of Plains culture, and was both very ancient and environmentally conditioned.

The earliest buffalo hunters used methods consistent with those of more recent people of the area. Archaeology reveals an extremely mobile and changing population: people moved around on the grasslands; small settlements were established and abandoned; groups left, returned, formed alliances, or came into conflict. There were movements across and within the length and breadth of the Great Plains, and incursions from every direction beyond them.

Major influences and migrations came from the south and south-east, together with isolated movements of individual bands and tribes from other directions; but it was from the eastern Woodlands that the earliest significant movements came. Infrequently at first but in gradually increasing numbers, the Woodland hunters crossed the Mississippi-Missouri, and followed the smaller tributary streams and creeks on to the Plains and across the grasslands. They brought with them influences, particularly in the combination of farming and hunting, which resulted in a semi-nomadic life style and semi-permanent villages; and by AD 300 some of these people had established themselves in the Rocky Mountain foothills of Colorado. Here they were linked through trade with the flourishing Adena-Hopewell cultures that centred in the Ohio Valley and with which many of the historic Plains tribes can be connected.[17]

Although the migrants comprised numbers of separate and unrelated groups whose movements spanned a very long period, it is unlikely that they considered themselves as distinct cultural groups. Indeed, it is hardly conceivable that 'cultures' and 'epochs' can exist within traditional Indian frameworks since life was thought of as a series of interrelated events: a great migration from one state or condition to the next. The ancestors were 'The People' just as present and future generations are and will be 'The People' too. In some ways this is more realistic than categorizing North American cultural periods since these did not suddenly spring up and flourish, then wither and disappear.

By about AD 500 the Adena-Hopewell people had established a vast trading complex that reached from the Atlantic coast to the Rockies, and from the Gulf of Mexico to the Great Lakes, although their roots lay in a much earlier period. The Adenans continued and elaborated on previous Woodland life styles: there are connections, for example, between them and the people who made beautifully worked banner- and bird-stones as early as 3,000 BC. Such stones were used as weights on atlatls, or spear-throwers, which effectively increased the length of the thrower's forearm so that he could project the spear with greater velocity and accuracy. Those from the Woodlands are remarkable in the way that the texture and form of the polished stone has been integrated into the design of the finished article. Other ancestors were probably responsible for working raw nuggets of copper into plaques and ornaments in the Great Lakes region about 1,000 BC.

Yet the Adenans did differ from these earlier cultures in their apparent preoccupation with death. They were one of the first mound-builder groups, erecting conical earthen monuments over clay-lined or log tombs in which the bodies of two or three individuals, painted with red ochre, were deposited. Their more important mounds were inside massive enclosures formed by ridged walls of compacted earth and, although circumstances may not be so fortuitous as to place them in the same archaeological time span, it may be in these that the cultural origin can be found for linear earth embankments that extend over hundreds of yards on parts of the Plains. Incised shell gorgets excavated from the Plains earthworks belong to a later date than Adena but certainly point to an Ohio Valley conception.

Right: The same close relationship with their environment that led the Indians to mark sacred areas with rock carvings and paintings also led them to believe that certain prominent features of the landscape, particularly tall bluffs, were favourable spots for establishing communion with the spiritual forces that governed the movements of the world. Medicine Mountain in Wyoming, shown here, has long been regarded as an especially auspicious locality; circular stones of unknown date but of some antiquity trace the outline of a sacred Medicine Wheel on the top of its high plateau.

Some of the Adenan enclosures, if not all, probably had a cult significance as they do not always contain mounds; and, since many are circular, they are often referred to as Sacred Circles: another expression perhaps of the psychic unity that pervaded the universe and was so important to the Plains nomads. Occasionally mounds were built in complex, figurative forms with no burial association, reaching their ultimate expression in the Great Serpent Mound of Adams County, Ohio, where a huge earthen snake uncoils over some 1,500 feet along a hill-top overlooking a small river. This is probably the finest and most effective image of its type, showing the supreme ability its builders had in capturing grace and beauty on a massive scale, and was used as a marker, a deliberate contrast to the surrounding landscape, by which the Adenans made a very direct and obvious statement of their belief.

A similar image occurs in a second, less spectacular, mound; and also in the form of an abstract reptilian bird incised on somewhat enigmatic shale and wood tablets found in mounds associated with this culture. The tablets are minute in comparison with the colossal earth serpents; but the powerful and emphatic use of form and shape is again dominant, and space is occupied in an equally impressive manner though on a lesser scale. In mythology the serpent is associated with water and female forces, symbolizing passive powers, and this peaceful implication was reflected in Adenan society. There were many local expressions, each with a characteristic development, and there is nothing to suggest that the culture was expansionist or attempted to subjugate or dominate neighbouring groups.

However, it did expand. With growth it became so transformed that we

19

refer to the later period as Hopewell, a name which, like Adena, derives from a particular mound group but is used as a general term for several culturally similar complexes. It was Hopewellian people who extended Adenan trade routes which then spread across the Plains to the Rockies.

The nature of this trade did not involve the westward movement of large numbers of people from the Ohio area, since it was conducted on an individual basis of gift exchange: a Hopewellian family might obtain raw materials from another family in a different area in exchange for finished articles. Nevertheless, the sedentary nature of Hopewell culture was not a barrier to the rapid advance of Woodland influence. With the growing importance of cults surrounding the dead, goods began to be made which served only to accompany the deceased, and the degree of honour implied by these seems to have been related to their quantity, quality and rarity. This created a search for unusual materials combined with an insistence on constant production which stimulated Hopewell traders to travel further than their Adenan predecessors had done, and in the process introduced new ideas and merchandise to the people with whom they came into contact. Both copper and marine shell, for example, have been found together with articles of Hopewell manufacture in Plains sites, and small clay pipes made on the Plains were modelled after the typical tubular stone pipes used for communal smoking in Ohio.

Archaeology, of course, reveals only limited material aspects of a culture – those which withstand the passage of time – but it is reasonable to assume that Hopewell influence was not restricted to trade goods. When the form

Left: The Snake River, which runs from the Yellowstone National Park into the Columbia River, derives its name from the Snake Indians, better known as Shoshoni, who used the snake as a 'totemic' image. Environmental conditions and features of the landscape in some parts of the north-western Plains were similar to those in the northerly regions of the Eastern Woodlands; and when the Blackfoot tribes, whose Algonkin language links them with the eastern groups, expanded westwards in the distant past they displaced the Snake Indians.

Right: A slate pipe made in the nineteenth century by the Santee, or Eastern Sioux, depicting the spirits of a couple and a horse. Eastern influences, among them pipes and smoking rituals, spread to the Plains from the Woodlands beyond the Mississippi. Pipes could be used to make offerings of smoke in which the prayers of the people were carried to the metaphysical forces occupying an ethereal region, and so they were frequently carved with forms representing powerful spirit-beings or with creatures that acted as messengers between humans and these beings.

of the pipe was introduced it is likely to have been accompanied by tobacco and smoking rituals; some of the Hopewell burial practices, and presumably their rituals too, were expressed on the Plains in a less ostentatious manner; and the first evidence of corn agriculture here is at semi-nomadic village sites in Kansas which bear unmistakably Hopewellian characteristics.

Plains influence is also suggested at Hopewell sites in the east. Apart from the presence of materials such as grizzly bear canines and obsidian which almost certainly came from areas close to the Rocky Mountains, ornaments have been recovered which use hand symbolism that was carried on into later Woodland cultures but was particularly important on the Plains, and the distinctive topknot hairstyle of Plains shamans appears here on fine effigy pots made as mortuary vessels.

The mounds themselves became larger and more complex, some of them containing the ashes of several hundred dead; and the contrast between these massive, solid earthworks and the delicate bird claws, snake heads, hands and so on that were cut from transparently thin sheets of mica that are almost too fragile to handle reveals the great versatility of Hopewell artisans. The tremendous empathy they showed for the natural qualities of such diverse materials is evident from the artefacts associated with these burials.

Among the more frequently found objects are stone pipes which support the figure of a bird or animal on a flat platform. These utilize shape and space to create an illusion of movement: a puma crouches as though it might spring at any moment, while a snake coils sinuously around the bowl of another pipe; elsewhere a turkey buzzard pauses and glares around, a hawk rips at the flesh of another bird, or a spoonbill duck rests and clutches a fish it has just caught.

As Woodland influences spread to the grasslands, they were modified and adapted by local environmental conditions. Agriculture, for instance, could not be so intensive in the drier Plains climate; and the stratified social frameworks that had developed in the east as the consequence of a relatively stable agricultural economy were rejected. Plains communities, including recently

arrived migrants, adopted democratic, tribal systems that may have been established by the early buffalo hunters.[18]

Thus Plains Hopewell culture, in common with that in other areas where trade had resulted in the adoption of some eastern traits, was a distinctly local expression. Since they had never attempted to establish political cohesiveness, the Ohio groups diversified as their populations increased and outgrew the mound complexes – which were heaped over with earth and ceremonially burned to the ground on abandonment. Their influence waned and the cults weakened.

Identifiably Hopewellian centres continued to develop independently for many centuries, and some of these gradually evolved into new culture complexes. From this proliferation of small mound-builder groups, one of them,

Left: A stone pipe from the Mississippian Culture of the South-East (AD 700 to 1700), where birds such as ducks and hawks, as well as wolves and other animals, were popular subjects for a form of tubular pipe.

Below: This Mississippian Culture embossed copper head dates from about AD 1000 and may be intended as a portrait of a prominent warrior. It clearly shows the forked eye symbol and ear spool that became conventionalized representations of the aggressive Southern Death Cult. Between AD 1200 and AD 1600 Southern Death Cult beliefs flourished on the Plains periphery at Spiro Mound in Oklahoma.

the Temple Mound Culture of the Mississippi Valley, eventually superseded the others to become the major source of influence east of the Mississippi around AD 900, some four or five hundred years after the Hopewell peak, and from here they expanded north and west.

As their name implies, they no longer built mounds as simple statements of belief or in connection with burials. Theirs were vast temple complexes where the summits of rectangular, flat-topped earthworks, some sixty to a hundred feet high and grouped around open plazas, supported wooden buildings in which sacred, eternal fires were kept burning by a special caste of priest-rulers. These served as ceremonial centres for city-states with populations of up to ten or fifteen thousand, comprised of a number of small communities in stockaded villages of thatched houses surrounded by fields of squash, beans and corn.

Combined with an aggressive south-eastern element, the cultism of these Mississippians became particularly brutal, and included sacrifices, ritual beheadings, and the display of severed enemy heads on platforms erected around some of the mounds. Monster pots and effigy heads, as well as shell gorgets illustrating ritualistic decapitations, have been found in burial chambers. In place of the graceful Hopewell carvings that connected man with the animal spirits, the figures on Mississippian pipes are often kneeling creatures and threatening demi-gods, some of which triumphantly clutch trophy heads. Skulls, weeping faces, red-crested birds symbolizing war, and especially the 'sun-wind' cross motif representing the sacred eternal fire, were synonymous with the later Mississippian period that is commonly referred to as the Southern Death Cult.

The attitudes expressed in the Cult may have arisen with improved agricultural techniques: man controlled his crops to a greater extent and was less dependent on nature; therefore he could assume an antagonistic stance rather than a conciliatory one. This was the antithesis of Plains belief and an impossible attitude to adopt within the harsher realities of Plains environments, and it is significant that the most westerly point of Death Cult expansion, which took the form of mass migrations of entire communities, was in the Oklahoma region on the grassland periphery. Caddoan people, who were full participants in the Cult, built Mound Spiro here; but apparently some form of cultural barrier existed and the excesses of the Mississippians never penetrated further.

Spiro, then, may have marked both the cultural and environmental limits in which cultism could be fully expressed. Mississippian migrants did, however, move on to the Plains. Although they introduced new strains of corn and beans that were capable of withstanding frost and would mature in the shorter growing season, hunting and gathering also played a major economic role. Adapting to a grassland habitat, they abandoned their villages for several months each year when they engaged in annual or semi-annual buffalo hunts; at these times they lived in a manner that was virtually identical to that of the nomads.

This type of cross-cultural influence was in part the result of an active trade that had developed between the nomadic hunting bands and the small villages that were based on the rivers and streams; but a thirty-year drought struck the North Platte River in Nebraska during the mid-1400s and was followed elsewhere by a series of droughts that spanned almost half a century. The flexibility of the nomads would have allowed them to avoid the more serious consequences of this; for the farming communities though, with crops that were only marginally adjusted to the environment in any event, they proved disastrous: by 1500 villages were abandoned; their occupants had moved east.[19]

Competition for the more favourable, fertile river areas in the restricted lands into which they moved culminated in open hostility. Ditches and

palisades were thrown up around the clusters of houses to protect them and an internecine war, which the nomads generally avoided, engulfed the village populations. When relations stabilized they coalesced on the Missouri into fewer but larger communities. Although the origins of the communities lay both south and east, their life-style was an amalgam of that of the older cultures which had waxed and waned on the Plains. Some, at least, of these groups can be considered very ancient inhabitants of the area: Adena-Hopewell influence is evident, as is a modification of Mississippian tenets caused by a rejection of the overtly aggressive elements that had characterized the Death Cult.

The more important of the village tribes during the historic period were the Arikara, Hidatsa and Mandan on the Upper Missouri; the Pawnee tribes in the valley of the Platte River; and various Siouan-speaking groups – the Ponca, Omaha, Iowa, Oto, Missouri, Osage and Kansa – occupying the area from the Middle Missouri to its confluence with the Mississippi. Their economy was divided about equally between the cultivation of crops and products of the hunt; all of them spent a considerable part of their year in pursuit of the buffalo herds, at which time they lived in hide-covered tipis and adopted a nomadic way of life. In a sense, their permanent villages of earth-covered lodges corresponded with the traditional river camp sites of the nomads: both provided a fixed reference to which they could return.

Nomadic boundaries, however, were broader since they were not dictated by the necessity to plant and harvest and were limited only by the environment and the migratory habits of game animals. Nomadism, therefore, more accurately expresses the complete freedom and independence that was characteristic of life on the Great Plains.

In the north was the powerful confederacy of Blackfoot tribes: the Siksika, Kainah and Piegan. They had lived on the Plains for a long time but their traditions refer to movements from the east and south, and their language suggests an eastern origin. During the historic period, which is roughly since the seventeenth century, they had expanded their territories to the south and south-west of the South Saskatchewan River into Montana, and ranged over a large tract of country centred in Alberta on the Red Deer, Bow and Battle rivers.

To their east and north-east were bands of Ojibwa, Assiniboine and Cree, whose Woodland origin is quite clear since they retained some eastern culture traits and had close relatives still living there; while on the western Plains south of the Blackfoot lived the Crow, who had only recently separated from the Hidatsa, one of the village tribes on the Upper Missouri, and established themselves in the upper basins of the Yellowstone and Bighorn rivers.

Further south were the Arapaho. Their migrations are typical of the whirl of tribal movements and divisions that occurred across the grasslands. When first seen by Europeans they were north of the Missouri, but as they moved south the tribe split. One division, the Atsina, decided to stay in the north where they joined the Blackfoot confederacy and are known as the Gros Ventre, a name given by early French traders to the Big Belly River, now the South Saskatchewan, on which they lived. The other, larger part of the tribe moved into the country between the North Platte and Arkansas rivers in what are today the states of Wyoming and Colorado.

Shortly after their arrival here the Arapaho were joined by the Cheyenne who have a well-documented record of a migration from western Wisconsin and Minnesota, where they farmed and lived in villages of earth lodges, via another earth-lodge settlement on the Sheyenne River in North Dakota, to the Black Hills, and thence south, having abandoned farming and villages and become nomadic buffalo hunters. A northern Cheyenne group remained near the headwaters of the Platte River, while the remainder formed

Left: The carving on this soapstone pipe, which was recovered from Spiro Mound, is generally assumed to depict a warrior beheading his victim; this was a common custom in the South-East, from whence the Spiro occupants had migrated.

a southern division which settled on the Arkansas plains.

With the Cheyenne, in their move from the Woodlands, came several tribes that are linguistically related and are often referred to collectively as the Sioux. Part of this group settled between the forks of the Missouri and Mississippi where they retained much of their agricultural tradition and are known as the Santee or Dakota; but many of them crossed onto the Plains as true nomads where they established a loose confederation of seven tribes called the Teton, or Lakota. Although considering themselves as allies and relatives, the Teton tribes – Blackfoot Sioux (unrelated to the northern Blackfoot), Brulé, Hunkpapa, Minneconjou, Oglala, Sans-Arc and Two-Kettle – were autonomous and did not constitute a political or economic unit. Between them they ranged over an area bordered by the Platte River in the south, the Missouri in the east, north to the Yellowstone, and west to the Teton Mountains. Two tribes, the Yankton and Yanktonai, stayed in the Dakotas between the Missouri and James Rivers and formed a third dialect division.

Other movements came from the west. The Shoshone and Comanche are related to the tribes of the Great Basin of Utah and Nevada and had crossed over the Rockies. In the region around the Black Hills they met the Kiowa, who are perhaps the descendants of some of the earliest nomads since there is no indication that they ever lived outside the Plains. They stayed in this vicinity until the expansion of other tribes forced them out: the Shoshone to the valleys of the Grand Tetons and Wind rivers, the Comanche ranging through the areas of Texas and Oklahoma, and the Kiowa into New Mexico. The Kiowa were also closely associated with a small Athabascan-speaking group, the Kiowa-Apache, who functioned as members of the tribe at major ceremonies but had no language similarity and communicated entirely with sign language.

As well as the tribes living year-round on the grasslands, there were a number of peripheral groups that made regular incursions into the area for buffalo hunting and shared many Plains culture traits. Included among these are the Nez Percé, who lived near the Snake River on the Idaho-Washington-Oregon border but used hide tipis while hunting east of the Rockies and regularly wore Plains-style clothing. They, together with the Cayuse Indians of Oregon, gained a reputation among Plains tribes as horse traders and breeders and are credited with developing the western saddle horse known as the Appaloosa. North of the Nez Percé, and inter-mittently at war with the Blackfoot who had overrun their traditional hunting areas, were the Kutenai; while further south, in Utah, Colorado and New Mexico, were scattered nomadic bands of Utes and Apaches.

This constant round of relocations and incursions was still continuing as recently as the end of the eighteenth century when the Sarsi came south from their far northern homeland on the Athabaska River to join the Blackfoot confederacy. Both history and prehistory indicate continual movement and change, while the concept of motion is implicit in Plains myth through use of the term 'migration' to suggest altered circumstances of any kind. Movement is also inherent in the natural forces, and it was the character of the environment that dictated the character of Plains nomadism which was to reach its typical expression among such tribes as the Blackfoot, Teton Sioux, Crow, Cheyenne and Arapaho.

Left: Rapid wind erosion of soft soils has created the rugged sculptured forms of the Badlands that run through parts of Montana, Wyoming and South Dakota, turning this region into a desert wasteland that supports sparse animal and plant life. Even the Indians avoided it, and early European travellers, following the Missouri through the mauvais terres, commented on their uncanny stillness and quiet, and the absence of large game.

27

LIFE ON THE PLAINS

In its sheltered wooded valley with the tipis tucked well back into a grove of cottonwoods and banked high with brush, a Plains Indian camp was secure against all but the most severe winter storms. During these long, dark evenings the people traditionally stayed close to the fires listening to the Elders, or Grandfathers, telling the old myths and tales. Their ancient traditions of the beginning of time, about the sun, moon and stars, the making of the earth, and the powers of the animals, Wind, Cloud, Thunder and Lightning, always followed the same formal order since they were about sacred forces and no one could alter the manner in which they worked. But they had different emphases according to whom they were being told.

Children were encouraged to follow the moral values that the legends explained, to heed their warnings against greed, avarice and irresponsibility, and to show respect for their elders. Tales of wolves (the symbols of warriors), of the mythic hero Scar-face, or the Twin Boys who defeated evil on Earth showed the young men that it was their duty to protect the community; while the women of their age group had the value of a virtuously led life held up to them as an example, for it was through virtue that they could reach honoured positions in major ceremonials.

Each speaker had his favourite introductions and narrative style which sometimes took the form of jokes about the mannerisms of another speaker whom he would mimic to laughter and shouts of approval from his audience. This helped break the formality of legends that defined the spiritual path the people should follow and which often contained practical rules of cooperation that enabled them to face difficulty together. As these were stories about the acceptance of nature and of ways of coping with the environmental conditions of the area, they frequently referred to the transient qualities of life on the Great Plains and emphasized the fact that the people had always roamed. Seasonal weather variations and the migrations of game dictated that they must move and it had always been necessary to be able to adjust quickly and to retain the flexibility and mobility that were essential to survival.

Even today, many of the tales look back to an early period when pedestrian nomads walked across the grasslands in the wake of the buffalo herds, and stress the difficulties of nomadic life and the paramount importance of the ability to move freely. So essential was this that the pedestrian hunters could make no allowance for anyone who was unable to keep pace, and in spite of the reluctance to abandon one of their members, the conditions they faced sometimes permitted no alternative. There was always a pressing need to travel to areas where game was available and often the infirm or aged, knowing their immediate family would expose themselves to danger by lingering behind to care for them, implored their relatives to leave:

I am old, and too feeble to march. My children, our nation is poor, and

Left: A Blackfoot man's shirt probably made in about 1820. It would have been worn only by an exceptional warrior on special occasions and is said by the collector, Herzog von Württemberg, to have been worth the equivalent of thirty horses in 1867. The groups of painted stripes represent a war record and are crossed with arrows and tobacco pipes, while hoofmarks — representing ponies captured on raids — form a line along the inner edge of the stripes. The Blackfoot sometimes transferred ownership of this type of hair-fringed shirt, when both the seller and the buyer, who had to have an indisputable prominence in the tribe, enhanced their prestige through public recognition of their achievements.

it is necessary that you should all go to the country where you can get meat, – my eyes are dimmed and my strength is no more; my days are nearly all numbered, and I am a burthen to my children – I cannot go, and I wish to die.[1]

As the relatives departed the wind would have borne the thin notes of a death song to them: a song, choked with emotion but full of pride, that told of a lifetime's achievements and of the preparation for a long, last journey since, even in death, movement continued.

The mobility of these groups centred on the dog, the Indians' only domestic animal, for although movement was dictated by other factors, the dog,

Right: This buffalo robe, made by the Hidatsa in about 1850, has the characteristic 'box and border' design of a woman's garment and would have been worn with the head to the left so that the pattern was seen horizontally. Nearly all painting of this nature was done by women (men restricted themselves to pictographic representations of war and hunting exploits or, sometimes, to designs with a sacred significance), and was accomplished by pressing paint into the surface of the hide with porous buffalo bone brushes, which resulted in an indented effect.

Far right: The fleet and sure-footed ponies used in war and hunting were selected for their qualities of independence and vitality; these qualities were recognized by the Indians in the wild horses that roamed the area. The Elk River Basin on the border of Montana and Wyoming shows the type of natural landscape that was ideally suited to the wild horse and to the equestrian life of Plains tribes.

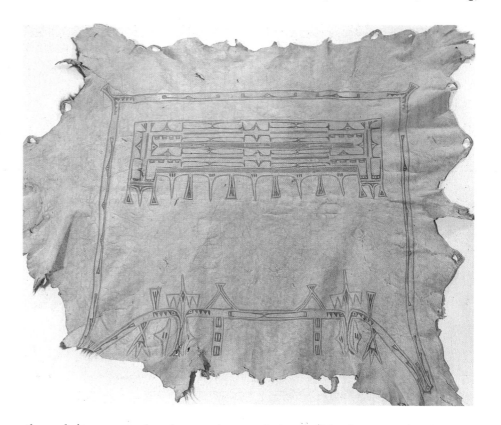

through its use as a burden-carrier, made it possible. Strong animals could carry as much as seventy-five pounds on the travois – an A-shaped wood frame that was fastened to a crude pack saddle over the dog's shoulders and dragged along the ground behind it. The weight, quantity and size of material possessions were all geared to this capacity: tipis, for example, were small since a cover made from six to eight buffalo hides, forming a dwelling of ten feet or less in diameter, was a maximum travois load.

The essential role of the dog in camp movements gave this animal a particular significance, and those owned by the women were highly regarded and praised for their size and strength since it was on them that the band's ability to move its belongings depended. A man, too, was proud of his dogs, giving them names which reflected his own heroic deeds such as 'Took-away-his-shield'; dogs often accompanied Crow and Cree war parties who used them to carry packs of spare moccasins if they expected their journey to be a lengthy one; or they had a function in hunting, as among the Blackfoot who trained them for bear baiting and for flushing smaller animals out of undergrowth or from their burrows.

The close relationship between man and dog was a frequent theme in myths. In one of these tales the dog follows the people, who have migrated from an underground world, and offers his material self as a sacrifice so that disease may be averted. He said (referring to his spirit, invested in future generations) of dogs: 'I shall always remain with the people. I shall be a guardian for all their belongings'.[2] This story illuminated belief in the dog's curative powers, which were thought to derive from the sun, as well as its role as a guardian – in which it was undoubtedly effective: early European explorers frequently found their way into an Indian camp barred by the bared fangs of its canine population. The Indian attitude, however, is perhaps summed up on Crow sacred pipes, which always have a single eagle feather attached to them to represent the dog's tail 'because the dog is the protector and friend of every person in the world'.[3]

They were also given a sacred role, especially by the Sioux and Arapaho, in rituals that involved feasts of dog meat. Dog feasts might also be given

to show respect for prominent guests from other tribes when, as in all matters of duty and honour, the Indian gave only his best. His favourite, most faithful dog was selected for the occasion and as the meal was served a speech was given in which the animal's loyalty, courage and faithful service were extolled.

Although dogs continued to be important, their burden-carrying function became less essential when the horse frontier spread along the old, traditional trade routes from the Spanish stock-raising settlements that were established in the Southwest during the seventeenth century. The impact that the horse had on Plains cultures was remarkable.

One of the major effects was economic. Equestrian hunters were able to travel further and faster in their quest for buffalo than had their pedestrian predecessors, and were capable of tackling larger herds since they had the mobility to do so. Once the travois was adapted to the horse greater quantities of meat could be transported, much of which could be dried and taken to the winter camps in the stream valleys. This reduced the risk of starvation if buffalo were scarce and permitted the size of the hunting bands to increase without running too great a risk of being unable to support themselves. This in turn brought about changes in the social order.

Heads of some of the families began to enjoy hitherto unheard-of prestige and status as these substantially bigger communities contained members

31

who were unrelated through either blood or marriage. The status of group leaders, which was reflected in a wealth of new goods, larger tipis and a dramatic increase in the number of material possessions, increased with their generosity, since it was primarily based on the number of people who chose to follow them; people gravitated towards the more generous ones, to those who loaned or gave horses for the hunt or to help move camp, but to maintain their positions they required horses.

These were initially obtained through trade. Kiowa and Comanche traders were riding painted ponies into Kansas in the 1680s, and the Wyoming Shoshone – who only obtained their first horses about 1690 – had already begun to supply the Blackfoot on the northern Plains by the early 1700s. Although trade could possibly have satisfied the economic demand – it has been estimated that the average Blackfoot family of eight (two men, three women and three children) needed twelve horses to move camp comfortably[4] – rapid changes within the societies caused horses to become equated with achievement. Young warriors, eager to prove themselves, were soon supplementing the herds of their own group by raiding those of their rivals, and skill at raiding quickly became an accepted means of gaining social recognition.

As a consequence, one family might possess only two or three horses and be dependent on borrowing from others or be forced to rely on dogs when moving its belongings, which were necessarily few, while another owned herds far in excess of its requirements, although both these examples were relatively rare. For most people the horse effectively lifted the restraints that the limitations of the dog had previously imposed; it made life easier, more comfortable and more secure, but most important of all it allowed a freedom and independence of movement that was closely akin to the motion the Indian observed in his environment and which placed him on a more equal footing with the natural forces.

The speed with which the pedestrian nomads became equestrian can be credited to the Plains Indian's affinity with, and profound knowledge of, animals and animal behaviour: he accepted every animal as a living being with particular individual characteristics, and had no misconception that he was superior in any way. Because of this attitude Plains horse culture flourished, and when George Catlin was a guest of the Comanche he stated: 'I am ready, without hesitation, to pronounce the Camanchees the most extraordinary horsemen that I have seen yet in all my travels, and I doubt very much whether any people in the world can surpass them'.[5]

He left this vivid description of one of their warriors, performing a feat in which all were equally accomplished:

> . . . he is able to drop his body upon the side of his horse at the instant he is passing, effectually screened from his enemies' weapons as he lies in a horizontal position behind the body of his horse, with his heel hanging over the horses' back; by which he has the power of throwing himself up again, and changing to the other side of the horse if necessary. In this wonderful condition, he will hang whilst his horse is at fullest speed, carrying with him his bow and his shield, and also his long lance of fourteen feet in length, all or either of which he will wield upon his enemy as he passes; rising and throwing his arrows over the horse's back, or with equal ease and equal success under the horse's neck.[6]

They were able to do this by dropping their weight into a short, hair halter braided into the pony's mane and looped under its neck; the trick, however, was used by the Comanche in displays of skill, which Catlin witnessed, rather than in actual warfare.

Catlin was obviously impressed, for in a sense the horse had become an

Left, above: The horse revolutionized Plains Indian methods of transportation and a complete complex of riding gear was developed. High-pommelled and cantled saddles were adapted for carrying goods and were used mainly by women, although the parade saddle shown here, a rare type in which the pommel carries a realistic carving, belonged to the Santee Sioux Chief Cub Nose.

Left, below: Hair was the 'seat of the soul' and thus linked with a person's spiritual identity and existence; consequently, much attention was lavished on hair decoration. The Sioux hair ornament shown here, with quills and downy eagle feathers attached to it, was worn at the back of the head.

Below: Elaborate hair-fringed war shirts and leggings were reserved for displays and rarely used in combat. Tassles of scalp hair, some of them from enemies whose souls the warrior had 'captured', form a fringe on these Crow leggings.

extension of the man: there was a unity between animal and rider of which the Indian was acutely aware. He saw this as beauty and expressed the aesthetic quality of a pony's movements in poetic phrases:

> My horses, prancing they are coming.
> My horses, neighing they are coming;
> Prancing, they are coming.
> All over the universe they come.
> They will dance; may you behold them.
> A horse nation, they will dance.[7]

This attitude still persists. An Indian will select a favourite parade pony for the way he 'dances'; because 'he knows that he is beautiful, he walks sideways and throws his head to show how beautiful he is'.[8]

A similar beauty was recognized in the herds of wild horses that roamed the entire area but which were concentrated in their greatest numbers in Comanche territory on the southern grasslands, where environmental conditions – the climate, short grasses and rocky foothills – were virtually identical to those of their original Andalusian homeland. Although these ponies were small they were also powerful, possessing the tremendous endurance of their Barb ancestors. Their nervous vitality created motion even when the herds were grazing quietly, and there was a wildness and vivacity, a feeling of controlled energy, in the spirit of a free stallion that exactly

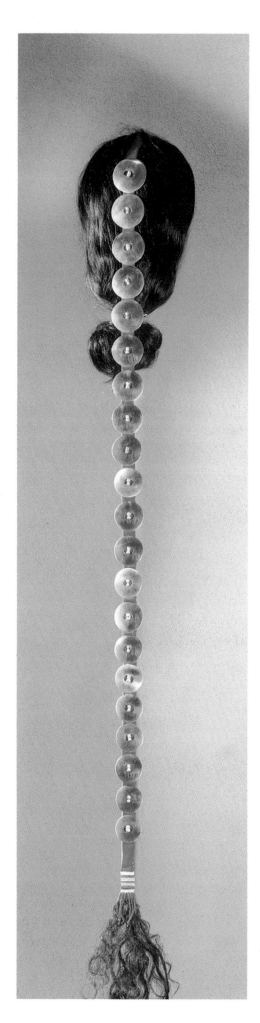

matched the Indian temperament. The combination of these two proud and independent spirits was fully expressed during the so-called 'war parade': horseback displays in full costume that usually took place at large gatherings and were associated with impressing important guests from other tribes with the power and solidarity of the host tribe's warriors. These were conscious demonstrations of tribal identities and proof of victory in the fight for survival on the Plains; they were designed to impress and never failed to do so.

In precise formation, forming long lines or great concentric circles, the parade was a 'whirling wheel of colour and motion', offering momentary glimpses of matched, black-tipped eagle-feather headdresses; spectacular painted shields and feathered lances; painted ponies with zig-zag lightning designs and white hail spots, symbolizing their power to ride unharmed through the 'rain, hail, and lightning of enemy fire'; and ermine or hair-lock fringes that trimmed the seams of buckskin shirts and leggings embroidered with porcupine quills.[9] This whole mass raced in a dazzling, dizzying exhibition of men and ponies and paint that evoked admiration and hushed respect from the guests before whom it was presented. The complexity of the war parade was stunning, and although each individual carried symbols of a personal spiritual experience which emphasized his individuality and helped him attain his status as a warrior, its organization demonstrated that each depended on the others for mutual support.

Some of the men wore wolf-skin cloaks that indicated their prowess as scouts for war and hunting parties, since the cunning and perseverance of the wolf was transmitted to them through wearing its hide. Others derived their power from the buffalo and had headdresses of split and polished buffalo horns; or received it from the chicken hawk and used its feathers as the symbol of a transfer of power.

The wing and tail feathers from the sacred eagle symbolized outstanding war honours 'because the eagle is the chief of the birds. It is the most powerful, can fly the highest, and yet it can see everything that happens on the earth',[10] and it was from these that the crowns and trailers of war bonnets were made.

The gentlest breeze set these black-tipped bonnets in motion. Their sweeping, graceful curves echoed the long, slow, powerful wingbeats of an eagle in flight, while the downy 'breath' feathers that trimmed their brow bands shimmered. War bonnets were imbued with spiritual force and stood out as conspicuous emblems of the leaders and prominent men against the single or few feathers worn in different ways, cut or split and painted, with which most individuals displayed their status. A single eagle feather suspended majestically from the bridle of a pony was a restrained statement, but no less forceful than the more flamboyant expression used elsewhere. The parade was an emotive confirmation of life, bringing together the forces of man and nature and directly symbolizing the motion that animated every part of the Plains environment; and in which man was able to be a full participant because of the introduction of the horse.

At the same time as horses spread from the southwest, guns were being traded in from the northeast. Even though these early firearms were less effective hunting weapons than either the bow or lance, they were nevertheless eagerly sought and most tribes began to acquire them from Indian intermediaries long before they had contact with white traders; but the gun was useless without powder and shot, which could only be obtained directly or indirectly from the trading companies, contact with which resulted in a continuous exposure to other goods of European manufacture, mainly iron, metal awls, beads and trade cloth.

These simplified many tasks – cutting heavy buffalo hides and applying quillwork embroidery, for example, were far easier with metal knives and

Plains Indians were quick to assimilate the influence of **European trade**, continuing an ancient pattern of cultural diffusion and adapting trade items to uses that were purely Indian in character. Many of these trade goods, particularly in the early days of contact when they were difficult to obtain, were incorporated into regalia and costume worn on special occasions, or given 'sacred' meanings.

Left: Men often wore German silver hair plates in a graduated series strung on a leather strap, as a hair decoration, like this one dating from about 1910; and women wore a similar ornament hanging from their belts. Silver was introduced to the northern Plains soon after 1800, and worked into bracelets, brooches and other ornaments. In the 1850s it was superseded as a trade item by German silver, which is an alloy of copper, zinc and nickel.

Right: This traditional form of porcupine quill and feather hair ornament, made by the Sioux in about 1890, includes a mirror plate in its design. Similar mirrors were used extensively by the Sioux as signalling devices during their wars with the US.

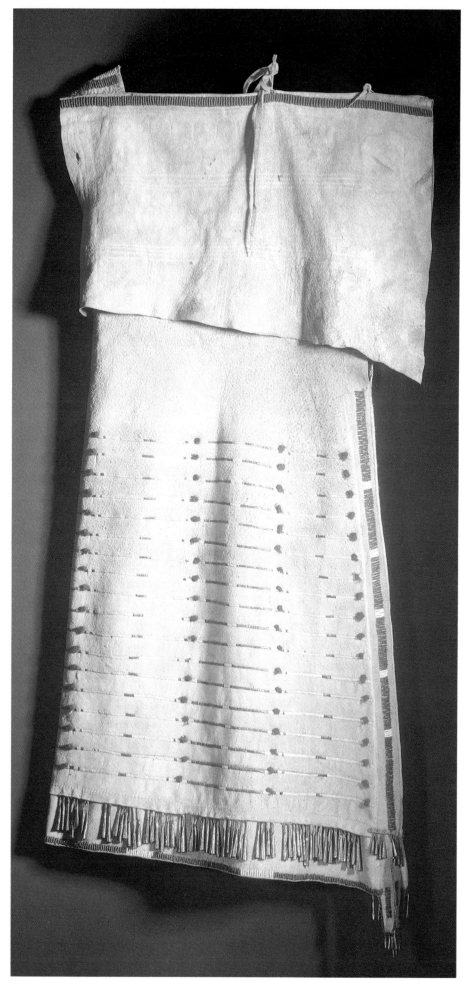

Left: The simplicity of this very early Sioux woman's dress adds to its aesthetic charm. It dates from about 1830 and is of a style identical to that of two Cree dresses collected by Lewis and Clark in 1804. The cape-like upper part of the garment, to which the longer skirt has been sewn, was fastened by means of a leather thong on the right shoulder and has a leather strap inserted on the left. Quilled stripes and red tassels, together with the metal cone fringe on the skirt and the beaded border of the cape, show the Plains Indians' preference for horizontal rather than vertical decoration, a predilection that continues to this day on clothing that is often made from cloth rather than skins and in which a fully beaded yoke replaces the earlier cape.

Right, above: The rawhide used for parfleches and other items that required semi-rigidity was extremely tough and durable, but difficult to work. Early hide examples were made using bone awls and needles, but when iron became available through white trade it was eagerly sought for this purpose. Short lengths of iron were set in antler or bone handles and filed to a point to make more efficient sewing awls like the one shown here. Similar tools were also used for making loops that went part-way through tanned animal skins to permit the attachment of porcupine quill embroidery or beadwork.

Right, below: Although this parfleche was collected from the Sioux, the style of the painting on it suggests that it was made by the Arapaho or Cheyenne, from whom the Sioux probably obtained it by way of trade. Such bags, used as containers for pemmican (dried buffalo meat), were widely traded and often formed part of the gift when food was ceremonially presented to members of visiting tribes. Parfleches were carried over the saddle on journeys, or occasionally on the travois, and in camp they formed a colourful addition to a tipi's furnishings.

awls than with bone tools – and acted as such a stimulus for Indian material culture that the transformation from small, poorly equipped pedestrian communities to colourful, expressive equestrianism was so sudden and complete that the first Europeans to visit the tribes of the Upper Missouri could describe them as:

> undoubtedly the finest looking, best equipped, and most beautifully costumed of any on the Continent . . . nothing in the world, of its kind, can possibly surpass in beauty and grace, some of their games and amusements – their gambols and parades. . . . of such tribes, perhaps the Crows and Blackfeet stand first; and no one would be able to appreciate the richness and elegance (and even taste too), with which some of these people dress, without seeing them in their own country.[11]

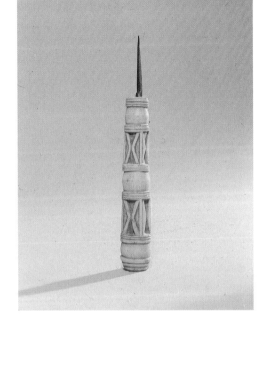

The Crow, in particular, acquired a reputation for self-assurance and self-confidence. Although they were a small tribe, they openly vaunted their daring and bravery – sometimes in a haughty manner – and their pride was reflected in the men's habit of growing their hair to extraordinary lengths. When He-who-jumps-high, a Crow warrior, mounted his pony, his long hair reached the ground.[12] Hair was only worn loose on parades and ceremonial occasions, when small balls of pitch were placed in rows at regular intervals to keep it in place. At other times it was tied and bound with lengths of fur or trade cloth. Crow women wore their hair shorter with a centre parting, painted red, in a typical Plains women's hairstyle. Both men and women dressed their hair daily with bears' grease to give it a jet-black lustre 'like a raven's wing' and perfumed it with sweet-smelling herbs.

The attention that men paid to the length of their hair was exceptional, yet it was really only an exaggerated form of a common custom by which their vanity and pride was expressed. Blackfoot warriors, for example, combed a narrow lock over the bridge of the nose, cutting this square. The Crow wore the hair over their foreheads cut short and brushed back to create

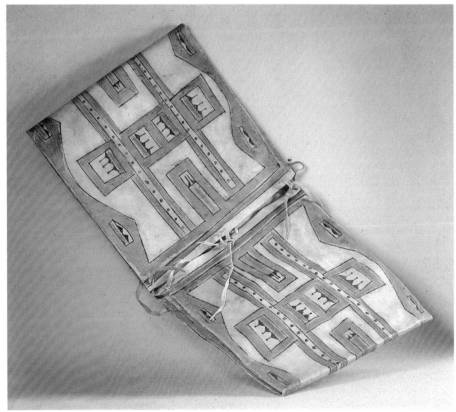

an effect so characteristic that it was used as a tribal mark for their warriors in Sioux pictographs. And some Arapaho men, following the Crow lead in having the hair over their foreheads standing upright, cut that over the temples into a zig-zag, and tied that at the back of the head into a thick braid.[13]

Although the splendour projected by the Crow was so noticeable that French trappers referred to them as 'handsome men', there can be no doubt that the Blackfoot were responsible for some of the most aesthetically impressive costume on the Plains. They frequently employed ermine where other tribes used feathers or locks of hair, and these white furs made a powerful and effective contrast with their darker deerskins.

For everyday purposes, clothing of the same style and cut was worn but without such extensively applied decoration. A breechcloth and moccasins sufficed for the men in warmer weather. On cooler days they would wear a deerskin shirt, cut so that it retained the original shape of the skins and with rows of porcupine quill embroidery covering the seams along the outside of the arms; long skin leggings, again with quilled seams, that reached from ankles to hips and were tied to the belt; and a buffalo hide robe.

Women wore dresses of deer- or mountain sheepskin reaching below the knee and supported by straps over the shoulders; these had separate sleeves that could be added in winter when they were tied with skin cords at the back of the neck (these eventually became incorporated into the dress as a beaded yoke). They also wore moccasins and leggings, although these were shorter than the men's and only reached the knee, and, of course, wrapped themselves in buffalo robes – or trade blankets – to keep out the chilling Plains wind. Numerous personal ornaments were used – especially necklaces, earrings, and hair ornaments – and these were made from a wide variety of materials including bone, shell, hair and feathers, and from trade goods such as beads and cartridge cases.

Obviously there were tribal differences. Cheyenne women, for instance, wore skirts and capes after a Woodland fashion; and the cuts of moccasins were so dissimilar that an experienced tracker could tell from their imprint to which tribe the wearer belonged. Blackfoot, Crow, and Cree Indians, whose northern homelands were subject to extremely bitter winter weather,

Right: The relatively high rate of infant mortality led most Plains tribes to seek special favours from the Sacred Powers to protect their children during their early years. The Pawnee traditionally cut a cradleboard from the centre of a living tree, thus preserving the 'heart of life', and used this as the supportive base for a skin baby-carrier in which the infant would be shielded from harm. Additional protection is sought through the design carved in the upper third of the board which, as well as being a very beautiful and rare example of Plains relief carving, is a symbol of Morningstar who gave the design to the Pawnee and whose supernatural power watched over the child.

Far right: With increased mobility many tribes abandoned the heavy wooden cradleboard in favour of a baby-carrier with a lighter base of rawhide, like that which supports this Sioux example with embroidered quillwork. The actual container is made from soft skins and has four tie strings to hold the child securely. The infant would be wrapped in moisture-absorbing cotton or dry moss for comfort.

supplemented their normal dress with fur-lined moccasins and mittens, and fur caps with ear flaps; and they painted their bodies with bears' grease as an additional insulation against the cold.

The richly decorated parade and war costumes, with their paint, beads, quills, cut fringes, elk's teeth, feathers, fur and hair – some tribes occasionally even beaded the soles of their moccasins so they could be seen when they rode on horseback – were considered to have spiritual power and were never worn as a matter of course, nor were they usually taken into battle; tokens of them were carried instead. When not in use they were kept in special, painted containers that had symbolic meanings or ceremonial significance. Cylindrical rawhide bonnet cases contained the fine eagle feather headdresses, and shields were dished so that their pendent feathers could be folded back into the concave surface when placed in their covers. Numerous other bags with long rawhide strip fringes were used for other articles of importance.

During moves between camps these containers and their contents, which served as indicators of the family's achievements, were proudly carried by the warriors' wives. Long fringes mingled with the decorative trimmings of martingales and streamers of coloured quillwork were visually striking seen against the colours of the ponies, the softly tanned skin clothing of the women, and the rich texture of buffalo robes thrown over their saddles. Even the horse travois was carefully packed so that the bundles on top showed their painted surfaces.

Through visual symbols, individual and family status and achievement were immediately recognizable. Details of costume, such as the manner in which a feather was worn or the type of trimming applied to a war shirt, referred to specific acts that an individual had performed; other items, eagle feather trailers fastened to war bonnets, for instance, might refer to the achievements of a family group.

Before any of the symbols could be used, a person's right to them had to be formally accepted by the community. Personal records were exposed to public scrutiny through demonstrations and proclamations of achievement; on these an individual was judged. Honour gained through the recognition of accomplishment meant that pride – if taken to mean a proper respect for oneself, and a sense of one's own dignity and worth – permeated Plains social relationships. To be accepted on the basis of personal merit was important to every member of the tribe regardless of status, and self-respect prevented the Indian doing anything dishonourable. Honesty was honoured as much as brave and selfless acts, and honour and social position had little connection with roles of authority. In fact, even the title of chief was honorific rather than authoritative and there were generally several in a band.

The role of chief was complex, but among all Plains tribes his powers were advisory and he held his position of influence only through recognition by others of his social conscience. The Arapaho statement that 'if a chief was unsatisfactory, he was not respected or obeyed, and so gradually lost his position . . . the bravest and kindest-hearted men became chiefs naturally' [14] can be applied in a general sense throughout the area.

His responsibility was clearly defined by retiring Cheyenne chiefs when they acted as advisors to their successors:

We have advised you and placed every man, woman and child of the Cheyenne tribe in your care. When it is necessary you will help not only your own tribe, but all other Indians. You have been appointed on account of your bravery, character and courage. In the future you will cause no disturbance or help to cause a disturbance among your own people. [15]

Proven ability as a capable leader was also a prerequisite for chieftainship, and usually demonstrated by assuming responsibility for the safety of small war and hunting parties. Among the Northern Shoshone ' "little" chiefs attained their dignity by the performance of warlike deeds';[16] the Crow believed that 'prestige depended primarily on martial glory . . . in his record for war exploits he is the foremost of living men [and] in the estimation of the Crow he therefore takes precedence';[17] while the Blackfoot held that 'deeds of the warpath were essential to the production of a head man, for in them was the place to demonstrate the power to lead'.[18]

Nevertheless, a prominent chief was rarely an active warrior. As the 'guardian and defender of the social order in its broadest sense',[19] his life was dedicated to the preservation of peace and harmony within the community and his presence there was deemed essential. He could neither abrogate nor delegate responsibility; he had to stand firmly behind all he said; he had consistently to uphold every promise; and he had to act on advice after discussion with the other chiefs of the band. Whereas warriors were young men between their late teens and about thirty or thirty-five years of age, a chief was more frequently an older man of fifty or so with considerable experience in handling difficult situations.

Although he had no formal jurisdiction, he would be called as an arbiter if disagreements arose within the band. By explaining the danger to others that dissent created, he attempted to talk the antagonists into taking a solemn oath, sealed by smoking a pipe together and which neither would break, that the dispute was forever closed. In everything he proceeded by tact and persuasion. His authority rested solely on personal influence; but as a member of the council, the collective body of chiefs and prominent men which discussed matters of community concern, he played a major role in decision-making and could aspire to the position of head man. This was an outstanding chief who had assumed additional responsibilities for convening council meetings, presiding over them, and acting as their spokesman.

Though there were distinctions of rank there were no hereditary classes – although the children of distinguished men, called Minipoka or 'outstanding children' by the Blackfoot, enjoyed some privileges[20] – and while the ownership of horses and other property made a chief's position easier to attain because they could be used in practical demonstrations of his generosity, lack of them did not preclude anyone from aspiring to leadership.

Many of the tribes had virtually identical tales of Boy-Heroes in which a poor boy, entering an alien camp but too proud to ask for food, is adopted by an old woman who becomes his 'grandmother', herself too proud to accept help from others. Although both are desperately poor they refuse to exercise their right to enter any tipi in the camp, where they could be certain of receiving food and assistance, preferring to pitch their tipi apart from the others so that no one will realize their distress and pity them. At the boy's request she makes him a bow and arrows, so he can provide for them and thus not receive her aid without giving something in return. These weapons are given supernatural power and whenever the boy shoots an arrow he kills game. This means that during a period of scarcity they are able to invite all the community to eat, thus ensuring the people's survival. Eventually the boy becomes a prominent chief who protects the band.

Similar tales were regularly told to children, instilling a belief in the respect and honour that could be gained from selfless acts that benefited others, but the same attitude could be found among all age groups and at all social levels. Anyone not prepared to exert him- or herself for group considerations was looked down on. Such a person was considered pitiable or perhaps treated with contempt, but was rarely ostracized: refusal to help, even in a case of blatant laziness, went against the moral liability that the community assumed for its members. Sanctions could, nevertheless, be

Above and right: Small beaded or quilled buckskin pouches containing the baby's umbilical cord were fastened to the fronts of cradles as 'playthings' for their occupants, and worn later in life as charms to avert ill-health and ensure long life. It is sometimes claimed that the pouches were made by a grandmother during the woman's pregnancy and that their form does not therefore indicate the child's sex, but other references state that the umbilical cord was made into a charm four days after delivery and that the amulets representing lizards or turtles (right) were given to girls, while boys received those representing snakes (above). The protective power of these charms, however, lay in their contents, and although several have been placed in museum collections, nearly all were opened and had the umbilical cord removed before their owners would part with them.

brought to bear on erring members. If the admonishments and entreaties of the immediate family went unheeded, a chief would be asked to intervene. He appealed to the person's better nature, pointing out the distress that he caused his relatives and the hardship he imposed on those who had to provide for him, and resorted to public ridicule if this approach met with no success.

The strongest commonly held obligation was to one's relatives, and family ties tend to emphasize the integrated nature of Plains social life. A close family, always camping together and occupying several tipis, might include grandparents and great-grandparents, unmarried brothers and sisters, parents and children; possibly totalling thirty or more individuals, each of whom had a mutually supportive role.

Elderly members could be cared for and looked after (the horse travois making the practice of abandonment unnecessary) and their knowledge and experience made them invaluable advisors to the young. A boy gained his first experience of hunting small game close to the camp under the tutelage of his grandfather, who also made him his first bow and arrows and taught him about the myths and ceremonies; while grandmothers spent much of their time with the girls, beading dresses for buckskin dolls, making play tipis, and helping the mother instruct her daughter in the art of dressing and tanning animal skins. Like grandparents everywhere they spoiled the children, and there was a particularly close bond of affection between these generations.

Supplying meat and protection was the duty of the men, and their wives were responsible for the household and moving camp. In fact, men had little say in matters concerning the home: the woman owned the tipi, household furniture such as buffalo-robe bedding and backrests made from peeled willow rods, as well as the kettle and tripod used in cooking; the parfleche containers of dried meat were hers, as was any meat her husband secured while hunting. In spite of the subordinate female role presented to the outside world – women walked a few paces behind the men when together in public, and men wore the most elaborate and colourful costume, sat in council, became chiefs, and boasted of their sexual conquests – women ruled the tipis and wielded considerable behind-the-scenes influence in any major tribal decisions. In some tribes, where residence was matrilocal, it was the man's direct responsibility to support his wife's relatives rather than his own.

Even in patrilocal societies, marriage extended obligations to other families with whom there was an interdependent relationship that was maintained through gift exchanges and mutual assistance. This began when marriages were validated by an exchange of goods, which were distributed among the respective relatives, but could continue for several generations as a marriage was often considered to be a union between families rather than individuals and might be arranged for this purpose. Many marriages, however, were romantic ones and folklore is full of references to girls secretly making moccasins for the youths of their choice, to Arapaho men wrapping themselves in borrowed robes or blankets to conceal their identities while courting from fear that the parents would reject their advances, to visits of youthful warriors to girls' tipis when the families were asleep, to love flutes and charms, elopements, and to Blackfoot couples going 'berry-picking' together.

A general belief that it was 'good to get more relatives' endorsed the extended family. It made a number of hunters available and, in the event of their making a large kill, there were several women to prepare the meat and hides. This type of organization, in which the relatives acted together as an economic unit, was essential on the Plains where resources were plentiful in summer and autumn but scarce in winter; it was imperative that there was a large group of people with definite responsibilities who could pool their skills. Also, children could be adequately provided for, should something happen to their parents; and rarely did anyone, through age, illness or misfortune, find themselves in the position of having no close relation to turn to for assistance.

The obligations of family and relatives were clearly defined and constantly reiterated, often by reference to the spiritual powers that guided man's actions and ultimately controlled his destiny. Tabus observed by a woman during pregnancy – such as refraining from certain 'harmful' foods and not sitting with her back to the sun, the Life-giver – protected her unborn child and brought spiritual assistance not only for a long, healthy life but for one

Right and far right: Although Plains Indian children were very independent and made a wide range of makeshift toys themselves, a large number of dolls was made by indulgent old women for their granddaughters. Many of these dolls were kept into adulthood. The painstaking care and attention to detail that went into their manufacture, obvious signs of the loving affection grandmothers had for their grandchildren, are evident in the Sioux buckskin horse doll (right), which has geometric beadwork and an attached saddle blanket, and the Sioux human doll (far right) which reproduces a woman's riding equipment and adult costume with great precision.

that would be lived 'the right way': in harmony with the environment, the Sacred Powers, and with his or her fellows.

Childbirth itself, although an important event, was attended with little ceremony. The woman, assisted by midwives who may have had spiritual sanction to administer herbal medicines that eased delivery, withdrew to an isolated tipi that men, including her husband, were forbidden to enter. An appeal to the Sacred Powers on the child's behalf was made by a woman whose age gave her both the right and the duty to do this, and she preserved a piece of the umbilical cord in a small beaded pouch that the child retained throughout its life. A boy's pouch would be in the form of a stylized snake, a girl's in that of a lizard; both promoted health and well-being through association with the powers of these animals.

Thus a child entered the world under the guidance and protection of sacred forces; but it was not until a naming ceremony accompanied by ear-piercing had been performed, usually when it was a few days old, that it received a 'human' identity. The stillborn and babies that died a day or so after birth were neither named nor mourned; as 'spirit-children' they returned to the other world from whence they would be reborn. Naming also carried obligations. It was an honour to be asked to give a name and boys generally received theirs from respected warriors or men with claims to supernatural power, while an old woman of irreproachable morals and who had probably been active in tribal ceremonials was asked to name a girl;

the child had a responsibility to live up to the expectations of this noted member of the community. Some people received power to confer a name in a dream, the medium through which sacred forces expressed their wishes, and to be given this was considered particularly beneficial.

Although women rarely changed their names, except perhaps on a namesake's death, men regularly did so on the performance of creditable deeds in war and hunting or the receipt of visionary powers. Those of the men were accordingly linked with achievement: the chief's might be more dignified, and those associated with war deeds or visions were essentially different in character. Because of its personal content, and as a man's achievements were already obvious in his attitude and behaviour, it was an extreme insult to ask a person his name directly; nicknames were commonly employed among friends, and 'not to have heard a man's (real) name even before meeting him was said to reflect upon his good standing among the people'.[21]

This formal approach was also expressed in other areas of social etiquette, and reached its most exaggerated form in the practice of avoidance of particular near relatives. This was an act of utmost respect; it was made from courtesy, but strictly adhered to and demanded by tradition. Brother and sister, for example, would never be alone together after puberty and barely spoke with each other, discussing only serious matters of immediate importance, yet they were extremely close throughout their lives: he decided her marriage prospects, excercised greater influence over her future than the father, and was responsible for her protection even after she married.

A man adopted similar but more extreme behaviour towards his mother-in-law: conversation between them would be conducted through a third party, since they would neither speak to nor look at each other. During a period of crisis, however, such as severe illness, they could turn to one another for direct aid and, once the danger had passed, were free of restrictions and able to converse, although the relationship between them was never very relaxed. Other relatives that he either avoided or treated with formal respect included his daughter-in-law, wife's grandmother and female cousins; while his wife observed similar restrictions, though not so rigidly, as far as his corresponding male relatives were concerned.

With his wife's sisters and brother's wife, whom he would be expected to care and provide for if anything happened to their husbands or immediate family, his behaviour and attitude were the exact opposite. As they were 'distant wives', prospective conjugal companions as the second wives in polygamous marriages, an exceptional degree of familiarity existed between them. Familiar behaviour also governed Crow contacts between the sons and daughters of fellow clan members. These 'joking relatives' attempted to humiliate each other publicly and, even when faced with a situation showing him in such a ridiculous light that he 'felt like sinking into the ground with shame',[22] a man had never to become angry with anyone who stood in this relationship to him. Indeed, any hint of anger only served to increase the extent to which he would be subject to ridicule, and it was therefore a matter of pride not to show discomfort.

A popular story is told of such a joke played on a member of the Crow tribe's Bad Honours clan, whose name 'Bad Honours' is itself a humorous designation, and which had a reputation for foolishness.

One of them saw another Crow wearing beaded buckskin leggings with red fringes. He asked how they had been made. The owner told him to take the leggings to his wife and have her cut them after the same pattern, then he should kill a buffalo, bring its bones home, boil them till the grease rose to the top, cool the grease, plunge his leggings into it and place them under his bed on the ground. 'The next morning, when you get up, they will be just like mine.' He followed these directions, but when he got up the next morning his leggings were so greasy that he did not know what to do with them; he hung them up and sent for his advisor. When the man saw the leggings he gave him his own.[23]

It was because of this that a member of the clan, whenever he met one of these relatives, would be greeted with: 'He is one of those who boiled his leggings'.

There were often practical reasons for the joking relationship, since humiliation was one means of chastising a person for a reprehensible act or one which broke the norms of social etiquette, and in these cases it was a 'familiar' relative who had a public duty to proclaim the miscreant's wrongdoing. Even so, the point at which friendly and serious joking diverge was indistinct.

Plains social organization, then, was subject to rigid rules of propriety which demanded expected modes of behaviour between very large groups of people, but was realized through quite extreme differences and complex relationships. This was complicated further by the band system in which each of the hunting communities, or bands, was linked with several others through a common origin and together formed the tribe.

The band was a social entity: a definite group consisting of a series of families united both politically and economically under the leadership of a band-chief and council and averaging about three hundred members, although there was considerable variation on this. Each had a name, generally referring to some peculiarity of a past or present leader or of the group as a whole, which implied a bond of blood and/or friendship under which collective responsibility was assumed for the actions of any individual member. Since families were usually too small to offer adequate protection and tribes too large to operate economically for extended periods under the conditions of Plains environments, the band was the basic unit to which a person belonged.

Yet affiliation was not absolutely fixed. Through marriages there were many relatives who normally lived in other bands but could be considered as candidates for inclusion in the blood-friendship bond; the increase in band populations created situations in which some people would follow an aspirant to leadership and form a splinter group; and it was even possible for a community to founder on the death of an influential head, when its members would join their relatives elsewhere. Comanche bands actually relocated in entirely new areas and changed their names on the death of one of their prominent members.[24]

Even so, most of them had considerable stability as the closest family ties were usually within one's own group, and camps were located in definite areas; a named band under the leadership of a particular chief would occupy certain places, and others always knew where they could be found. In many ways the band supported the existence of the extended family through the protection and stability it offered, while the family established the band by voluntary adherence to its structure and leadership.

The security offered by the band was of essential economic importance in winter when unpredictable and often extremely harsh weather could make it impossible to hunt or travel. Because of this the groups moved into their winter camps before the cold weather set in and while food and fuel resources were still readily available. Various animal signs indicated whether winter would be early, and by watching these, plans could be adjusted accordingly. Many winter camps were near a 'piskun', or buffalo-jump – an abrupt cliff edge or vertical river bluff over which a small buffalo herd could be driven and killed – to ensure a plentiful supply of meat and

Right: Every man carried a decorated pipe bag made from deer or buffalo skin, which, like this Sioux quillwork bag, contained pipe, tobacco, tamping stick and 'strike-a-light'. Even though smoking purely for pleasure was uncommon on the Plains, the importance of pipe-smoking rituals cannot be over-emphasized: any act of ceremonial or social significance required a pipe to be smoked. Warriors seeking spiritual power offered smoke from the pipe to the Sacred Powers; sacred acts were solemnized by smoking, generally with elaborate codes that dictated how the pipes should be handled and in which directions they were to be passed; pipes were used to seal pacts of friendship or oaths, and to indicate commitment to join in any group activity; and even the visitor to a tipi first smoked with the tipi owner before exchanging greetings and engaging in conversation. For major rituals the sacred Medicine Pipes were used, but on other occasions the individual's pipe sufficed.

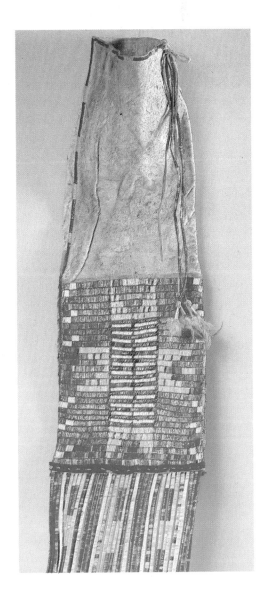

hides close at hand and to minimize the problem of transporting supplies.

Proceeds from this form of hunting were distributed evenly and the fat and dried meat from the herd, supplemented with dried fruits, roots and berries and whatever fresh meat could be obtained, formed the staple winter diet. Failure to find the herds before they dispersed in late autumn meant that the stores of dried meat would become depleted, and should this coincide with a protracted spell of bad weather the entire community could easily face the very real threat of starvation.

Winter hunting was potentially very dangerous, since a bright, clear day might be dramatically transformed if the north wind drove a blizzard over the mountains on to the Plains. Temperatures dropped sixty or seventy degrees Fahrenheit (thirty or forty degrees Centigrade) in the face of these icy winds; mists swirled before them and drifting snow so altered the features of the land, muffling sounds completely, that all sense of direction was lost.[25] When the Ma-kai-peye, or charge-storm, raged, even the dogs, used to the hardships of scavenging and capable of withstanding almost any extreme, stayed in the circles of firelight or huddled tightly against the lee sides of tipis.

Winter was consequently the least nomadic part of the year. For five months (November to March) the bands remained virtually immobile, never undertaking a journey that could not be completed by the afternoon of the same day and changing camp solely if local resources became so scarce that their survival was threatened.

The only time the bands were united in tribes was during summer, when the massed tipis of several hundred families were pitched in vast camps that were visible at great distances over the flat, open grasslands. A full council of the different chiefs and head men was then convened under the authority of a tribal head. Of course, there were variations on this generalized schema of band organization: all the Cheyenne, for example, were subject to the same tribal council of four ex-chiefs and forty current chiefs elected from the various constituent groups; whereas the Piegan, Kainah and Siksika, who are collectively known as the Blackfoot, considered themselves to be completely distinct divisions, had separate tribal heads, did not recognize any overall leadership, and were not always on terms of friendship with each other.

Nevertheless, in summer the full range of tribal social activity was evident and the band system was temporarily replaced by an exceptionally strong centralized authority. Fundamental to this authority was the control exercised by warrior societies – groups with ceremonial and militaristic roles that drew their memberships, on the qualification of age, parental affiliation or achievement, from several bands – or occasionally by clans and gentes, who were appointed by the tribal head or council to serve the community.

They were empowered to enforce order by punishing virtually any social transgression. The severity of punishment depended upon how seriously the transgressor's act affected the welfare of the group; it usually took the form of counselling, and if this failed to bring improvement, of whipping the offender or destroying his property. But the purpose of the action was rehabilitative rather than punitive, and should there be no repetition of the offence and no cause of further disturbance, the offender was reinstated as fairly as possible and given presents to atone for the whipping, and new goods to replace those destroyed.

The societies also assumed control of the summer hunt, acting on the authority of the council and with the guidance of a shaman, and no one hunted without their specific approval, since a premature move could frighten the herds from the area. Quiet was maintained throughout the camp from the moment that scouts reported buffalo nearby; dogs were

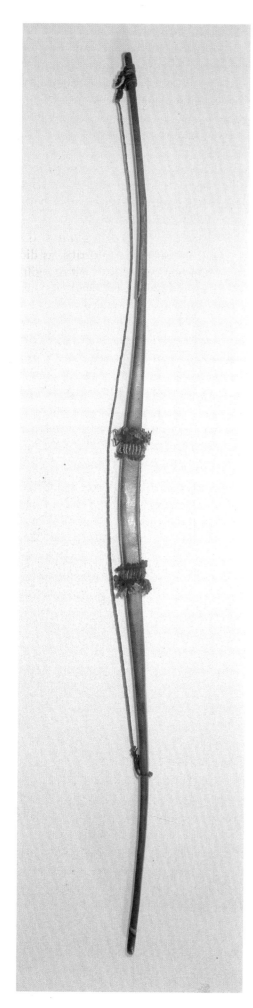

muzzled and parents charged with the responsibility for keeping young children from screaming.

Actual organization of the hunt rested with the shaman, whose ritual was associated with calling the buffalo. He was a central figure as his powers came from all the birds and animals and were believed capable of influencing the winds that drove the herds. Through concentrating his knowledge, power, and belief in the strength of his spiritual helpers, the shaman made himself answerable for the hunters' safety. This responsibility was not undertaken lightly, for buffalo hunting was dangerous and danger increased with the size of the herd; his preparations placed him in direct control of the largest hunt of the year, involving men from several bands who pitted their skills against massive numbers of animals.

The powers inherent in the tokens he employed were ancient ones that had been used in pre-horse days to assist hunters in the surround. This was a manoeuvre when they encircled the animals which, finding no direction of escape, milled around in a confused mass while arrows and lances were used against them. Although the surround on horseback was used to some extent in later years, the chase was more popular. This was a headlong rush in which man and beast engaged in a deadly game. The fast and sure-footed hunting pony, or buffalo-runner, would bring its rider alongside an enraged buffalo, remaining level just long enough for the arrow to be released, and then veer sharply to the side and safety. Leaning forward, concentration fixed on his quarry, the hunter depended for his success and safety on the runner's sagacity and skill.

These horses were special, trained from the time they were very young and selected for their courage and reliability. Training was so thorough that they reacted instinctively; it was an Indian custom to refer obliquely to the pony's ability and training by crediting it with successful kills, which reflects the almost complete dependency that the hunter had on his buffalo-runner to bring him close enough for his weapons to be used effectively.

Spiritual aid in the hunt was also sought. Particular methods of feathering, or incised and painted markings, were used on arrows as insignia of the hunters and arrowshaft-makers, ensuring straight flight and imparting the power to strike accurately. After the chase, hunters located their own kills through examining the marked arrows which symbolized their individual powers.

The bow, too, received lavish attention and careful manufacture. Frequently less than three feet overall, the Plains bow was designed to obtain the maximum power in the shortest possible length, thereby making it less unwieldy for use from horseback; in the hands of the Indian it was capable of sending an arrow completely through a buffalo. Its power was related to the tenacity of the quarry and its efficiency is amply proven as most men retained them for hunting long after guns became readily available. Many of them were of high aesthetic merit. They might be wrapped with rawhide and decorated with dyed porcupine quills or beadwork. Strips of sinew might be glued to their backs to increase elasticity before the whole was polished to a brilliant gloss; while white laminated bows of horn or antler, used by the Crow and Blackfoot and obtained in trade from tribes beyond the Rocky Mountains, were highly prized and frequently had coloured horizontal bands of quillwork, and tufts of horsehair fastened to their ends. Sometimes an additional symbolic meaning was imparted by a covering of rattlesnake skins, giving the power to strike swiftly and silently, and such weapons were often used in ceremonial contexts. Several tribes, however, valued above others bows made from Osage Orangewood, or *bois d'arc* as the first Frenchmen in the area called it, since these were light, flexible without the need for sinew backing, powerful and durable. They were often bent into a double curve which, apart from its function of adding impetus to a thrown arrow, was of exceptionally elegant form.

The significance of the buffalo hunting bow is perhaps demonstrated by the fact that many warriors carried two bows: one was purely functional with little decoration and quickly made, and therefore easily replaced; but several weeks may have been spent in perfecting the other, which was used only in the buffalo hunt or on particular, special occasions such as on parades, when it was carried as a signal mark of pride, achievement, honour and beauty.

When a hunt was over and the men had finished the butchering work, the travois would be laden with meat and hides. The women led the pack horses back to the camp, which then bustled with activity. Some of the choicer cuts of meat were given to privileged members of the tribe, in recognition of the support and assistance they gave the community: the shaman, whose powers brought success, received prime buffalo ribs, as did the chiefs who would use their shares in feasting important visitors; gifts were sent to men who had loaned ponies for the chase, and social contacts with people from other bands were strengthened and renewed.

Although a tremendous amount was immediately consumed or given away, a large quantity of meat, cut into thin strips and hung on racks that were characteristic of camps after a hunt, was dried in the sun and stored for future use; other meat was cooked and pounded together with fat, and sometimes with berries, to make 'pemmican' that would keep several months; and vast numbers of buffalo tongues, perhaps five hundred or more,

Left: The buffalo-hunting bow reflected, in a linear format, the Indians' sense of perfection and aesthetic refinement. Most powerful was the re-curved bow, which employed a double curve to increase its power so that it had enough force to send an arrow completely through a buffalo. The Crow example seen here is made from Osage Orangewood — a straight-grained timber ideally suited to bow-making but only available in limited quantities through trade — and would have been valued highly. It has sewn rawhide, a cut fringe and beadwork forming the handgrip, and a twisted sinew bowstring that would have been stretched to the right when the bow was in use. Such bows were reserved for buffalo hunting and for carrying in parades, inferior bows being used at all other times.

Right: Tipis were not only dwelling places but also symbols of home life and representations of the creative power contained within the Sacred Circle, whose form they echoed. Toy tipis were often replicas of a full-size tipi and bore similar decorations, as in this Sioux example made of buckskin with beadwork decoration and tin cone dangles.

were set aside for the ceremonies and feasts that would be held at the end of summer when the ceremonial circle-camp was formed.

Anticipation of future needs was an important aspect of summer camp activity, and the greater part of the work resulting from the hunt was in processing hides that would be finished later in the year. All the preparation was done by women, who were constantly engaged in the difficult and laborious tasks of scraping skins and removing the hair with elk-antler or bone tools, or with a heavy, flattened section of rifle barrel hafted to a short wooden handle. Treatment of hides varied from simple cleaning through to elaborate procedures of smoking and tanning that produced tones ranging from cream to nearly black.

Some untanned skins made a flexible, lightweight, waterproof and virtually unbreakable rawhide which could be used for making anything that required semi-rigid strength, from the large rawhide envelopes, or parfleches, used for storage, to shields, rattles, drums and lacing thongs. Advantage was taken of the shrinkage that occurs in rawhide to bind stone heads to war clubs, and to make wood frame saddles: the wet hide was sewn into place, completely covering the frame, and as it dried it tightened about the joints, preventing them from loosening in use. Other skins, subjected to a number of curing processes, always remained soft even after becoming repeatedly wet.

An important use of the softer hides was in making tipi covers. These needed to be replaced every two or three years, a task traditionally undertaken at the summer camp because of the large number of readily available hides. Women gathered in 'sewing bees' under the supervision of an experienced elderly woman who directed how the skins should be cut and sewn. About fourteen were required for an average-sized cover, and when these had been carefully trimmed, pieced together and sewn with sinew thread, they could be stretched taut over a pole framework to make a dwelling that comfortably housed a family of eight; larger ones were made for prominent families that entertained frequently, or to accommodate the ceremonial meetings of the warrior societies. The Blackfoot are reputed to have made covers so large they needed forty skins and could only be transported in sections; when erected for a feast or celebration this massive tipi held perhaps a hundred people.

The tipi is perfectly adapted to the Plains environment and a nomadic way of life: it is warm in winter but cool in summer, can be taken down or erected in a few minutes, weighs little and is easy to transport and simple to make, yet provides almost absolute security against the elements. Its practicality is a result of its simplicity. Although little more than a tilted cone – so pronounced in Crow tipis that they are nearly perpendicular at the rear – with a front seam that is pinned together to leave a space as a smoke escape hole before the crossing of its poles, the tipi shape encourages convection currents which can be controlled by adjusting smoke flaps – extensions of the cover on either side of the smoke hole that are moved by means of long poles fastened to their tips. This keeps the interior smoke- and draught-free, while the form of a cone allows water from sudden downpours to run off and provides no grip for strong winds that are a constant threat on the Plains. Weighted with logs or stones to prevent the pegs from pulling, a tipi will withstand gales that uproot trees.

It also had an unmistakable presence, both in its shape and in its decorations. Interior linings, which helped vent fumes by being fastened to the poles in such a way that a flow of air passed between it and the cover, were embellished with geometric patterns in paint and quillwork, or with pictographic representations of the occupants', or extended family's, war exploits. Similar pictographs were painted on the outside covers by the Sioux, while the leading edges of Arapaho tipis regularly had circular quilled or beaded

Above: Many scholars have read representative meanings into Plains Indian designs — joined triangles, for instance, are said to be 'dragonflies' and single triangles are 'tipis' or 'mountains' — yet the Indians were rarely so simplistic. Naming a design element was convenient but bore little connection with any symbolic meaning it might have. In this Gros Ventre buffalo robe the symbolism is typically subtle and abstract: viewed with the head to the left, as it would appear when worn, the robe bears sixty-eight horizontal and six vertical stripes of dyed porcupine quills which are crossed at intervals by bunches of red wool; and the decoration illustrates the fertile and productive period of a woman's life.

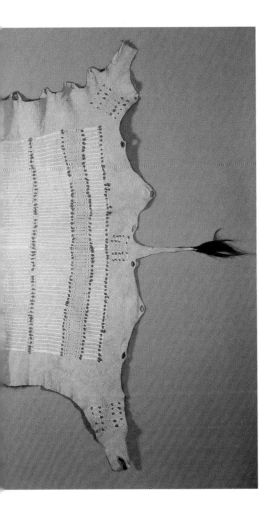

ornaments with horsehair tails fastened to their centres applied to them.

Paintings of visionary experiences, since they were symbols of spiritual powers, could only be used by people with a specific right; but even the undecorated tipi had some sacred significance and symbolized the way the Indian conceived the world. Its floor represented the earth, the walls the sky, and its poles the trails from Earth to the Spirit World.[26] The circular ground plan was to the Indian the perfect form, and many tribes cleared a space between the place of honour at the rear and the central fire that was sacred to Mother Earth and where incense – sweetgrass, cedar or sage – was burned so that its fragrant smoke would carry the prayers of the people to the spirits above.

A clear distinction was made between the summer hides used for tipis and other items that needed to be relatively fine but were exposed to continual wear – exceptionally fine work being done with thinner but less durable deerskins – and the thick, heavy winter furs that served as bedding and robes. The refinement and delicacy of beautifully worked buffalo robes illustrates the skill that was passed down through the generations. Many, bearing designs in brown and white against the off-white colour of the fleshy side of the hide, are superb examples of the art of painting on skin in which the Plains Indian excelled.[27]

Some of the finest robes, with very restrained motifs consisting purely of parallel rows of quillwork, were made by 'guilds' since quillworking was controlled by ritual sanctions and required a right to practise. The guilds were an important part of the social framework: young women became apprenticed to them and studied the intricacies of their craft – in which porcupine quills had to be dyed with plant and berry juices, or often by boiling them together with trade cloth to transfer the colour, then softened, flattened, and sewn individually into place – rising by degrees to prestigious social positions. Even when trade goods became easily available and beads replaced quills in elaborate costume decoration as they could be used to cover large areas quickly, the old guilds continued to be active and the practice carried over into the Southern Cheyenne Beadworkers' Guild that specialized in ceremonial beadwork.[28]

Although there were men and women whose superior skills were sought by others outside their own families, much of Plains design was on an intensely personal level where the 'meaning' of any particular motif was known only to the person who made it. By utilizing all the natural resources of the environment – its colours, rocks and stones, reeds, grasses, earths and clays, and the feathers, skins, furs and bones of its birds, animals and reptiles – the Plains Indians created an art form that was adapted to no-madism, and which linked them as individuals with the movement they saw expressed in the world around them.

But even though they took advantage of all these different materials and thought abstractly of the environment and its various forces as a unified whole, in practical terms it was always the buffalo that remained central to life on the Plains. In addition to its use for food, clothing and shelter, its sinews made fine cordage and bowstrings, and the hair was braided into ropes. Hammers, fleshing tools, arrowshaft straighteners, dice and gambling sticks could be made from the bones and hoofs; horns were boiled and moulded into ladles and bowls, or used as powder flasks; while skulls were important in ceremonies. A yellow paint could be obtained from the gall-stones, and this was mixed with buffalo fat for use; tails made tipi ornaments, the paunch a water bucket, while ribs were lashed together as makeshift sledges and the tips of horns formed spinning tops in children's games.

Because it provided for almost all of the needs of Plains communities the buffalo was believed to be sacred, and it was through the Sacred Buffalo that the people were able to survive.

THE WAR COMPLEX

Before the fur-trade demand for robes and pelts caused a decimation of the buffalo and beaver populations, the most obvious reason for contention on the Great Plains had been access to wood and water, since these were extremely scarce in some regions and both were essential to the survival of the nomadic communities. Because the sheltered valleys, where wood and water were available, were also gathering places for game which, although plentiful, had uncertain migration patterns, conflicts frequently developed from disputes over access to hunting areas and the preservation of hunting rights.

While these factors undoubtedly contributed to strife, particularly so when groups moved into or through new areas and utilized resources to which an 'original' occupant already laid claim, they do not in themselves give sufficient reason for the pervasiveness of a 'war philosophy' in Plains culture. A small elite body of warriors could almost certainly have acted as a strong enough deterrent to protect the interests of band or tribe, at least as far as the larger tribal groups were concerned, but instead every man was a warrior to a greater or lesser extent: if not an active one he was either an adolescent trying to achieve this status or an elderly man whose social position was largely based on his previous war record. Martial success was crucial to a man's place in society and the recounting of war honours featured strongly in ceremonial contexts. In addition, children acted out the exploits of famous men in their play, and young boys struck the carcasses of game animals as though they were dead enemies while their sisters danced with wolf and coyote hair in lieu of scalps. Elder brother encouraged younger to perform rash acts in battle for the glory this would bring, warriors boasted of the courageous feats they had accomplished, and the man with the most brave deeds to his credit was looked up to and respected wherever he went.

This suggests that the causes of war were complex and deeply rooted, and not wholly attributable to immediate material motives. Indeed, material considerations appear to recede even further into the background when the pattern of Plains warfare is looked at in greater detail: in particular by the fact that tribes as such rarely fought battles – most conflicts were restricted to the activities of individually organized war parties; but also that defensive warfare was of secondary importance, that war parties were more frequently formed in summer (though not exclusively so) when travel was easier but material pressures less acute, and that traditional 'enemies' were those tribes that could be thought of as more or less equal in strength regardless of whatever threat they represented. The Arapaho actually claim to have

Left: The eagle feather war bonnet, symbol of the outstanding warrior and a source of spiritual power and inspiration, utilized an ingenious method of rawhide strap attachments that made the feathers' movements echo the eagle's wingbeats, thus imparting the eagle's gift of graceful and noiseless approach to the wearer, in this case a Sioux warrior.

fought mostly against the Utes because they were the bravest (after themselves) and next with the Pawnees because they were the fiercest.[1]

Arapaho attitudes can be taken as fairly typical, and it was not unusual for a war party to travel a considerable distance – sometimes three or four hundred miles – to make a provocative attack in the heart of a rival's territory. Their gain, in terms of horses captured and so forth, was negligible in comparison with the effort needed to achieve it and the danger that had to be overcome. In a similar way, any acts of extreme courage – such as killing an enemy in his own camp, which was obviously far more hazardous than doing so outside its boundaries – were not only devastating blows to an opponent's morale, because they challenged their ability as warriors, but offered convincing proof of the antagonist's daring and superior skill.

In a wider context, this concept of overcoming excessive danger, of challenger and challenged, can be seen to derive from the nature of the environment where survival was threatened by potentially dangerous and certainly very powerful natural forces, and where tribal strength, if it was to be seen as an effective force, had to be continually 'tested' against equally powerful opponents. If a person, and by extension a tribe, felt himself to be weak he easily succumbed to any force that he considered stronger, whether a human, environmental or metaphysical one; on the other hand, a strong individual or tribe could resist pressures that most other people would consider intolerable.

Under constant pressure to prove himself the Plains warrior would fight bitterly if necessary, neither giving nor asking any quarter, whatever circumstance he was faced with; for many men it was preferable to die bravely rather than return alive from battle and admit a compromising defeat. The collective attitude was no different from the individual one and a community faced, say, with starvation would stubbornly cling to life, refusing to give in although all hope was apparently lost. The same stubborn refusal to admit defeat meant that encampments, though temporary, might be defended to the last man against a surprise attack. It is this assertiveness and persistent determination to win through – in many ways a will to live, to survive against even impossible odds – that characterized Plains warfare and had so many parallels in other spheres of Indian life.

War had both material and immaterial objectives: the protection of resources on one hand, and the establishment of a personal and tribal identity on the other. Thus the small war parties – which were ideally suited to the flat, open spaces of the Plains where a large body of warriors was easy to detect – went against their foes from the necessity of proving that they were able to survive as an identifiable tribal group and not from desire to reduce enemy numbers or gain a material advantage over their opponents. The Crow Indians, whose geographical position placed them between the confederacies of the Blackfoot and Sioux and in control of the richest hunting areas on the Upper Missouri, can be used as an example to illustrate this general point.

Crow attitudes were sometimes haughty and overbearing: they spoke disdainfully of both Blackfoot and Sioux, whom they considered enemies, and freely boasted of their 'victories' over them. The forcefulness of their character was in part a compensation for their being the numerically weaker group, having fewer than half the warriors of either confederacy; yet in spite of this they waged incessant war against them and also against the Northern Cheyenne, to the extent that early ethnographers expressed doubt that the tribe could sustain the losses of its fighting men and still retain an independent tribal identity powerful enough to protect its territorial claims.[2] To the Crow, however, this kind of challenge was an essential means – in fact the only means open to them – by which this identity could be retained, since it proved that they had the ability to strike back and this acted as a means of proving tribal worth as well as being a deterrent that prevented the other tribes dominating their hunting areas.

Obviously there was a minimum size below which a tribe was unable to resist outside pressures. The Gros Ventre, for example, relinquished all territorial claims and placed themselves under the protection of the Blackfoot confederacy after losing some 75 per cent of their population in a pre-1800 smallpox epidemic. Similarly the Kiowa-Apache, who had migrated through the length of the Plains with other Apache groups some few hundred years earlier and who inherited the same fierce independence of all these northern Athabascan-speakers, were forced to ally themselves with the unrelated Kiowa when the Apache tribes scattered on reaching the southern Plains. Their alliance was really a licence to hunt and camp as they wished within the territorial limits of the stronger group: they hunted freely in Kiowa-dominated country and attended Kiowa ceremonies, yet even though their population always remained small they kept their status as an independent nation and never came under the jurisdiction of the Kiowa tribal council.

Alliances between large tribes were usually very unstable and short-lived: the relationship fluctuated between periods of close friendship and open hostility, sometimes between all members of both tribes but often involving just factions within the tribes. Much of this was caused by the autonomy of the bands; it was quite common for one band to consider itself at war with another tribal group while other bands of the same tribe still remained on friendship terms.

As tribes followed their own patterns of nomadic movement and their

territorial claims expanded and contracted, the balance of power between them constantly shifted. Tribe pushed against tribe; weaker groups were forced to relocate and so brought new pressures to bear elsewhere, while stronger ones secured boundaries that encompassed larger areas.

These tensions were played out over the entire space of the Great Plains, and also affected marginal groups that entered the grasslands on periodic hunts or to trade. Consequently there was a complex and changing pattern of different pressures and struggles of varying intensities. Over long periods of time the migrations of the nations would presumably have followed the lines of least resistance, since these offered possibilities for establishing camps and settlements, and as the smaller groups formed alliances they too became party to these power shifts.

Because the band system created similar tensions within the societies, flux and motion were expressed both internally and externally. Factionalism might cause tribal splits, with explosive movements away from the original tribal centre of power, but separate groups also merged to form cohesive units that had a more significant power base. Warfare, born from and nurtured by the transient nature of Plains life, in turn contributed to the nomadism of the tribes.

Unfortunately, the Indian narratives of warfare in pre-horse and pre-gun days – mainly the reminiscences of an aged Piegan chief called Saukamappee (The Boy) of battles that took place when he was too young to have been a very active participant – are atypical and inconclusive. He does, however, describe one encounter when two equal forces met and neither could establish superiority. Apparently a large body of Blackfoot warriors, comprising several hundred men, met a similar force of Shoshone and the two groups formed parallel lines facing each other, each man concealed behind a large shield. Although the battle lasted all day, with showers of arrows released by both sides, no one was killed and when it grew dark the parties retired, neither side being able to claim a victory.[3]

Yet at the time the Blackfoot were moving into Shoshone-held hunting areas and forcing that tribe out, and presumably the Shoshone would not have left as the result of such indecisive encounters; there must have been other battles. The usual pattern of warfare was probably similar to that of the post-horse period, when continual harassment by small mobile groups of warriors could eventually have made the enemy camps untenable.

Since early information is so meagre it is necessary to look elsewhere for an example of how the assertive character of the Plains warrior was expressed in a 'war' context before the horse was introduced, as the acquisition of horses quickly became a prime motive for war exploits. This can be found in the Indian concept of 'gambling', a term they used to refer to any act or undertaking that involved risk of a loss of any kind – material or even prestige or status – and which does not have the limited and rather negative implications that it has in European society today.

The Plains Indian spoke of war as gambling and gambling as war, linking the two on the basis that superiority had to be established as proof of a person's worth through a form of rivalry that always involved potential risk. He saw this risk as being greatest when the natural balance between opposing forces was disturbed, and in either war or gambling his intention was to prove that his own resources were equal to those by which he was threatened since it was only by doing so that he could avoid 'defeat'. Defeat in an actual war situation could have fatal consequences, and by analogy it was thought a disastrous outcome to lose in a gambling game where the 'stake', although also wagered in material goods, was the warrior's own worth that he was attempting to establish beyond doubt. Just as he sought out his strongest foes in war, so he gambled with the man whose skills most nearly matched his own.

The mythological Twins, who represented or controlled the opposing natural powers such as day and night, winter and summer, male and female, also controlled the oppositions of war, of defence and aggression and of challenger and challenged, and 'comparison of origin myths discloses the primal gamblers as the divine Twins . . . always contending, they are the original patrons of play, and their games are now played by men'.[4]

All the games emphasized an individual's power and ability; for even though a society or a group of friends might assist, the actual rivalry was played out between two people – the challenger and his opponent – and war was very similar. Many men might be involved in a conflict, but the battle itself took the form of a series of individual encounters.

Gambling was clearly equated with war and one of the more popular gambling activities was the hand game, which was conceived as a warpath. In spite of its basic simplicity – the 'hiders' of one team concealed marked sticks or bones in their hands, while an opposing team guessed which held them – it involved a conspicuous show of skill and a single-minded sense of purpose. Chance was always present, even if not vocalized, since the outcome was considered to be dependent on the assistance of supernatural forces that were only indirectly under the control of the players.

The playing (hiding) team sang and 'drummed up power', beating time on a tipi pole laid on the ground in front of them, the players swaying hypnotically to the insistent rhythm peculiar to gambling songs: low, deep chants that increased in volume and intensity as the power of the team was concentrated into the hands of its two hiding members. Their words formed an echoic rising and falling pattern of nonsense syllables interspersed with taunts that were intended to disconcert the opposition's guesser. Following the song with the motion of his body, the hider moved his hands with bewildering rapidity as he deftly changed the pair of sticks from one to the other, sometimes behind his back or beneath a buffalo robe, and passed them back and forth between himself and his companion. Skill was reflected as much in the grace of his movements as in his ability at concealment and in confusing his opponent. Members of the other team sought to defeat him: 'one would recount how he took a scalp, leap upon the shoulder of the player, grasp his hair, flash a knife, etc., he all the while handling the sticks'.[5] If his war deeds were true, success being credited to metaphysical help, they would give him strength to overcome the power of his rival when 'he crossed into enemy territory to follow the trail (of the sticks) and find them'.[6]

The origin of this game is recorded in a myth where the creatures of day gamble against those of night. The day animals want perpetual light and the night animals perpetual dark, but although the sticks remain in the possession of one or the other team for long periods so it appears they will

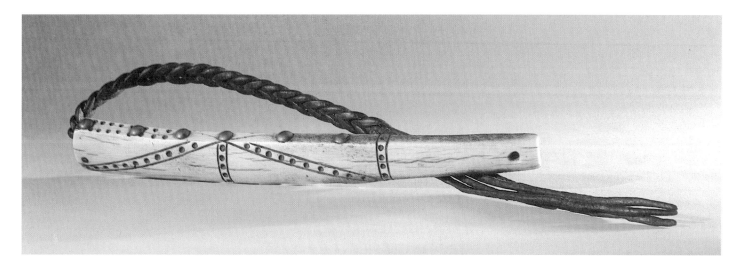

Right: Hell's Half Acre, Wyoming, is the location of sulphurous springs and site of a prehistoric piskun, or buffalo jump, with architectural evidence that the piskun incorporated a corral into which the buffalo were driven prior to slaughter. The Plains warrior often credited his success in hunting to the personal assistance of the same spiritual forces that aided him in war, and considered the activities of war and hunting to be closely related.

Left: To give him protection in battle and the ability to achieve his objectives, the warrior sought a vision in which power was granted. Horse effigies, such as this example from the Blood tribe of the Blackfoot confederacy, were often used as War Medicines to gain success on horse-raiding expeditions, when they were taken into combat strapped on the visionary's back.

win, the result is inconclusive and day and night continue to alternate. Its inconclusiveness is important because it parallels the relationship between traditional enemies: that although the balance of power shifts from one to the other, giving a context in which individuals may excel, the essential equality of the opposing forces will always, ideally, restore equilibrium.

War and gambling are also connected with hunting traditions (because hunting was also seen as a challenge and was intimately associated with survival) where spiritual powers are invoked to bring success. In one hunting tale the chief of all the buffalo challenges a man to a race in which the man will win back his wife, Buffalo-woman, if successful but forfeits his life should he lose. Although the buffalo-chief has the help of the swiftest earth animals and most of the birds and other creatures, the man wins with the assistance of magpie, eagle and hawk, all flesh-eating birds associated with war. He has power over buffalo thereafter. A second version of this tale pits Old-Man-Coyote against the buffalo-chief known as Lone-Bull, and Lone-Bull is killed by being tricked over the edge of a cliff: the origin of the piskun method of hunting.[7]

Very old traditions of many tribes associate a hunting ritual used in calling buffalo with the hoop-and-pole game, which was played as a challenge between two prominent warriors who were supported by the songs of their team mates, often fellow members of warrior societies. It was called 'mock-hunting' by the Crow, 'shooting-the-buffalo' by the Sioux, and 'buffalo-game' among the Cheyenne.[8] Young boys, playing a variant of it, actually pretended that they were engaged in a buffalo hunt. A small hoop was rolled along a course marked by a log at either end, and the players attempted to pierce or catch it on arrow-like poles. In its original form the hoop was probably a simple one of buffalo hide stretched over a frame of willow or other pliable wood, but as the game developed in complexity these became more elaborate. Many are exquisitely made, of fine delicacy, compact size and careful finish, and have from five to seven rawhide spokes, each of which is decorated with a different colour of beads, paint or quills.

In many gambling situations when a team gained a point it sang 'Crazy Dog Dance songs, songs of reckless bravery, self-abandonment on the war-

Right: This Horse Medicine, also from the Blood tribe, bears traces of the red and yellow paint that its owner received in his vision. A black horsehair scalp and two arrows with red leather points are fastened to it as symbols of power. When it was collected the owner also gave the Medicine song associated with it:
The man spoke first: You see my horse.
He has magic powers.
Then the horse spoke: I have magic powers.
I have magic powers.

path. Men careless of death sang such songs before they set out for the country of the enemy, sang such songs before they went into battle, before they broke into the enemy camp'.[9] As these songs could normally be used only by prominent and established warriors, especially at the height of a battle, they indicate the fervour of the game and emphasize its importance as a war exploit.

Perhaps the clearest instances of the war-gambling concept are shown in competitions held between members of rival warrior societies, in which the opponent was seen as an enemy and the game as war. A team combined its power, as a war party might, to gain victory but the 'fight' was essentially between two individuals; spiritual powers were invoked, often the same ones that influence war and/or hunting; boasting of war honours was an important part of the gambling, and these may have been re-enacted in mock battles; 'officials' were elected to various roles on the basis of their war records, with specific functions assigned to men who had been in analogous situations during conflicts; and defeat resulted in the losers having their prestige and status as warriors derided in songs, or provoked the organization

63

of a war party so that success could be sought and honour regained.

Gambling in these situations had an aggressiveness and fierceness behind it that comes very close to the emotion that found its outlet in war. People became caught up in this atmosphere, particularly young warriors, adopting antagonistic postures of challenge and insult which might be combined with a fanaticism that drove the individual to a point where he could gain, or lose, practically everything. The material aspects, even though a man might be left destitute, constituted but a small part of the stake: he placed his pride and his ability to stand as an equal before others against similar qualities in his opponent. This perhaps sums up the warrior's outlook on life: rising to insult and challenge, he was prepared to take the most drastic course if this gave him an opportunity to establish his identity as a warrior and to demonstrate his full potential.

Inter-society horse races held at the summer camps were typical of this type of rivalry. A prominent warrior, dressed as he had been when performing a brave deed in battle and mounted on a painted pony, made a speech in which he denigrated his rivals, claiming they were 'as nothing' and challenging them to prove otherwise by defeating his society in the race. As these were annual affairs both societies had, in anticipation, held secret trials where a fast pony with plenty of stamina had been selected, preferably one with an appearance that belied its ability so that people would be induced to wager heavily.[10]

Much of the excitement of the horse race came from the bets laid against it – which could be as high as the right to the use of a painted Medicine-Tipi; yet even families with few valued possessions wagered quivers of arrows or parfleche cases of dried meat, because the value of these could sometimes change social relationships quite drastically: by gambling away the rights to powerful spiritual tokens a man effectively gambled with his status and position.

This, of course, has an analogy with the type of losses that could be incurred in warfare; but war symbolism was also obvious and direct. The start line, for instance, was a furrow marked on the ground between two upright lances that were the insignia of the warrior societies (and which represented a vow not to turn from a challenge) or was between two piles of rocks erected by men who had used rock fortifications on a war party; while if the start was signalled with a gun, then this could only be fired by someone who had used a gun to kill an enemy.

Stamina and endurance were as essential for success as speed; over a distance of as much as four miles, several hundred yards might separate the riders at the finish: a disparity that was often credited to the illicit use of 'horse medicine', which was believed to influence the outcome by causing an opponent's mount to stumble, run slower or become breathless. Its use in this context was so feared that race horses were closely guarded for several days prior to the event to prevent its being applied. The practice of horse medicine was in the hands of horse doctors, who formed an organized cult among some tribes and, although they openly treated sick, injured or exhausted ponies and undertook selective breeding by gelding stallions, they also had secret and powerful rituals associated with war and hunting.

Bundles of herbs from which the doctors derived their power were carried into battle tied on a pony's halter, where they were known as a 'war bridle'; or a token rubbed with them and dropped in front of a herd was believed to make buffalo run slower during the chase. This method was similar to one employed in horse racing: a competitor's pony could be prevented from running past by throwing a quirt (a riding whip with a braided rawhide thong and a short handle, often of elk horn) which had been treated with the herbs in front of it, or slowed by dropping the quirt in its tracks. The same whip might be taken to war where its influence was directed against

Left: The Sioux shaved horn war bonnet and eagle feather trailer symbolized the collective deeds of the followers of a particular war leader, and the right to wear it was bestowed on the man who, by common consent, was the outstanding warrior of the group. This right was given in a ceremony at which each feather was held up while the deed it stood for was recited; the feather was then handed to the bonnet-maker for sewing into place.

the enemies' horses to delay pursuit.

In any of these contexts the metaphysical powers of the doctors, realized through the use of the herbs, were sought to impair the performance of an opponent – represented by an enemy, competitor, or a buffalo – and this is really a quite significant feature of the war complex, since it implies that a warrior's personal qualities could not be enhanced: he rose or fell as a consequence of his own abilities and skills, obtaining a degree of protection because he was assisted and guided by supernatural forces that worked to his opponent's disadvantage. As the opponent was often similarly protected, victory over him was also proof that the victor was powerful enough as an individual to overcome the weakening effect of the forces being directed against him.

The metaphysical forces that governed success in gambling could be appealed to for success in war and hunting, either directly through invoking similar powers, or indirectly by association. War was therefore part of a larger complex: it was a fight to maintain the existence of the individual, family, community and tribe, and was expressed in terms of overcoming a challenge. This philosophy governed mans' relationship with man and also with his environment; it permeated the entire social fabric.

A man's social position in the community depended largely upon his martial achievements; the bravest warriors became men of distinction, but selfless acts also gained a man honour. Bravery was recognized in speeches and narratives, or displayed through symbolic costume details and insignia, face and body paint, and in songs and dances. But it was mainly within the context of the warrior societies that a man's status was publicly acknowledged. Through a series of ranked positions, these societies both recognized achievements and conferred prestige on individuals, while membership and rank predetermined behaviour during conflict so that society organization had a profound effect on the character of Plains warfare even when the society was not directly involved.

Their nature was integrative since membership cut across band divisions and kinship units, and each of them usually had an indefinite number of lay members and a restricted number of 'officers' who directed and managed society affairs and were elected because of their exceptional bravery and courage. Affiliation was based either on age, when all members were young boys, unmarried active warriors and so forth, or on initiation, which was frequently at the society's invitation. Typical of the former, referred to as 'age-graded', were those of the Blackfoot, where a man gave property to the owner of society prerogatives in exchange for membership; the original member transferring into the next highest group. These also make evident the differing degrees of martial involvement of the various age groups.

The youngest of the Blackfoot societies (within the Piegan division of the confederacy), the Pigeons, was composed of youths who had never been members of a war party: they were 'men without power' and usually about fourteen years old, although age was reckoned in terms of achievement rather than years. It was within the Pigeons that they prepared for adulthood and the acceptance of a warrior's duties.

With the acquisition of power – usually derived from a vision – they became 'men who went to war', members of the Mosquitoes, until they had proven their ability in conflict and earned the right to join the Braves, or 'all-tried warriors'. This society was very powerful as it consisted of established, active and experienced warriors, forming the principal fighting force of the tribe.

The origin of the Braves was credited to Red Blanket and his wife Generous Woman, who missed one of their travois dogs when the camp moved. Red Blanket went back to look and met a dog-spirit which showed him the songs and dances he was to use to form the society. Because of this, members

Above and right: A degree of psychological power could be gained over invisible or dangerous forces by representing them in a visible form. On the leggings (above) and shield (right), 'tadpole' figures are painted to indicate bullets and give the user of the object protection from the weapons of his opponents. It was believed that this protective power was absorbed by the owner of the object, who did not necessarily wear or carry it in battle, provided that he observed certain ritual restrictions. In the case of the shield, the warrior's most sacred and valued possession, a tabu forbade it ever touching the ground. The painting of the bear represents the 'shield spirit' that invested the shield with the bear's supernatural power.

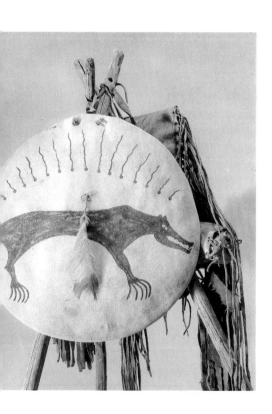

of the Braves (or Brave-Dogs) imitated the actions of dogs: they left a camp when everyone else had gone, as this animal is supposed to do, and travelled slowly so as to arrive last. This was really a mythical explanation for the practical function that members had during camp movements. Travelling behind the main body of the band or tribe exposed them to danger, since there would be no warning of the approach of an enemy, and it was their duty to protect the rear. As the groups were at their most vulnerable during moves, every member had sworn to act bravely in battle: 'a Brave-Dog must always face the enemy, no matter how much he feared them . . . he could not turn back, unless one of his relatives drove him back like a dog'.[11] It was usual for leading members to vow greater acts of courage than others, and distinctive regalia and paints were worn which indicated their position and the degree of bravery that these implied, and the society paint worn by all Brave-Dogs marked them out as among the most honoured of the tribe's warriors.

Immediately above the Braves in the Blackfoot series were the Crazy-Dogs, whose members were such prominent warriors that they are often referred to as 'chiefs'; but more powerful still were the Kit-Foxes. When parading in public they marched as a war party, and in their individual dances the members jumped from one side to the other 'because the fox never goes straight. His tail always seems to guide him'.[12] Although spoken of as a characteristic of the fox, this action was typically used when charging directly at the enemy in battle since the movement confused his aim, and by demonstrating it publicly the warriors established the fact that they had all performed this dangerous feat in a conflict.

Older men joined the Bulls, the highest in rank and from which all war bonnets are said to originate, while women might belong to the Matoki, or Buffalo society. The women's society is interesting because of the war-hunting concept and the division of male and female roles: whereas the men's dances and ceremonies emphasized war, those of the Matoki were re-enactments of a buffalo drive and their dance lodge a symbolic corral at the base of a piskun.

The Crow and Cheyenne had societies that were similar to the Blackfoot in many respects except that membership was not based on 'age', although there might be some system of grading within individual societies. Fixed affiliation meant that societies could consider themselves as equals so that more extreme rivalry developed between them than was possible in an age-graded system with its hierarchical series and changing memberships. The function of rivalry may have been to channel intra-tribe tensions into an open situation, thus preventing them being expressed in an anti-social or covert and less controllable manner that might have weakened tribal authority.

Humiliation did, in fact, function in war as a tribal and society unifier. It was used against the man who performed a cowardly act – the degree of cowardice often judged in terms of the obligations accepted with society membership – and this spurred warriors to greater bravery both for the individual acclaim and because their actions reflected on the standing of other members. Society vied with society, with the threat of ridicule if they did not acquit themselves well. The threat was a very real one: historical records and verbal traditions both suggest that minor groups with society structures were sometimes forced to dissolve through humiliation when their members did not display the fearlessness expected of them.

Other powerful groups ceased to function probably because their members were too brave. Blackfoot Crazy-Dogs had a motto: 'It is bad to live to be old; better to die young, fighting bravely in battle';[13] and the most fearless of all Cheyenne warriors became Dog-Soldiers, or Dog-Men-Warriors, with four of their number literally singled out as 'the bravest of the brave'.

With this kind of thinking governing their actions it seems likely that some societies ceased to exist because all their members had been killed.

In many ways the ideal of the warrior was one of reckless bravery since most societies included members who were 'expected to die in defence of the tribe',[14] although these men were exceptions and were idealized rather than emulated by the majority of warriors. Other men, pledged to sacrifice their lives in combat as the result of an inconsolable personal loss, actually separated themselves from the community by talking and acting 'crosswise': that is, they said and did the opposite of what they meant. Their reversed actions made them among the fiercest of Plains warriors since instead of retreating when defeat seemed inevitable they would fight more bravely.

Cheyenne Inverted-Warriors, or Contraries, had a sacred obligation to speak and act in this manner as a man became a Hohnuhk'e, or Contrary, only when Thunder, in the form of the Thunderbird, appeared to him in a dream or vision.[15] Unlike other people they were in constant readiness for battle but only watched if success seemed certain; if the warriors were defeated, however, it was their responsibility to charge the enemy and fight until they were killed or their opponents routed. It is said that their closer contact with the Sacred Powers gave the Contraries a purity of thought and action that was usually denied to man.

There was obviously a tremendous incentive for a warrior to act bravely, partly from recognition of this in society honours and partly from tribal pride in his successes, which was readily given because the tribe's reputation as an effective force that could defend its camps and hunting areas was based on individual achievement. When the prestige associated with war honours and the need to demonstrate tribal strength to ensure survival are taken together with the volatile temperament of the Plains Indian, it is certain that war parties were regularly out searching for the camps of their opponents.

War parties were far from being uniformly successful. Often one would return having failed to find the enemy camps, or because they were too strong to be safely attacked, or because the war party's presence had been prematurely detected. Perhaps one of its members had been killed and regardless of the cause of death, the mission then abandoned. It would also return to bring an injured comrade back even though no war honours had been gained. But when a conflict did occur it took place within an elaborate code of conduct that all warriors adhered to and respected, and in which an individual's success was measured in terms of the number of 'coups' he had counted.

The coup, literally a 'blow', was the basis for a formal system of progressive war honours that reflected the degree of danger a person has successfully overcome; but they were not necessarily connected with overtly aggressive acts. Among the Blackfoot 'to ride up, jerk a gun from an enemy's hand and get away without injury to either party was the greatest deed possible',[16] and the Crow recognized that 'taking a scalp was evidence of a killing but did not rank as a deed deserving special notice',[17] since it could be taken from the head of a dead foe without incurring physical danger.

The coup-proper was only one of the deeds on this scale. It was the dangerous act of touching an opponent with the hand or with an object held in the hand: often, but not essentially, with a special striped lance known as a coup-stick. When witnessed and deliberately performed – accidentally touching an enemy or striking him in the course of fighting was not a coup – it was an honour of such importance that warriors not infrequently attempted to claim coup before they made any effort at killing, injuring or disarming their opponent.

While the history of coup-counting is vague, it was highly systematized by the time Europeans arrived and was presumably practised, probably in a limited form and more in connection with war trophies, by pedestrian

Right, above: This detail from a Shoshoni painted buffalo hide gives a good indication of war costume. The mounted figure has a long feather trailer indicative of his high status, and rides a painted pony whose tail has been tied up for war, while the posture of the standing figures is suggestive of a war or society dance. Immediately in front of the rider are two men who appear to be wearing long sashes of the 'no retreat' type that show they have made vows to stand fast before an enemy.

Right, below: Among the Blackfoot, a high position in a warrior society might be marked by the wearing of a war cap surmounted by buffalo horns. Feathers taken from flesh-eating birds are used to emphasize this warrior's power of overcoming his foes.

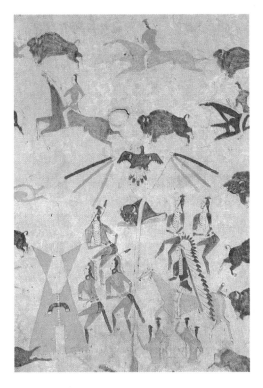

warriors. Horses may have made the coup more important: a mounted warrior dashing into the midst of the enemy's forces simply to touch an opponent hardly bears credibility in the light of European standards of warfare; but to the Indian it was an act of spectacular daring, of fearlessness, and a demonstration of superiority that struck not at the opponent's life but at his confidence and morale. It suggested that the enemy could be struck with impunity by a warrior who had no need to protect himself.

In addition, the possibility of counting a series of coups on a single enemy (they were usually counted either three or four times, in a descending order of merit), or of gaining prestige by capturing his shield, horse, weapon, or the token he carried to symbolize his spiritual helpers, and rescuing a fallen comrade, all of which were ranking war honours, meant that each man was acutely aware of events happening elsewhere at the battlescene even though he fought as an individual. This kept the fight concentrated, and warriors were able to support each other; yet it also meant that there were numerous instances of men, having fought and killed an opponent, losing their claim to honour when a fellow tribesman formally touched the body and counted coup before them.

The principle of counting coup and the general pattern of a war party is described in a tale called 'The Boy and his Horse' in which a poor boy has a vision where he obtains from a rock a wonderful (supernatural) horse. Although worthless in appearance, it has the ability to transform itself into a grey war pony that enables the boy to perform miraculous deeds.

On his first war party the warriors tried to make him go back because his weapons were poor and he only had an old horse, but the boy insisted on following them until they reached an enemy camp where forty warriors were selected to make the first attack; the main body of men waited in the ravines, ready to rush out and terrify the enemy should the forty be pursued, while the women waited elsewhere, the boy with them. He took an opportunity to slip away unnoticed; his horse transformed into the war pony, and when the warriors lined up waiting for the command to charge the boy joined them, unrecognized.

When they charged he passed everyone, was first to enter the village, struck an enemy wearing a war bonnet, and then returned to the women where his horse resumed its old form. The women thought he had been there all the time, and when the war leaders called everyone together after the battle to ask who it was that struck the enemy with the war bonnet, another man, who also had a grey horse, claimed that he had done so. A friend of this man had touched the enemy with a club just after the boy knocked him down and claimed a coup.

Returning to their village, the warriors performed a sham battle so that the people who had remained behind would know they had been victorious; they gave their war cries, sang war songs, and rode up to the village where the war leaders announced that a man had knocked down an enemy wearing a war bonnet and that another had counted coup. The whole camp sang and danced for these two warriors. During that night the boy had a dream in which his horse told him he would go on four successive war parties and in each would gain greater success than in the preceding one.

On his second war party he was again mocked because of the poor appearance of his horse, but once more it transformed itself and he was first to reach the enemy, killing one man just outside and another in the camp with his spear. Two other men claimed his honours, and the people rejoiced because an enemy had been killed in his own camp. The boy dreamt again, and this time his war pony told him to paint a downy eagle feather yellow and to take the paint with him when he next went out with a war party.

A council of war was called and they decided to make another expedition.

This time the boy painted his horse: on the shoulders, hips, ears, and a little at the root of the tail; he also painted his own body and his spear. Again he was first at the camp, killing two men near the village and another in the village itself, before returning to where the women were hidden. When the war leaders asked for claimants for the boy's deeds several men stepped forward. The one who claimed the honour of killing the enemy in the village was given first place.

At the fourth war party, again the boy rode in first, his horse painted yellow, killing several enemies; then he went to the south of the village where his horse neighed and all the ponies in the camp broke their ropes and ran to him. The loose ponies also came and the boy drove this great herd back to where the women were waiting. This time everyone saw him and realized that it was he who had been performing the great deeds. When the chiefs heard about this they called a council, where the boy claimed his honours and was made a chief. Although they sent for the man who made the false claims, he knew the honours were not his and would not come, and shortly afterwards he fell sick and died.[18]

This tale sheds light on a number of typical features of a war party: the warriors attempt to dissuade the inexperienced and poorly equipped boy from participating; a camp is made immediately before the attack and a select group of proven warriors is chosen to enter the village, the others remaining behind to offer support if necessary while non-participants are hidden in a place of safety; there is a rendezvous after the battle (so the party can return in a body) where honours and coups are claimed and distributed; a mock battle takes place before a triumphant entry to the home village, when the warriors act as though they are attacking it – giving war cries and singing war songs; and the war leaders announce each man's honours which are then celebrated by the whole tribe. It is unusual only in that it exaggerates the number of false claimants to honour and that women accompanied what were exceptionally large war parties (which is contrary to the general practice of small war parties consisting only of men).

The customary roles of various 'authorities' are also specifically stated: the chiefs remain behind in the camp and form a chiefs' council which has power to confer the civil honour of chieftainship; whereas the war council's function is to organize the war party. The war leader has jurisdiction over the warriors when they are away from the camp, and his duties are concerned with the safety of the whole group. In battle itself the individual turns

Above: The supernatural power of the bear is reflected in a Blackfoot knife which has a single-edged metal trade blade set into a hilt made from half a bear's jaw. Although referred to as a scalping knife, this type of heavy-bladed knife also served as a utilitarian tool on the warpath for a variety of purposes, including skinning game, as an eating implement, and for cutting wood and brush. The superb sheath is decorated with dyed bird quills, which were used earlier than porcupine quills, and it has a leather fringe to which metal cones have been attached.

Above, right: This Crow shield, which bears a black-painted bear paw as a symbol of its maker's patron, is made from the tough neck skin of a buffalo bull. Shrunk with heat until extremely dense, the hide could stop an arrow or spear thrust and, used skilfully, could deflect bullets from muzzle-loading rifles. With the advent of more powerful breech-loading guns the shield's practical use as a defensive weapon became less important, and warriors relied more on the protective power of the painted vision image to ward off the enemies' bullets.

for protection to his spiritual helpers: the boy (and we can assume this held for the other warriors too) paints himself, his pony, and his weapons in accordance with instructions received in a dream (vision). Warriors compete to be first to enter the opponent's camp, 'first place' goes to the man who kills an enemy in his own village, and honour is attached to striking the man wearing a war bonnet (which indicates his high status as a leading warrior) even though someone else claims coup, while the killing of other men is given much less prominence. Taking horses is also classed as a war honour. It is significant that the highest ranking acts were those that indicated a warrior's 'power' rather than those that materially damaged his opponent. A false claimant, however, is called to account and shamed: he falls sick and 'dies', which symbolically states that his status as a warrior – which implies honour, reliability and honesty – is no longer recognized.

In many similar stories the characteristic and distinguishing attitudes, actions and beliefs of the Plains warrior are consistently revered; they were narrated in front of children, giving social approval and encouragement to younger generations to emulate the achievements of 'heroes', since the more avidly these aims were pursued at an individual level then the greater the tribal reputation as a deterrent power and the stronger its ability to ensure tribal security.

A war party was generally initiated by the war leader, who usually wanted to go to war for some personal reason and gathered whatever support he could from among the tribe's warriors; on expeditions involving large numbers of men he may have been chosen and appointed by the war council. As the number of supporters was almost entirely dependent on this man's reputation and popularity, the size of war parties varied very widely. To fulfil his role he required spiritual sanction which was obtained by seeking and obtaining a vision that guaranteed the safety of the men in his charge, for which he would be held accountable. Since war was always conceived as an opposition of forces, both natural and supernatural, so the war leader could not hope to lead his men to success unless he had spiritual asistance that was greater than the power of individual warriors.

The warpath was thought of as the sacred (ceremonial) red road and before anyone could follow this path they formally had to leave the white road of peace, on which violence was inadmissible.[19] On leaving their home village the warriors therefore set up a new camp, perhaps erecting only a single token tipi, which marked their withdrawal from the community. This camp also acted as a meeting place for the party's participants and it was here that the first wolf (war) songs were sung and where tabus governing actions between the members and safeguarding their relationship with the Sacred Powers came into force.

As the tabus prevented the warriors from becoming angry, engaging in dispute, or using harsh language, they had a practical function in quieting any dissension that might arise during the warpath, which was fraught with danger and where feelings often ran high. They remained in force until the warpath was formally closed when the participants returned to their own village and resumed the path of peace.

A second ceremonial camp was set up when they entered enemy territory as a request for supernatural guidance that would lead them to their objective; and a third, which symbolically asked for additional assistance at the moment of greatest danger, was made immediately before the attack. It was at this pre-raid camp that individual warriors appealed to the Powers who had appeared in their visions to grant the protective power they had promised, and applied the war paint that was considered the personal gift of the Sacred Powers.

The attack varied from waiting about the outskirts of the camp for any

opportunity that presented itself to lightning dawn raids and pitched battles; but the objective was always limited and there is no evidence that any war party, having carried out an attack, even though this may have been on an enemy group met by accident and whether successful or not, ever proceeded further to locate a second encampment. To Indian logic the conflict was decisive: success established their supremacy and there was nothing to be gained from further hostilities; while defeat, even the loss of a single man, broke the ceremonial order of the warpath – which built to a climax in success not defeat – and necessitated their return.

Although the general procedure was similar, distinctions were made between different types of war party depending on the amount of ceremonial organization required: the more the tribe as a whole was involved then the greater the ceremony. Two basic forms were distinguished: the scalp raid and the horse raid. Motivated by social pressures to gain credibility as a warrior a man had little choice but to join a war party at some time in his life, even though this was entirely voluntary, and when he did so he either went to war to kill enemies or to take horses.

Scalp raids were held irregularly and might be separated by periods of several years as they were usually initiated on the death of a close relative, not necessarily as a consequence of enemy action, and were intended to alleviate suffering and end a period of mourning. The war leader and many members of the war party were often mourners and revenge may have motivated them, although it is unlikely that this was ever the main reason since punitive warfare over extended periods was completely unknown. In fact, with the exception only of the Sioux and Cree, the scalp (indicative of a killing) was subordinated to other forms of war honour. A Blackfoot warrior, for example, when recounting war achievements, spoke of the number of coups counted and the ponies and guns he had captured but rarely mentioned scalps; while the number of scalps taken was not usually a measure of a man's prowess. It is therefore necessary to look more closely at the meaning of the scalp to understand why these raids took place.

The scalp, a small circular patch of hair from just behind the crown of the head, from the centre of which warriors braided a narrow lock of hair (the scalplock) that was hung with beads, feathers and spiritual tokens as a provocative challenge to an enemy, was synonomous with a person's identity or soul: it represented the immaterial or metaphysical part of his being. The capture of a scalp was therefore proof of spiritual rather than physical death, and although the taking of this hair trophy, by running the point of a sharp knife around the patch of hair and tugging violently to loosen the skin by which it was attached, was extremely painful it was by no means fatal. People who had been scalped alive were greatly feared as the 'living dead'. Attitudes varied, but it was rarely that a person who had been scalped and survived could be re-integrated into the society since his or her identity as a living human had been taken.

Their captured soul could be taken into the enemy's village, in the form of the scalp, when it became servile to the group's own deceased in a 'spirit world'. In effect it was a spiritual replacement: one 'death' was replaced by another, or several if the deceased's status warranted it, and suffering was alleviated by making the enemy suffer instead. Placed on the graves of the recent dead or given to bereaved widows, scalps symbolically ended a period of mourning and might then be either discarded or retained to serve a secondary purpose – as war charms which gave the holders power over the souls of their enemies. Stretched on wooden hoops, many are delicately trimmed with beads or quills and hung with copper cone pendants and claws from birds of prey.

Mourning sometimes took violent forms. In the depths of sorrow, widows and widowers would gash themselves with flint knives, cut their hair, wear

Above: When on the warpath, the leader of a Crow war party would regularly sit apart from the others and smoke the pipe he carried, in an attempt to establish communion with the Sacred Powers whose advice he sought. Horse hoofs marked on the tubular bowl of this example indicate that it was used during horse-raids.
Right: Shields generally had soft buckskin covers which might themselves have supernatural power. This cover, made by the Plains Cree in about 1820, gave protection through pictographic images of the owner defeating his opponents, and might often have been carried into battle instead of the heavier shield.

old clothes and generally neglect everything: forgetting to eat, not caring about their appearance, letting the blood from their wounds dry on the skin, and having no regard for their own safety. Some had to be physically restrained from taking their own lives or those of others, and it was often in this situation that a man swore vengeance and formed a war party.

Yet, strangely in view of the extremes to which mourning might be taken and the idea that captured souls served those of the deceased, there was little concern with what happened to the soul after death. Although there was a universal belief in some form of after-life, the dead, when their fate was given any thought, were generally supposed to exist similarly to the living. Elaborate ceremonies, however, might be held to hasten the departure of the souls of prominent chiefs and warriors. Catlin was told of one particularly important Omaha chief, named Black Bird, whose burial ceremony complied with his request

to bury him on the back of his favourite war-horse, which was to be buried alive, under him . . . He owned, amongst many horses, a noble white steed that was led to the top of (a) grass-covered hill; and, with great pomp and ceremony, in presence of the whole nation, he was placed astride of his horse's back, with his bow in his hand, and his shield and quiver slung – with his pipe and his *medicine-bag* [a skin bag containing tokens of supernatural powers] – with his supply of dried meat, and his tobacco-pouch replenished to last him through his journey to the 'beautiful hunting grounds of the shades of his fathers' – with his flint and steel, and his tinder, to light his pipes by the way. The scalps that he had taken from his enemies' heads could be trophies for nobody else, and were hung to the bridle of his horse – he was in full dress and fully equipped; and on his head waved, to the last moment, his beautiful head-dress of the war-eagle's plumes. In this plight, and the last funeral honours having been performed by the *medicine-men* [shamans], every warrior of his band painted the palm and fingers of his right hand with vermillion; which was stamped, and perfectly impressed on the milk-white sides of his devoted horse.[20]

The band's interest was in ensuring him a safe spiritual journey and not in any future existence that he might enjoy. The Plains Indians' concern was with the living: even the taking of a scalp was a confirmation of life – at least from the taker's point of view – rather than an involvement with death.

Horse raiding had a different purpose – to take horses – and was subject to less rigid ceremonial control than scalp raiding, partly because it involved smaller parties of warriors who attempted to enter and leave an opponent's camp undetected, but also because it had less spiritual significance. Much has been made of the horse raid's economic motive, and while it is true that this was of importance to younger warriors who needed to accumulate herds with which they could back a rise in social position – and who, indeed, were the most active raiders as a result of this impetus – there were many men who participated even though they had more than sufficient ponies for their needs. Neither would economic reasons alone justify the frequency with which such raids took place. A nineteenth century account states that 'except during the bitterest weather of the winter, war parties of Blackfeet were constantly out, searching for camps of their enemies, from whom they

Left: Crow Heart Butte, Wyoming, receives its name from a legend in which the heart of a fearless Crow warrior was impaled on a stick by his opponents, and carried before the Crow war party to intimidate them. It has been the scene of many tribal battles and the setting for numerous narratives of war exploits.

might capture horses'.[21] This may overstate the case, but it does make it obvious that horse raids were regular occurrences unlike the periodic raids for scalps.

An Indian quotation shifts the emphasis from simple acquisition. They spoke of 'taking' and said that 'taking a horse is not the same as stealing it. We took horses from our enemies; it was a challenge in the same way as fighting them. They would do exactly the same to us. They challenged us and tried to prove themselves too'.[22] Horse raiding was seen, to some extent, as another method by which the warrior gained superiority over his enemies and proved his ability to meet a challenge.

There was also a strong element of honour involved. Buffalo runners or war ponies were picketed outside their owners' tipis at night where they could be protected from raiders. It was a tremendous affront to a warrior's prestige and self-respect to have his highly trained and favourite horse taken literally from the threshold of his home, and without it his ability to hunt and fight was seriously disadvantaged.

The man who took it obviously acquired much more than an ordinary horse, for the buffalo runner's proven abilities and intensive training made it worth a dozen other ponies which could be easily run off from unguarded pasturages outside the camps. In fact, most horses secured on raids were run off from these pasturages by inexperienced warriors – when even a small party could take as many as one hundred head – while only the most highly regarded men actually entered the camp.

The prominent warriors emphasized their achievements by narrating tales of their own war experiences, many of which were lively accounts of heroic deeds and narrow escapes. Henry and Thompson, who witnessed such story-telling at the turn of the eighteenth century, wrote that the Piegan took such delight in relating their adventures in war, and the details were so vivid that they seemed to be fighting the battle over again. These stories were always told as re-enactments, so they gave an exaggerated view of successful war exploits. The wealth of tales gives an impression of an aggressive and hostile nature, whereas we now know that many tales were handed down through the generations and the narrator may have had no involvement in the conflict that he spoke of as having just taken place.

Although there are reports of great brutality from the Plains — of dismemberments, mutilations and horrifying treatment of the corpses of enemy dead, practised by Indians against both Indian and white victims — most of these are from a time when the tribes were being affected by the advance of Europeans who brought previously unknown diseases, especially smallpox and measles, that swept through the Indian nations and killed vast numbers of people within weeks. Often, before the tribes had recovered from one onslaught, disease hit them again. This caused an imbalance between the tribes and broke the natural relationship they had with their environment. When the white frontier then pushed tribes to the west, they became reactionary and hit back with an aggressiveness and hatred that was alien to their culture.

That this wave of aggression affected contacts between tribes and was not solely directed at white intrusion was simply because the Indian was making a desperate stand against a situation that was not of his choosing and which he could not control. It was made more intense by the fact that he was being pushed into ever smaller areas, and it was from this that brutality and destructiveness were born. Yet, somehow, he managed to retain his belief that war was a sacred activity, although it now became channelled in new directions which give an impression that it was conceptually separated from other aspects of life, and rested uneasily with a belief in harmony, balance and the inherent goodness of the natural world.

This had not always been so, and war was previously integrated completely into the cultural ethos – its ceremonial organization, coups and war honours, the roles of warrior societies and individuals and their conduct and attitudes, the regalia and insignia, tokens of supernatural patrons, and its connection with hunting and gambling, were all directed towards the single goal of meeting the challenge of survival. With survival threatened so drastically and severely, it is not surprising that energy was thrown wholeheartedly into a war effort to meet this challenge and overcome it.

Left, above: This pictograph of a horse raid contains a wealth of ethnographic data. A Medicine headdress of buffalo horns is shown at lower left; the warrior at upper left has a 'stand-up' bonnet of a type associated with the Horn Society and originating among the Blackfoot; and the upper figure at centre right wears a single exploit feather.

Left, below: The fine texture of the human hair on this scalp, which has been stretched on a wooden hoop, suggests that it was taken from the head of a child. White beads used on the reverse to form a Morningstar symbol point to a ceremonial significance.

Below: This unique Sioux horse effigy depicting a war pony was probably carried in celebratory dances by a successful warrior. Carved holes are marked in red paint to imitate bleeding bullet wounds, indicating that the effigy was used to honour a favoured horse wounded in battle.

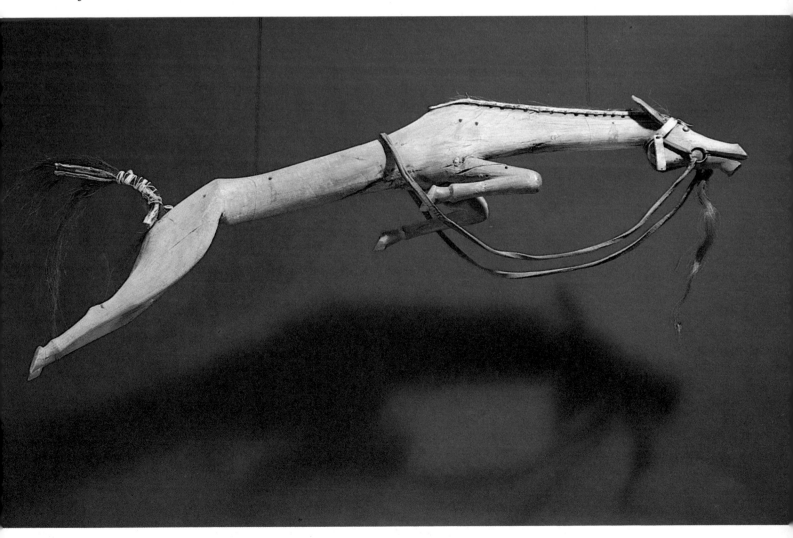

MEDICINES
AND MYSTERIES

Potent metaphysical forces governed and regulated everything in the Indians' world. They resided in the land, the skies and the waters and manifested themselves in various ways: some were tangible and visible, as in the strength of a Plains thunderstorm or snow blizzard; others were subtle, invisible and immaterial, contained in a breath of wind or a shadow. They might be as minute as a grain of sand or as large as the universe; they could be solid and unchanging, as rock, or constantly appearing in different guises or making their presence known through animal intermediaries. All were mysterious powers that transcended the ordinary and were beyond normal understanding; man could, however, communicate with them by living in a sacred manner, through following the prescriptions and proscriptions laid down by the Sacred Powers in dreams and visions.

Faithful adherence to the dictates of the Sacred Powers brought a deeper knowledge of the mysterious nature of the world and closer communion with the forces that controlled it, resulting in benefit in the form of a receipt of power. Power was everywhere and in everything, for without it nothing was able to exist. Although the power granted to man was held by individuals it was expected that it would be used for communal good: to promote the health, well-being and spiritual strength of family, kin, friends and nation by the performance of sacred ceremonies and the observance of ritual tabus.

So essential was this to both individual and community that Captain Bonneville, who travelled among the north-western tribes in the early days of the fur trade, commented:

> Simply to call these people religious, would convey but a faint idea of the deep hue of piety and devotion which pervades the whole of their conduct. Their honesty is immaculate; and their purity of purpose, and their observances of the rites of their religion, are most uniform and remarkable. They are, certainly, more like a nation of saints than a horde of savages.[1]

Left: Landscapes like this — Medicine Mountain in Wyoming — inspired the Plains Indian, who sought in them a metaphysical explanation for human existence. It was on such mountain peaks that spiritual forces manifested themselves in visions; and it was here, too, that Indian relics, graves and memorials bore evidence of the spirit-contacts of past generations that ensured growth, prosperity and harmony for the generations that would follow.

The reason for the devotion that struck Bonneville so forcibly was that life itself was thought of as sacred: to be lived, and sometimes sacrificed, in exercising the power that man had been given. The manner in which this was done was deeply personal and varied from simple private observances to ritual acts involving large numbers of people from different bands. However, when French trappers first made contact with Plains societies they saw power being used by shamans in a very obvious way during curing ceremonies and, drawing an analogy between the shaman and their own physicians, called it *médicine*, a term which came into general usage to refer to power in any of its forms, whether connected with cures or not, and which can best be translated as 'mystery' or 'life-force'; although it should be borne in mind that even inanimate objects, since they have a metaphysical

Above: This canvas altar, which would formerly have been made of painted buckskin, is part of a Blackfoot Horse Medicine bundle used during ceremonies intended to increase wealth in horses or as part of a horse-doctor's secret rites. In use, the red half was placed to the north to represent both this direction and day time; the south was black to symbolize night. Sweetgrass incense was burned on a horsetrack marked outside the north-west corner of the square, so that the bundle's contents could be purified in the smoke, while the four feathers, symbolizing the four directions and the Sacred Powers who govern these, were painted red and black. Horse Medicine rituals were very sacred and only the horse-doctors and their wives were admitted to them; the right, or guest side of the tipi remained vacant during the ceremony.

Right: The eagle was the most sacred of all birds, and features frequently in ritual contexts as a Medicine Power. It was via the eagle that human wishes were conveyed from the Earth to the forces occupying the sky realm. The Crow eagle headdress (above) was probably a personal War Medicine that had been revealed in a vision. Although other birds and animals were also used for this type of headdress (depending on which creature had acted as messenger in the vision), to receive power via the eagle was thought to be particularly beneficial. The eagle wing fan (below) formed part of a Crow shaman's ritual paraphernalia. During cures the fan was employed to call on the eagle's sacred power for assistance.

existence, possess power. There is consequently a distinction between the Indian meaning of Medicine and our restricted application of a similar term to specify medical practice and healing.

The concept of medicine-power wove its way into every corner of the social fabric, and is basic to an understanding of the way the Indian viewed his environment and his relationship with his fellow-man, the birds and animals, natural forces and the supernatural world. Underlying the concept was a belief that the world was created in harmony; that all its oppositions were, in a perfect state, naturally and evenly balanced, and that man had a responsibility to maintain this balance by correctly carrying out his spiritual obligations. Failure to observe these, whether by accident or intent, resulted in imbalance and disharmony: offending the Sacred Powers, who brought retribution in the form of illness, disease, famine or disaster. Harmony had then to be restored and the imbalance corrected by placating the disturbed forces and counteracting the evil influence. From the belief in a perfect balance, it follows that a purely evil spirit could not exist since it would introduce an element of permanent discord. Actually each of the forces had a capacity for bad as well as good, but were generally beneficent.

The strongest of these forces, or Medicine Powers, was also the most vaguely defined. It existed simply as a nebulous source of creative energy that never appeared in visions and did not give power directly to man. Its identity is confused. The Blackfoot, for instance, often personified this supreme power as Napi, or Dawn-Light-Colour-Man, while the Crow referred to it as Bahkoore-Mahishtsedah, which literally means That-Above-Person-His-Eyes-Yellow, but also knew him as First-Worker; and both Napi and First-Worker may be spoken of as Old-Man.

However, the Crow state quite clearly that 'the people of old times referred to the Sun as Old-Man; he was the Supreme Being'[2] and the Blackfoot conception of the Sun was as 'the great centre of power and the upholder of all things [it was] the Blackfeet's supreme object of worship'.[3] From this we might assume that the Sun and Old-Man are the same and are identical with a benevolent creative Medicine Power; but a Blackfoot tale denies this by saying 'there was once a Great-Spirit who was good. Then Old-Man came along'.[4]

The separate existence of Sun and Old-Man is confirmed in ritual attitudes. Sun is the primary object of devotion, although not always directly addressed, whereas Old-Man is never invoked in prayer; and Sun is rarely believed to be anything other than absolutely good (in myth he might attempt to use his power, not always successfully, in punishing the people for showing disrespect), while Old-Man has a reputation as a trickster and is especially noted as a seducer – it is often said that a man who continually chases women is trying to be like Old-Man. The many different antics the tales credit him with reveal him as 'powerful but also impotent, full of wisdom but at times helpless . . . a combination of strength, weakness, wisdom, folly, childishness and malice [that] encompasses all the virtues and sins of mankind; he is not considered to be perfect, but has all human characteristics'.[5]

It appears then that Old-Man and Sun may be dual aspects of a single Medicine Power. Old-Man is seen organizing the world and initiating human frailty, and perhaps giving a purpose and power to all living things; while Sun, as an obvious symbol of light and a life-giving force, acts as a renewing power that ensures man's existence and survival. In addition this theory has the advantage of linking both the Crow concept that Medicine derives from First-Worker and the Blackfoot concept that it is *natoye*, of the sun, with the tenets of other tribes such as the Cheyenne, who believed that all power came from Maheo, the Great Mysterious One, and the Sioux, who held that the supreme power was Wakan Tanka, the Great Medicine.

Although the details may be complex and elusive, the principle is quite simple; all power traces back eventually to a single obscure source, which may or may not be named, and that as it emanates from this source it divides and subdivides almost indefinitely.

This principle was set at the beginning of the world, when the creative force placed something of himself in each part of his creation. He made the Earth feminine, directing her to be the greatest power in the lower world where she was to give sustenance to all growing matter and to the animals and creatures that lived on and within her. Her power was balanced by the Sky, a masculine force whose warm rains were carried by the sacred messenger Thunder to impregnate the Earth, from whose body sprang the grasses and trees that grew to maturity under the life-giving rays of the Sun. Sun's counterpart was the Moon, the ruler of the night skies, and when the tangible world was finally formed it paralleled the intangible supernatural world that lay beyond it.

The creation was made harmonious and all its separate parts interdependent so that they reflected the many facets of life that flowed back to form unity in the creator's own being, which was the seat of absolute harmony and, according to the Crow, consisted of all the vaporous elements that existed before the world was made. He then sent Old-Man (or Sun) to give the world the form by which people would know it. According to myths, which give symbolic form to beliefs rather than literal explanations, when Old-Man arrived on Earth he found it covered with water; the only living creatures were the ducks which he sent to dive for mud. The Blackfoot claim that the ducks were successful on their fourth attempt and that it was from this mud that Napi made the land before creating people. Crow tales state that First-Worker heard Wolf and Coyote howling but did not create them, and that these animals were powerful because they attained life without his help. He also saw a shining object on the ground and discovered it was a medicine stone and said that 'this is a part of the Earth, the oldest part of the Earth. This is a separate being, no wonder he is here already and is able to reproduce himself',[6] and this is the reason that stones cover the world.

A soul or spirit was given to each animate and inanimate thing which thereby had a spiritual as well as a physical existence; the soul was placed in the keeping of the immaterial powers while the body returned to Earth from which it was born. The only exception was the stone, since it was already part of the earth. In this way all the Sacred Powers were given different responsibilities, and their characters were linked with the animals, plants and so on over which they had charge. When the world was completed it was the likeness of the creative force which was the Universe Itself and everything within.

The way in which the responsibilities of the Sacred Powers were defined is extremely complex, but in essence the creative force or Great Medicine was believed to have four primary divisions, each of which contains four powers. The Sioux differentiated these as a Superior Power, its Associate Power, a Subordinate Power and a Spirit-like (although not a Sacred Power, the Spirit-like shares some Medicine characteristics). Because of this the Sioux shaman's name for the Great Medicine is *Tobtob Kin*, or four times four: it is four times four Powers which, considered together, are one.

An interesting comparison can be made here with the theories of the distinguished Swiss psychologist Carl Jung. Jung's work showed that the 'nucleus of the psyche normally expresses itself in some kind of four-fold structure' in which the 'invisible' part of a person's character (the anima) develops through four distinct stages; and that 'four times four represents totality'.[7] But the Plains Indians apparently have a four-fold structure that represents a collective rather than individual psyche and there is an active

81

Above: Few Plains animals matched the grizzly bear for strength and ferocity, and the warrior who received a vision of a bear was thought to acquire similar strength in the heat of battle. A female bear in an appropriately aggressive stance, with the head of a second bear emerging from the red field on the lower half of the shield, is shown in this Crow vision painting. The red hand coming from the bear's mouth may be a symbol of war, while real bears' ears are attached to the shield to provide a direct association with the physical manifestation of this supernatural animal. Attachments of this kind were sometimes removed and loaned to a member of a war party who had approached the shield owner with a request for spiritual help.

translation of the invisible into visible terms: the unconscious is effectively made conscious through Medicine.

The four divisions of the Great Medicine demonstrate this in a very practical way since they govern much more than spiritual attitudes. Sun (which is more powerful than the Sky even though it receives its own power from this source) is the Superior Power in the first division and all other Powers are consequently secondary to the Sun. It controls the four great virtues – bravery, fortitude, generosity and fidelity – and, through its Associate, Subordinate and Spirit-like, all the primary forces, drives and actions of man. Its symbolic colour is red, which is the Sacred Colour; and as the potency of the Sun is in fire and cannot be contained within anything else, it can not therefore be imparted to anything.

Skan, the Sky, is Superior in the second division from which all forms of power and movement are derived, and where the secondary drives and the qualities of the senses are controlled. Accordingly it contains the patron of directions and trails as well as that of wisdom, Medicine and magic. Its Spirit-like is the *Niya* which accompanies a person 'like a shadow' through life, with death as the consequence of its departure. Blue is the symbolic colour, and because of the importance of Skan this colour can only be used in a sacred context by an exceptionally powerful shaman.

In the third group is power to bring things into being and over those material things on which man is dependent. Earth, the All-Mother, who is ancestor of all material objects except the Rock and patron of everything that grows from the ground, of food and drink, and of the tipi, is the Superior. Her colour is green. Associated with the Earth is the Feminine, who harmonizes and mediates between man and the Sacred Powers, and the Four-Winds is the Subordinate, which acts as the Sacred-Messenger. The Feminine and the Four-Winds should always be addressed first in ceremonies since it is through them that mans' communication with the Powers is made possible. *Nagiya* is the Spirit-like in this division, and is the immaterial part of all material things other than man.

The Rock, or All-Father, is Superior in the fourth division, and is the spirit through which power is administered. He is the symbol of permanence, the patron of authority and vengeance, and of construction and destruction, and his symbolic colour is yellow. His Associate, *Wakinyan*, is the Winged or Thunder-Being that protects warriors, and as he is anti-natural he must be addressed through taunt and ridicule (the opposite of the intent): anyone in contact with this Power becomes a *Heyoka* and always acts in the opposite way to others. His subordinate, Whirlwind, patronizes friendly contests, while its Spirit-like, the *Sicun*, is a form of power that is given to man and distinguishes him from the animals. The Sicun is interesting because it is granted to man by the Sacred Powers, and although it is the most minor form of Medicine it may nevertheless have the potency of any of the Powers with the exception of Sun and Skan (neither of whom give power directly to man); this potency may then be imparted to material objects by a shaman, and these act as tokens of the Sacred Powers.[8]

The metaphysical powers are thus placed in a formal order which also relates them to the physical forces and explains the relationship between the tangible and intangible, and between man and the Sacred Powers. The significance of four divisions, however, is even wider. Tyon, who interviewed Sioux shamans between 1896 and 1914, wrote that they:

... grouped all their activities by fours. This was because they recognized four directions: the west, the north, the east, and the south; four divisions of time: the day, the night, the moon, and the year; four parts to everything that grows from the ground: the roots, the stems, the leaves, and the fruit; four kinds of things that breathe: those that

crawl, those that fly, those that walk on four legs, and those that walk on two legs; four things above the world: the sun, the moon, the sky, and the stars; four kinds of gods: the great, the associates of the great, the gods below them, and the spirit kind; four periods of human life: babyhood, childhood, adulthood, and old age; and finally, mankind had four fingers on each hand, four toes on each foot, and the thumbs and the great toes of each taken together are four. Since the Great Spirit caused everything to be in fours, mankind should do everything possible in fours.[9]

Just as there is one Great Medicine with four divisions, and one unit of life that has four periods, so there is one space above the world that contains four parts. This form of numerical unity, of which the four is the most apparent example, is very common in Indian belief. In fact, the Cheyenne believed that immediately beneath the vague but all-powerful life-creating force were four Sacred Powers, the Four Directions.

These were the *Maheyuno* who are the guardians of the semi-cardinal directions. Each has a distinct character: Southeast, where the Sun rises, represents life, light and renewal; Southwest, from where the spring rains originate to refresh the earth after winter, was the place of warmth; Sun paused after a day's journey at Northwest, symbolizing ripeness and perfection in the sense that the day had been completed or brought to fruition, before beginning his journey back to his lodge at the Southeast; while inertia, death, disease and cold weather were all associated with Northeast.

Although some tribes placed an emphasis on the cardinal rather than the semi-cardinal points, the importance of Four Direction symbolism was Plains-wide. The Four Directions were the same as the Four Winds, conceived as separate individuals but addressed as one Power, and are synonymous with the Four World Quarters, the essential divisions of the Sacred Circle. Everything proceeds in a clockwise direction that is referred to as 'sunwise' and considered sacred.

Thus, using the Cheyenne as an example and beginning at Southeast, the point of renewal, the Directions symbolize the nourishment of new life or growth (Southwest), completion (Northwest) which is the central part of the circular movement and represents maturity, and return via death (Northeast) which has to precede rebirth so the cycle can be repeated. Four divisions that together make a whole in which harmony and interdependence is symbolically stated is quite clearly being expressed.

The Four World Quarters also reveal some basic oppositions that are essential in Plains metaphysics: coldness and inertia oppose warmth and growth, while renewal opposes completion. Perhaps a deeper insight into Old-Man's character is now possible, for he too is a complex of oppositions: wisdom/folly, weakness/strength, and so on. Similarly, his link with the Sun has a corresponding basis: Sun is prayed to, Old-Man is not; in his role as Sun (Life-Giver) Old-Man is a devout person, but elsewhere his antics provoke mirth and represent earthly lusts.

Among most tribes an opposition of this type governs the entire Medicine world. The Crow divide this world into the Supernatural-Earth, whose ruling Powers are Wind, Fire, Water and Earth, and which includes plants,

Left: Dawn over the Bear Lodge Mountains on the Montana /Wyoming/ South Dakota border. The glow that preceded sunrise was considered an omen of good fortune as it presaged the birth of a new day, and was accordingly given mythological meaning and personified as 'Dawn-Light-Colour-Man'. He is synonymous with the Crow Indian deity First-Worker, or Old-Man, who was responsible for putting the world in order, and it was he who taught man to follow the sacred laws and observe the sacred ceremonies.

rocks and the souls of living humans, and the Without-Fires (the Sun, Moon, Stars, Sky and Thunder, all animals of earth and water, ghosts, dwarfs, and the souls of the dead). By this separation the forces of the Supernatural-Earth have material roles, subsist on power drawn from the earth, or directly affect earthly events; whereas the Without-Fires are immaterial, indirectly reliant on the earth, or have predominantly intangible roles. It is because of this division that a person's material body stays with the Earth-Mother at death, while the immaterial soul or spirit returns to the Without-Fires where it properly belongs.

The Crow use rather more imagery in accounting for this movement of souls than other tribes, as they consider the Without-Fires to be divided into two clans that gamble against each other using human souls as stakes. A person assumes the relationship of 'child' to 'father' when he receives a vision of a Sacred Power, and death is the consequence of the father gambling away the adopted soul. This then travels to the Without-Fires where it is 'eaten' (absorbed) by the victor in the game. Without its immaterial spirit the body wastes and dies. Thus the Sun, although a powerful Crow ally, was an unfortunate patron since he was a keen gambler but a frequent loser: the receipt of his power made someone a great Medicine-man (shaman) at the cost of a short life.

It is also within this context that the Crow come closest to any conception of an evil or malevolent spirit, in the form of *Istseremurexposhe*. He acts as a servant to the Without-Fires and is described as 'a spirit in human form with pine trees growing from the lower lids of his eyes, who arranges war parties, brings the enemies together, and leads the souls of the dead to the winning clan where they are "eaten". If no one is killed in battle he returns to his supernatural home, disappointed and tired'.[10]

Cutting across the division of Supernatural-Earth and Without-Fires is another pair of opposites: that of the Powers of Above (Sky-Beings) and those of Below (Earth-Beings). Each of these had a 'helper', generally a bird or animal, through which it usually communicated with man, and although the 'helper' possessed a degree of Medicine-power of its own it acted in this case as a mediator and was not considered to be the Sacred Power itself. Sun, for example, does not appear directly in visions but sends his first helper, the eagle. The eagle is in turn assisted by a hawk, which has three other hawk species as its assistants. Other creatures help different Powers: otter acts as the messenger for Morningstar, buffalo for Eveningstar, and rats, mice and snakes all assist the Earth.

Known to the Cheyenne as 'Listeners', since they listened to the vows people made, the Sacred Powers also made themselves known through animal intermediaries. The greatest of the Listeners-Above was the Sun, who represented masculinity and the male generative force. The Listeners-Below were ruled over by Earth, the feminine symbol, and these can be thought of as representing female procreative power. Through the sacred union of male/female the life-force, or power, was distributed among the people so that spiritual harmony can be thought of as the point of balance or compatibility between these inherent opposites.[11]

Natural forces were personified by the Blackfoot and ordered into Above-Persons, Below-Persons and Underwater-Persons. Thunder, for instance, a prominent Above-Person, is personified as a frightening old man or a gigantic bird; Wind-Maker, an Underwater-Person, rolls the surfaces of lakes to make winds blow; and one of the Below-Persons, Ground-Man, represents the powers of the earth. All of these, and others, appeared in animal guise when people saw them in dreams and visions – according to Blackfoot thinking the animal might actually be the Sacred Power which has assumed a different form – and it is said that dreams may be wiser than waking.

Right: In contrast with the snow-covered, glaciated ranges of the Bear Lodge Mountains, the Yellowstone River Valley was an extensively wooded area containing warm springs. Deposits of yellow earth found near these springs give the Yellowstone its name, and it was customary for Blackfoot women who possessed the requisite specialist knowledge to come here and dig the clays as a source of paint pigment.

Napi stated this quite clearly, for he told the Blackfoot:

Now, if you are overcome, you may go and sleep, and get power. Something will come to you in your dream, that will help you. Whatever these animals tell you to do, you must obey them, as they appear to you in your sleep. Be guided by them. If anybody wants help, if you are alone and travelling, and cry aloud for help, your prayer will be answered. It may be by the eagles, perhaps by the buffalo, or by the bears. Whatever animal answers your prayer, you must listen to him. That was how the first people got through the world, by the power of their dreams.[12]

Dreams were of vital importance to the Plains Indian, yet the distinction between ordinary 'no account dreams' and 'power dreams' tends to be rather vague; a person felt the power in one but not the other. As a consequence, dream symbolism was sometimes indirect and might be unintelligible to the dreamer, although the shamans, because they were highly trained and experienced specialists, could interpret the obscure imagery and explain its significance. Nevertheless it can be said that in general those dreams in which a Sacred Power or its messenger appeared had 'visionary' potential.

At times these significant visions occurred spontaneously, usually when the dreamer was under stress, but they were more frequently deliberately induced through voluntary acts of suffering. The most popular was ritual fasting, when a vision seeker chose some lonely, deserted place – often the top of a high bluff that was the home of eagles and where the relics of ancestors lay undisturbed — where he, or occasionally she, could concentrate completely on an attempt to establish communion with the Powers.

In this spot, where there was nobody but the seeker and the Sacred Powers but which was full of the mysterious forces of the world, exposed to the elements, weakened from the fast – and perhaps from loss of blood as it was not unusual to sever part of a finger or cut small pieces of flesh from the arms or legs – the supplicant appealed to the Great Medicine, asking that compassion be shown through the granting of a Medicine vision. He wept loudly, claimed to be a pitiable object, and regularly offered a sacred pipe so that its fragrant smoke would carry his pleas from the earth.

It was an intensely emotional and extremely solemn and pious act. It has been misinterpreted by many observers of Plains cultures as being indicative of an obsessive fear of the Sacred Powers, but it must be considered within the context of its social framework in which respect was shown through humility. The extremes of the quest were symbols of the deepest respect. In fact, it was often incumbent on the person of high status to display greater suffering than those of fewer privileges, and poor people were more likely than he to receive power dreams simply through falling asleep when tired as their situation was already a humble one. Mythology is full of references to poor boys who obtain power from unsought spirit contacts.

As power could only be granted by the Sacred Powers and, once received, imposed an obligation to perform ceremonies that maintained its potency, there was obviously no reason for pretending to receive such a vision as it would be impotent and have no protective strength; a man's presumption in claiming power to which he was not entitled might actually prevent him achieving a genuine vision, and it was in any case by no means certain that a vision quest would necessarily be successful and result in a receipt of power.

Although the appeal was frequently directed towards the Sun as the symbol of the Great Medicine, the Sun rarely appeared in dreams. Instead,

Above: Buffalo Heart Mountain in Wyoming had the same significance as a place of spiritual worship for the Crow as Chief Mountain had for the Blackfoot and Sacred Mountain, or Buffalo Butte, had for the Cheyenne. In each case the mountain was a prominent feature of the landscape that became a focus of supernatural power, thought to emanate from its summit. Anyone reaching the top would, if granted a power-vision, receive metaphysical strength that could be called on in times of tribal need.

one of the lesser Powers usually responded, as in this typical warrior's vision experienced by Lone Tree, a Crow Indian. He dreamt that he was surrounded by a hailstorm of terrifying violence that left a circle free around him. Into this space a giant white bird descended from the storm clouds; lightning flashed from its eyes and smoke rose when it touched the ground. After telling Lone Tree that it wished to adopt him, the bird was transformed into an eagle which flew back up into the sky. On the following night the hailstones, each as big as a fist, could be heard calling to each other: 'Whatever you shall ask, we shall do it for you. I am the High Thunder'.[13]

There is an interesting point in Lone Tree's identification of the High Thunder with the eagle. This bird was Thunder's messenger (as well as that of the Sun), and Thunder himself is seen as a gigantic bird, the Thunderbird, which is 'the big bird coming down from the clouds', whose eyes flash with lightning and who causes thunder when he moves his wings. The same spirit was the patron of warriors. By way of comparison, the following narrative of Black Elk, a Sioux Indian, also features this Power, and both men used the eagle as its symbol: Lone Tree carried the head of a bald-headed eagle with him; Black Elk painted a spotted eagle on his war pony and wore a single eagle feather across his forehead.

Black Elk's vision is, however, of greater significance: he was given power to doctor as well as Medicine that can be used in war, since the Sacred Powers that he contacts in addition to Thunder are exceptionally important ones. His dream had been received under stress when he was a boy and had

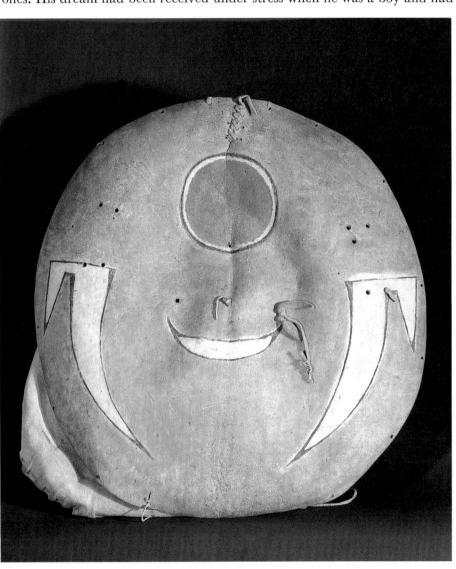

Most visionary experiences were intensely personal and, although their meanings were interpreted by shamans, their full significance was only ever known to the visionary. This was a gradual revelation that was completed at the end of a person's life, since he or she had then fulfilled the conditions of the vision by living and practising it. Anyone who failed to comply with the conditions, usually imposed in the form of tabus which were associated with the tokens, paintings and songs given in the original spirit contact, would never realize the full potential of the vision.

Right: The images on this Plains Cree shield seem to have a celestial origin. The central figures are probably representations of the Sun and Moon. Far right: An Assiniboine hand drum painted with a spirit design reminiscent of 'hallucinatory' images, in this case almost certainly the consequence of weakness and partial delirium resulting from a long period of fasting and thirsting.

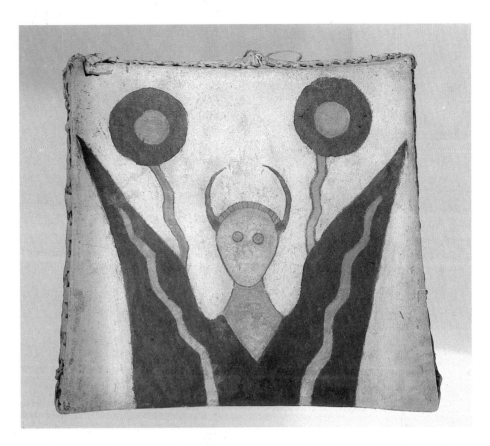

been taken so ill that all hope for his recovery had been abandoned. Black Elk described how he felt his soul separate from his body and fly up to the sky so that he was able to look down on his material self with a feeling of complete detachment:

> Flames were rising from the waters and in the flames a blue man lived. The dust was floating all about him in the air, the grass was short and withered, the trees were wilting, two-legged and four-legged beings lay there thin and panting, and wings too weak to fly.[14]

As he moved closer to the ground the bow he carried turned into a spear whose 'head was sharp lightning. It stabbed the blue man's heart, and as it struck I could hear the thunder rolling'. In explaining its symbolism, Black Elk said: 'I had been riding with the storm clouds, and had come to earth as rain, and it was drought that I had killed'.[15]

Black Elk also tells of being taken to a cloud which turns into a tipi whose doorway is the rainbow. Here sit the six Grandfathers, 'older than men can ever be – old like hills, like stars', who represent the Powers of the World: the four cardinal directions, Sky and Earth. Of these the first is the Power of the West who shows Black Elk the Thunder-Beings and tells him that they will take him to the 'high and lonely centre of the earth' so that he may gain understanding. In Black Elk's own words:

> While I stood there I saw more than I can tell and I understood more than I saw; for I was seeing in a sacred manner the shapes of all things in the spirit, and the shape of all shapes as they must live together like one being. And I saw that the sacred hoop of my people was one of many hoops that made one circle'.[16]

The centre of the world could be anywhere as it was not a physical place and was reached only in the spiritual consciousness. It was this movement towards a conceptual centre of understanding that distinguishes

Tokens of contact with supernatural visitants were often worn as personal ornaments, particularly in the hair or around the neck. These objects were not intrinsically powerful but were symbols that could be used with the proper knowledge and reference, usually in connection with distinctive face- and body-paint and a Medicine song, to ensure the close presence of a 'Sacred Helper'. Warriors frequently donned them as part of their preparation for battle.

Right: A Crow Bear Claw Medicine that would have been attached to the scalplock.

Far right: An Eagle Talon Medicine pendant and necklace.

Black Elk's vision: an awareness of the sacred nature of the world is imparted here, whereas Lone Tree simply obtained ability to contact the Powers and request their assistance. In their essentials all visionary experiences were nevertheless similar. They occurred in dreams or dream-like states, were effective only when a Sacred Power conferred benefit, and often involved a spiritual journey during which the purpose for which the power had been given was explained and demonstrated, and when restrictions on its use were imposed.

As part of these the beneficiary received 'instructions' which usually required him to make a Medicine bundle that represented the Powers he had been in contact with; and since Medicine-power was almost without exception received in visions, bundles nearly always had their origins in dreams. The principal part of a bundle was a token symbolizing the supernatural visitant: Lone Tree, for example, wore a necklace of large white beads to represent the hailstones in his dream. But as the acquisition of Medicine-power through a vision was a personal matter, the forms of their associated bundles could vary very widely.

Personal charms that were believed to assist in bringing success in war and hunting and which helped secure a long healthy life were undoubtedly the most common form. Simple braided buffalo hair ropes might be worn around the neck to link the wearer with the spirit of the buffalo, the animal on which the tribe depended for survival; strangely weathered rocks and ammonites – a rock yet not a rock – protected warriors and charmed game; while bunches of feathers, quills and beads were made into hair ornaments and fastened to the scalplock during battle. When not in use any of these might be kept in cloth wrappers or placed in a skin pouch to make a bundle; and sometimes the pouch itself – perhaps the complete skin of a hawk or kingfisher, or that of a weasel or other small mammal – was stuffed with sacred sage grass as the actual Medicine token.

Most bundles in fact contained, or consisted of, bird and animal skins. A man receiving power from the gopher used its skin in making his bundle. That of a Crow warrior who dreamt of the Moon automatically included an owl skin as the owl was Moon's first helper, while a dream of water required an otter skin because the otter was 'chief' of the water animals. Other bundles contained skins, sometimes of several species, appropriate to the particular power conferred on the dreamer.

As a consequence there were groups of superficially similar bundles linked with closely related powers: the connection between those of one 'type' however was, simply, that their owners had been contacted by the same or similar Powers; the bundles themselves, and the power inherent in each, belonged to individuals and often contained a complex of objects, such as beads, horsehair, or paint. The diversity of Medicine bundles can perhaps be better appreciated when it is realized that the concept was much wider than the strict definition of 'something wrapped up': simple charms, war shirts and headdresses, shields, lances, and even painted Medicine tipis, might all be grouped under this generic heading, and a single bundle could contain objects from a number of separate visions. No two were alike, and they ranged from expressions of hope through to Medicines that controlled sacred activities involving the entire tribe.

The powerful Hoop-Medicine of the Crow gave skill in locating the enemy and hence protected the band, and because it was received from Morningstar its willow hoop was wrapped in the skin of an otter: Morningstar's messenger. Eagle feathers, quilled pendents, braided scalplocks, beads, small animal and bird skins, and possibly a rawhide cut-out painted with the four-pointed 'star of understanding' were arranged around the hoop's circumference.[17]

Another form of protective power was obtained from a quite different type of bundle: the shield. On these it was contained in a painted dream-image that derived directly from a vision where the design was revealed floating in the sky; for which reason a shield must never touch the ground. These paintings are intensely personal, although they often feature symbols of the Sun, clouds and animals and may have tribal characteristics: Crow shields usually have a single animal figure with zig-zag lines representing a hail of bullets or arrows, while those of the Arapaho are commonly painted with the figure of a turtle since this creature was difficult to kill.

Even though the shields were made from heavy buffalo neck rawhide, which was shrunk with heat to about a quarter of an inch thick and strong enough to stop an arrow or spear thrust or turn a glancing bullet, it was the design rather than the shield itself that gave protection. The Cheyenne actually made shields which had only a crosshatch netted lacework and offered no physical protection at all.

Although the shield is specifically a War Medicine it functioned in peaceful times by granting security; and conversely, many Medicines that had apparently benign purposes were much used in battle. The Blackfoot Smoking-Otter, for instance, protected its owner by giving him a long life rather than superiority over his foes; used in a war context, it prevented the weapons of his enemies from causing him harm.

Other Medicines could be quite macabre though their function was not at all aggressive: for example, the potent and extremely sacred Skull Bundle of Braided Tail was the preserved skull of a powerful and successful Crow Medicine-man (shaman) who had died many generations earlier.

Decorated with sacred red paint, it was used as a medium through which his spirit could be contacted.[18]

The potency of any bundle obviously depended on the tokens it contained since these were directly representative of Sacred Powers, but the presence of powerful tokens was not a guarantee of a powerful bundle. The dreamer may have been deceived in his vision – the Sioux, for example, credited false visions to a mischevious spirit called *Iktomi* who had been banished by the other Powers because of his scheming and trickery and condemned to wander forever alone on earth, where he tried to fool men and disrupt sacred ceremonies[19] – or a shaman may have misinterpreted the symbolism, and it was also possible that power once given would be withdrawn.

Because of this, bundles were 'tested' to prove their efficacy. A warrior took his newly acquired Medicine on an expedition led by an experienced war leader, and if he returned unscathed – or, better still, had taken horses or counted coup – he credited this to his bundle's power. Should it prove unsuccessful it would be discarded.

Quite often, though, the failure was blamed on the owner himself for not having paid strict attention to the ritual details of ownership. This was because the bundle was a sacred object and its 'real' power lay not in its physical form but in the songs and paints that were given in the vision and with their ritual use, since it was this that connected the owner directly with all the mysterious forces of his environment. In Black Elk's case he saw himself in his dream 'painted red all over, my joints were painted black, with white stripes between the joints. My bay [horse] had lightning stripes',[20] and his power was only effective when he had ceremonially painted himself in this manner.

Similarly, an eagle feather in an individual's War Medicine might symbolize the gift of this bird's power to seize prey by pouncing on its enemy and imparted the 'power of flight, vision and noiseless yet swift approach, to the confusion of the enemy and his horses';[21] but this power had to be

Far right: The emphasis on bead decoration on the buckskin wrapper of this Crow Rock Medicine means it was probably used to obtain good health and luck. The Crow had many Rock Medicines in use, often elaborately decorated, and their specific purposes were very diverse. They were kept inside Medicine bundles that were opened at the first sound of thunder in spring, and again immediately before the onset of winter, when the contents were displayed in the 'Singing of the Cooked Meat' ceremony which was intended to bring good fortune to the tribe.

Right: Although used in a similar way to Rock Medicines, by being opened for tribal benefit at the first thunder, the Medicine Pipe bundles were far more powerful, their power residing in the decorated pipe stem. Shown here is the Blackfoot Thunder's Pipe which came as a gift from Thunder and was said to protect the tribe from enemies and sickness. There were about twenty Medicine Pipes in use among the three Blackfoot tribes in the 1870s; their owners formed a shamanistic 'fraternity' and were distinguished by distinctive top-knot hairstyles that projected over the forehead.

invoked through a precise application of paint, when the owner painted himself in the way that the Sacred Powers had painted when he saw them in the vision, and by following an exact sequence of songs. Benefit derived from a sacred ceremony, correctly performed.

The sacred nature of the bundle was reinforced by tabus, which were either decreed in the vision or stipulated by a shaman, and these were in effect at all times, even when the bundle's power was not being directly invoked. Often it would not be allowed to touch the ground, but had to hang on a tripod outside the tipi during the day and was moved at specific times so that it always faced the Sun from which it drew power. It could only be opened or appealed to after completing the appropriate ceremony, which usually consisted of ritual purification in smoke, painting and songs, and a smoke offering with a sacred pipe.

Henry and Thompson, commenting on smoking tabus among Piegan bundle-owners in 1811, wrote:

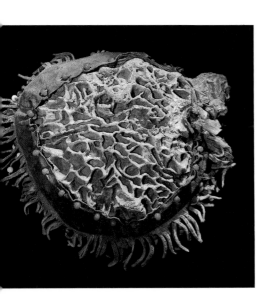

> Some of them will not smoke while there is an old pair of shoes [moccasins] hanging up in the tent; some of them must rest the pipe upon a piece of meat; others upon a buffalo tongue. Some will smoke only their own pipe, which they themselves must light; others, again, must have somebody to light it for them, and then it must be lighted by fire only; no live coal must touch it, nor must the coal be blown into a blaze. No person must pass between the lighted pipe and the fire.[22]

Other restrictions, which might involve eating, the type of noise that could be made in or near the tipi where the bundle was hanging, or correct forms of address, were binding on the owner and also on his guests: they were expected to be aware of the bundles in a man's possession and to respect the tabus in force, since breaking these was believed to turn the owner's power against himself, causing such afflictions as blindness or lameness, or possibly even death. The tremendous amount of inconvenience that tabus sometimes caused their owners was, in many ways, a test of the individual's preparedness to uphold the obligations and responsibilities that the possession of power entailed.

This responsibility was most marked in the 'tribal' bundles: although ostensibly 'owned' by a single person, the Bundle Keeper, his obligation was to maintain the bundle and its tabus on behalf of the tribe, and to open it at specific times in appeals that brought collective benefit. In fact, the ritual handling of this type of Medicine usually required both the Keeper and his wife, for she frequently played a major role in tabu observances – it was she, for example, who moved the tripod around the tipi during the day – and her co-operation in any bundle ceremonial was implicit.

One of the major tribal bundles, of great importance over the entire Plains area, was the Medicine Pipe. This varied in form between the extremes of restraint and simplicity: a flat, plain pipe stem with a tubular bowl of undecorated black stone; and the elaborate beauty of paired pipes whose long stems might be painted with coloured bands, trimmed with ermine and beads, and adorned with the brilliant feathers of the mallard or red woodpecker. Suspended from these could be strings and fringes, pendents of red-dyed horsehair, and splendid fans of eagle feathers that might also be dyed or painted red.

The Medicine Pipes were powerful and, although they had various functions, all played some part in establishing harmonious relationships: between man and the Sacred Powers, between men within the band, between the bands themselves, and between tribes. The Crow said that 'the Medicine Pipe was a pipe of peace; that he who owned it could travel from tribe to tribe and be received as a friend';[23] while 'of all the Blackfeet

95

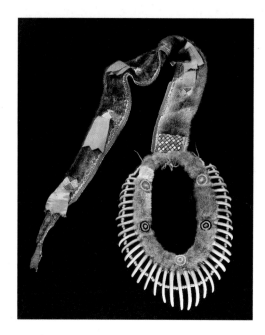

Above: Necklaces with a matched row of bear claws have long been used as a mark of distinction among Plains Indians. Although similar necklaces were used by many tribes, the number of men qualified to wear them through bravery resulting from contact with the Bear-spirit was limited; only a handful of the members of any tribe possessed the right. The necklace shown here was made by the Fox Indians, a peripheral group living on the fringes of Plains and Great Lakes cultures, and employs the claws of the now-extinct Great Plains grizzly.

Medicines, the Pipe is believed to have the greatest power, but it also brings the greatest burden'.[24]

A reason for this was that its power safeguarded everyone: it was smoked at the first thunder in spring for a general blessing, and could be opened in response to a vow taken by a man or woman to ward off danger by requesting Thunder's intercession; since the Pipe was handed down to the people by Thunder as a symbol of his protective power. Because of this the Pipe-owner was under obligation to the entire community and his failure to observe stringent tabus could be blamed for any misfortune.

Yet the pre-eminence claimed by Blackfoot Pipe-owners was disputed by the Blackfoot Beaver-men, the owners of Beaver Bundles, who asserted that theirs was the oldest and largest single bundle and therefore took precedence. Its size was considerable and no other Plains tribe had any bundle approaching even half that of the Beaver. Theoretically, every creature is represented in it, and, according to myth, each gave a song to Beaver when the bundle was first formed.[25]

The Beaver Bundle did not serve any specific function, being opened primarily as a general blessing, but its rituals were associated with many tribal ceremonies that renewed the 'wholeness' of the nation and ensured successes in hunting. Beaver-men, however, were credited with good memories as a consequence of the lengthy rituals (although no single individual could ever hope to memorize all the songs) and were highly regarded for their ability in forecasting the weather. As part of this role, they kept tally sticks with which they counted the passage of the moons and determined the changes of the seasons, and in this respect they were influential in deciding when camps should move; nevertheless, during moves it was the Pipe-owners that actually led the band.

Many major Medicines could be transferred to new owners through ceremonies in which the songs and paints associated with their rituals were taught. The role played by some bundles in the continuing integrity of a tribe meant that they had to be transferred. Among the Cheyenne the Medicine Arrow Bundle, or Mahuts, and the Sacred Buffalo Hat, or Is'siwun, together represented the unity of the tribe. According to their own traditions, supported by historical fact, the tribe has two parts: the original Medicine Arrow Cheyenne who migrated from the Woodlands and received power directly from the Great Medicine in the form of Mahuts, and the Half-Cheyenne (or Suhtaio) that have always been a buffalo-hunting people of the Plains and whose power lay in Is'siwun. They took on such a collective character that it became mandatory for every family of the tribe to attend their ceremonies.[26]

The person responsible for controlling the ritual power of these major Medicines was usually the Bundle Keeper, although in some groups his responsibility was limited to maintaining the bundle's good condition and ensuring its tabus were kept. The knowledge and use of its contents within a sacred context was invested in the Ritual Keeper who was invariably a man with shamanic ability but required the sanction of the Powers to hold office – generally being given this in a vision.

Shamanic visions were similar to others except that they were considered more potent by virtue of the fact that a Power with the capacity of conferring understanding had been contacted, and the province of the 'Medicine-man' was really concerned with the study of these mysteries and their interpretations. He was the philosopher among Plains Indians and, in terms of pragmatic philosophy, determined the meaning and truth of all concepts and tested their validity by their practical results. Thus he was essentially a man who conducted ceremonies and who was credited with special visionary powers.

Much of his knowledge was hidden in esoteric languages used by shamans' fraternities. Among the Oglala Sioux, for instance, most people referred to Medicine as 'wakan', a mystery, but the shamans might use the word 'akan' instead to refer specifically to those forces that derived directly from the Sacred Powers. They qualified this by saying 'this is akan, for no one of mankind can comprehend it',[27] thereby implying that the shaman, whose ability at understanding was not of mankind but of the Sacred Powers, had a sacred capacity for comprehension. It was because of this that the role of Ritual Keeper required supernatural sanction, whereas other Medicines might be readily transferred.

Most shamans, of course, had a role that was much wider than an involvement in bundle ceremonies; they had an important say in anything that required spiritual consideration, assistance or sanction. Depending on the power obtained through individual visions, they fixed the times for major sacred undertakings, led the way in camp movements, decided the most propitious times for hunting, attempted to influence the weather and foretell future events (by keen observation and close knowledge of the natural signs in animal behaviour and the environment), often directed warparties, advised the council, and doctored the sick; although in this last example they were most often called when other forms of treatment had failed or when the illness was believed to be caused by spiritual forces.

They had no particular function at such times as birth, marriage and death, beyond the fact that a family might ask an important shaman to officiate for reasons of prestige, as these occasions were generally considered to be the responsibility of the family concerned.

Right: The Blackfoot iniskim or buffalo stone bears comparison with the Crow Rock Medicines, but it had a more specific function in that it was originally used during rituals for calling buffalo. Most iniskim are fossil forms, particularly ammonites and baculites, but any strangely shaped stone or pebble might be given a Medicine designation and be kept wrapped in buffalo hair in a Medicine bundle. Larger rocks, also called iniskim, featured as sacred places where offerings were left. It is said that the buffalo stone became a sacred object a long time ago, during a winter when the Blackfoot were starving and the spirit of the Rock came to a woman in a vision, telling her where buffalo might be found. With the decimation of the buffalo herds, iniskim were popularly employed to promote general well-being and became widely distributed, almost every Blackfoot family possessing one.

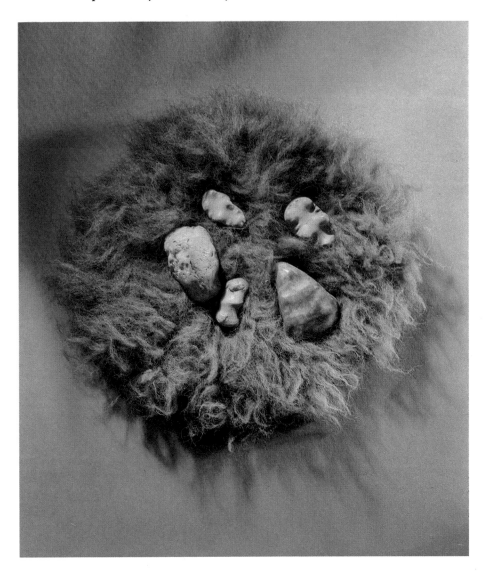

97

In strict terms there was a distinction between the shaman-proper, who directed ceremonies, and the doctor, who had power to cure; but these roles may have been combined in a single individual, and both were referred to as Medicine-men or women and used symbols of esoteric mysteries other than those contained in bundles. Catlin described the costume of a Blackfoot doctor during a curing rite as:

> ... the strangest medley and mixture, perhaps of the mysteries of the animal and vegetable kingdoms that ever was seen. Besides the skin of the yellow bear ... there were also the skins of snakes, and frogs, and bats, – beaks and toes and tails of birds, – hoofs of deer, goats, and antelopes; and, in fact, the 'odds and ends', and fag ends, and tails, and tips of almost everything that swims, flies, or runs, in this part of the wide world.[28]

Each of these was a token of Medicine-power so the primary helper of this doctor was obviously the Bear, with spiritual assistance deriving from the other creatures associated with the vision. Not everyone was as sympathetic as Catlin, and there are many traders' reports of Medicine-men using gesticulations and songs to conjure up their gods and demons. Yet the Indian never believed he was surrounded by spirits that could be ritually summoned. He felt that there was a unity between himself and the Sacred Powers: that they and he were 'as one', and that in this sense he *was* the spirit since 'he felt it in his mind; he could feel the power working in him when he doctored'.[29] In all instances of Indian Medicine usage it was power that was sought rather than a manifestation of the spirit.

Other than in dreams, the Sacred Powers were only manifest in the natural world in such things as wind, storms, particular animals, or in unusual events and behaviour: a person who lied or stole did so not of his own volition but because he was 'possessed' by a mischievous power – in other words he acted irrationally because the balance of his mind had been disturbed by some outside force, and rituals would be performed by a shaman to restore balance and hence normality. Indian notions of illness were nevertheless more subtle than a vague belief in malignant spirits. Sanapia, a Comanche Medicine-woman, conceptualized the nature of illness in the following manner:

> A healthy body is one which possesses a balance and calm throughout all its parts. When something causes this balance and calm to be disrupted, sickness results. Things in rapid and erratic motion or rapid and erratic motion itself are intrinsically dangerous to the human body: something moving rapidly or erratically in the body has caused an area of the body to become swollen. This swollen area is producing a toxic liquid which, if removed from the body, will relieve the symptoms of the illness. The cause of the illness is destroyed by the medicines which [the Medicine-man or woman] has endorsed with extraordinary potential.[30]

These Medicines could equally well be used for harmful as beneficial effect and, although few cared to admit their involvement, there were

Right: When a bird or animal appeared in a vision as a messenger of the Sacred Powers, the skin of this animal had to be secured as the medium through which power could be realized. This skin then featured as the main part of a Medicine bundle. In the Crow Eagle bundle shown here, the bird's body has been stretched and wrapped with trade cloth. Straps attached to the legs would have been used for fastening or suspending the carcass during the bundle rituals.

definitely grounds for suspicion of 'sorcery' where some shamans were concerned. But perhaps the greatest display of shamanic power, certainly the most dramatic, were the shamans' sleight-of-hand contests that the Crow called 'seizing one another's arms' (rendering an opponent powerless), in which their power was openly tested against one another through the performance of magic, conjuring and hypnotic tricks, usually before large audiences. Some men specialized in transformations: turning bark into tobacco and making Indian turnips or ripe chokecherries miraculously appear, which were then handed to their opponents to smoke and eat. The most spectacular feats, though, were those when a person's will was imposed on the rivals who were powerless to resist: one shaman 'would twist his blanket thereby causing the man opposite him to drop in a faint; then by untwisting the robe he would restore his opponent'; while another 'hopped round with peculiar movements of his left hand and all fell over towards the right side. Then he made movements with his right hand, and they all fell over to the other side'.[31]

How the tricks were accomplished – whether it was mass hypnotism, pure conjuring, or whether they really happened as a consequence of Medicine-power – was a mystery to sceptical Europeans who saw them and could offer no explanation. As tests of shamanic ability they were taken very seriously, since someone who was 'defeated' lost prestige and perhaps even his reputation as a Medicine-man.

The principle underlying the demonstration is highly characteristic of Plains Indian Medicine practice: that strength was related to proven potential and that power was only effective if it could be shown to work. A shaman who was unable to uphold his position against a rival was believed to be in contact with weaker Powers; people lost faith in a doctor who failed too frequently in cures, and refused to follow a war leader who suffered defeats and was unable to guarantee spiritual protection.

Throughout the environment the Sacred Powers could be seen fulfilling their varied roles under the auspices of the Great Medicine; and the spirit of man, the power of his belief, moved him to work harmoniously with these so that he might gain spiritual strength. In this way he accepted the 'reality' of every part of his world: of the intangible forces as well as their tangible expression; and of both conscious and unconscious, and material and immaterial power. Thus he acknowledged that nothing happened which did not have a 'real' meaning, although this might be an obscure one; considering the physical and metaphysical worlds as a totality in which even dream images were analysed and studied so that their meanings could be put to practical use, and recognizing the limits of his own potential by stating: 'It is from understanding that power comes; for nothing can live well except in a manner that is suited to the way the Sacred Power of the World lives and moves'.[32]

Left: Whereas the wing and tail feathers of the sacred eagle were obvious symbols of the power of soaring flight, and were used on war bonnets and pipes to connect men with the Powers above, the talons provided a more direct symbolic link with the bird's ability to strike at its prey. It is probably in this connection, from a power-vision that gave a warrior the ability to strike successfully at his opponents, that the talon is used on this Crow Medicine.

Right, above: Buffalo horns attached to this headdress suggest that the owner possessed virtues — particularly of stamina and endurance — which were comparable with the qualities of the buffalo. It was worn by a Blackfoot medicine-man and has a form characteristic of the Buffalo Horn Society. The Blackfoot classed such bonnets as Medicine bundles and considered them to be individually owned.

Right, below: The Medicine bundle shown here served to unite the members of the Weasel Chapter of the Crow Tobacco Society, since it acted as an 'emblem' that distinguished this Chapter from numerous other Society divisions. During ceremonies the bundle was opened and women danced with the weasel skins to obtain supernatural power, as promised by the Weasels in a vision, that ensured the fertility of the sacred Tobacco — a species distinct from ordinary smoking tobacco — and, by analogy, for the fertility and growth of the Crow tribe.

THE CIRCLE-CAMP

The Indians' belief that they were surrounded by metaphysical forces whose powers transcended the ordinary led them to look to these for an explanation of the nature of reality and being and of the origin and structure of the world. This explanation was contained in traditional myths and legends and was based on the supposition that life, as manifested in any form in the realm that man occupied, had an inherent opposition between its material and immaterial aspects. By maintaining a balance between these the integrity of the family, band and tribe was preserved, so individual activities throughout the year were directed towards the broad purpose of ensuring that the delicate relationship between the physical and metaphysical remained intact.

Governing this relationship was a concept of circular motion, since everything was thought to take place within a series of circular movements, each complete and functioning independently, that combined to form the Sacred Circle: the symbol of life and harmony and from which the essential life-forces emanated. Although granted privately to man in the form of individual Medicine-power, these separate forces could be integrated to renew the wholeness of the people in a national sense when brought together in a tribal context.

Before the tribes split up into their separate bands after the summer buffalo hunts, each of them held a great tribal celebration that was a composite of social events, sacred rituals and spectacular dances, songs and parades in which everyone participated. It was here that the existence of the nation and the spiritual unity of its members were demonstrated and affirmed.

The integrative nature of this camp – symbolically the circle encompasses all the physical and metaphysical forces – is expressed by Tyon, a mixed-blood Oglala, in his explanation of the significance of the Sacred Circle:

The (Oglala) believe the circle to be sacred because the Great Spirit caused everything in nature to be round except stone. Stone is the implement of destruction. The sun and the sky, the earth and the moon are round like a shield, though the sky is deep like a bowl. Everything that breathes is round like the body of a man. Everything that grows from the ground is round like the stem of a tree. Since the Great Spirit has caused everything to be round mankind should look upon the circle as sacred for it is the symbol of all things in nature except stone. It is also the symbol of the circle that marks the edge of the world and therefore of the four winds that travel there. Consequently it is also the symbol of a year. The day, the night, and the moon go in a circle above the sky. Therefore the circle is a symbol of these divisions of time and hence the symbol of all time.

For these reasons the (Oglala) make their tipis circular, their camp circle circular, and sit in a circle in all ceremonies. The circle is also the

Left: The painted elements on this buffalo skull, catalogued as Arapaho, have an arrangement more akin to Blackfoot concepts of metaphysics. Most Plains tribes used quite similar skulls in connection with circle-camp ceremonies, often as part of an 'altar' in the Sun Dance lodge, but the Blackfoot also used them in the sweat-lodge rituals, where they acted as a symbolic link between humans and the life-sustaining forces represented by buffalo. The painting forms a series of oppositions, such as day and night, north and south, or masculine and feminine, which the ceremonies centred on the skull attempted to unify.

symbol of the tipi and of shelter. If one makes a circle for an ornament and it is not divided in any way, it should be understood as the symbol of the world and of time.[1]

All these symbolic connotations were implicit in the circle-camp, which represented the totality of Plains Indian life: all the activities of the tribes, their beliefs and ceremonies, traditions, myths, customs, social relationships and so forth, were enclosed within its boundaries. It was the ultimate expression of everything the Indian considered essential to his existence, and provided an opportunity for all the members – men, women and children – to show a national commitment to tribal belief that could be restated each year; thus preventing a cultural hiatus between younger and older generations as well as ensuring that the yearly round of activities – which included collective and individual objectives – could be satisfactorily completed.

The circle-camp therefore had a function in bringing the tribe together in a situation where active social and ceremonial support was demanded from all. This was important on the Plains where environmental factors meant that a person was primarily concerned with the affairs of the band for most of the year rather than with those of the tribe. Its sacred character was underlined in a number of ways, obviously by the fact that it was formed in a circle but also by restrictions of a ceremonial nature and by particular rules of etiquette that governed the actions of and behaviour shown towards those members who had important ritual roles.

Many of the rules and restrictions have symbolic meanings that are frequently obscure. Although their symbolism may be difficult for us to understand, the rigorous and precise manner in which they were employed and the complexity of ritual events that had to take place in a certain structured and unalterable order suggest that the meanings are not only fundamentally important, but encompass the tribal past as well as being a source of inspiration for the future.

Though the various tribes differed in ceremonial organization the circle-camp always acted as a tribal unifier to renew tribal power, and there is sufficient similarity between the major ceremony of all the groups to refer to them collectively as 'Sun Dances', a name popularized in the 1830s and used in ethnographic literature since. It is, however, a term that can be misleading as the sun featured no more strongly than in any other Plains Indian ceremonialism, and although the Sun Dance was held by all Plains tribes – with the exception, until recently, of the Comanche – the Sioux were the only large group to give the sun any special significance: even among them this was restricted to a part of their complex where supplicants for power underwent self-torture in the 'Gazing-at-the-Sun-Dance' from which the generic term has been coined.

'Sun Dance' refers specifically to the historic ceremony of which we have records, but it is certain that there were older ceremonies with a similar purpose. The Sun Dance was actually a whole complex of events, a group of disparate rites, that the ritual attempted to unify into a structured whole.

As the Sacred Circle concentrated 'life-giving' or creative powers, so the Sun Dance had the express purpose of concentrating power in the circle-camp, from where it could be dispersed and distributed among the people as a life-force that would sustain them until the formation of a new circle-camp the following year. As power could not be arbitrarily summoned, it was gradually accumulated through minor ceremonies and activities that were considered necessary accompaniments to the Sun Dance. Preparation began when an individual pledged to sponsor the feasts associated with it and to act as the principal participant, many months before the circle-camp was formed.

The Sun's cycle of movement — from rising to setting — was often thought of as part of the Sacred Circle, in opposition to the Moon's movement at night, and it dictated the times of certain rituals. Above: The target motif, seen here on a Gros Ventre buffalo hide shield made in about 1860, was often considered a sun symbol and may have connected the shield owner with 'Sun-power' that safeguarded his life.

Right: Go-to-the-Sun-Mountain in Montana gained prominence in Blackfoot thought as marking the spot where the Sun descended at its cycle's end before its journey across the dark side of the Earth.

This person was a medium through which power could be channelled, and since this was a creative function analogous to birth – it gave new life to the nation – it was often filled by a woman, who is invariably known as the Sacred Woman or Medicine Woman. Even among tribes where a man

pledged the Sun Dance, a woman always had a very prominent part. Her role also symbolized a challenge successfully met, and to demonstrate her ability to meet opposition she customarily made her vow by appealing to the Sacred Powers for assistance at a time of personal stress or danger: among the Blackfoot, for instance, the Sun Dance could usually be initiated only by a woman's promise to 'hold a sacred Sun Lodge before all the people if health and strength were restored to her sick child'.[2]

Her promise was binding if the appeal was answered successfully – omeone else being required to make a similar vow and act as Sacred Woman should it fail – so that she was a person with a proven capacity for bringing beneficial metaphysical help. Moreover, she was someone who acted as a symbol of perfection: who had always retained high values in life and had not been led astray by human weakness. Only a person with an irreproachable moral character, who had lived a 'perfect' and consequently spiritual life, could set an example of this nature which, again, had to be a proven quality. It was very important that perfection was seen to be lived and it could not be taken as an abstract ideal that was desired but never achieved.

Even though other people made similar vows that committed them to

These buckskin tipi models, collected from the Cheyenne in 1904, show the types of sacred images applied to Medicine tipis. Bushy Head's tipi (top) had the power of the Buffalo. Buffalo tracks encircle it near the base and the crescent shapes represent buffalo horns. Bull Rib's tipi (above) linked him with the Elk, as is shown by the elk's head painted above the red shield. The striped pattern of Little Chief's tipi (right, top) is a more abstract representation of an intangible Medicine force. Shining Belly's tipi (right, above) bears images of Sun, Moon and Star, and the sacred Eagle that carried prayers from Earth to the Sky.

act as secondary participants or 'dancers', it was around the Sacred Woman, assisted by her husband, or occasionally by a surrogate husband who in some tribes was the actual pledger of the ceremony, that the Sun Dance centred. Their sacred duties were beyond the scope of individual endeavour; they required spiritual guidance and assistance which was sought through ritual seclusion and purification.

Seclusion was a requirement of the Sacred Woman, and from the time when the appeal was granted until the close of the circle-camp ceremonies – usually a period of several months – she rarely left her tipi except when travelling. Most of the time she spent sitting quietly, a buffalo robe drawn tightly about her and her hair hanging loose so that it covered her face in a symbolic gesture of withdrawal from the community, devoting herself to establishing and maintaining a spiritual contact.

Purification was demanded of her husband. He, together with the Sun Dance 'priests' (men with an intimate knowledge of the ritual but who, unlike shamans, did not require supernatural sanction to practise) purified themselves in a sweat-lodge, an oval pole framework covered with heavy buffalo robes in which water was sprinkled on heated stones to produce a cleansing vapour. This rid them of human 'contamination' and made their presence amenable to the Sacred Powers.

These procedures set this small group of people apart from others. They and the shamans, who had a parallel function as the conductors of ceremonies, were able to establish a connection between the Sacred Powers and the secular contexts – such as hunting – in which their supernatural aid found its outlet.

'Power' stemmed from the resolution of opposites including that between sacred and secular, and as the Sun Dance set out to integrate these oppositions on a grand scale, it is logical that its ceremonies should include both secular and sacred activities.

The Sun Dance usually lasted for four days of preliminary rites followed by four days of dances. During these a sequence of events was carried out in a definite fixed order, and although this order varied from tribe to tribe, there is enough procedural similarity for us to gain an overall impression from the typical ceremony of a single tribal group: the Blackfoot.

Among the Blackfoot the Sun Dance is known as the *Okan*, or Medicine Lodge, and, as is usual in tales of ritualistic origins, several myths are used when accounting for the various features of the ceremony. The myth of Elk-Woman contains the origin of an elkskin robe, buckskin dress and the *Natoas* (Sun Dance headdress) that were the essential parts of the Sacred Woman's regalia, and also explains why Beaver songs are sung at the Medicine Lodge – the husband of the first woman to use these articles was a Beaver bundle owner; while another tale, that of 'the girl who wished to marry Morningstar', contains the origin of the sacred digging-stick that belongs with the Natoas bundle and describes the special form the headdress should take, as well as defining the Sacred Woman's importance.

The first Medicine Lodge, however, comes from a more recent mythological period since it is said to have been held by Scar-face, the son of the girl who married Morningstar. He built this on his return from a journey to the Sun where he had killed seven enormous birds that threatened the life of Morningstar, his father. The number seven is significant because it represents conflict, or war; thus Scar-face's journey is really a warpath, and the myth symbolically points out that the purpose of both war and the Medicine Lodge is to meet a challenge successfully.

As for a warpath, certain ritual preparatory moves had to be made before the ceremony was considered to have begun; and for the Sun Dance the entire tribe made four moves on four consecutive days, each to a new camp site closer to that where the Medicine Lodge would be built.

Instead of following the usual informal pattern of moving camp, these ritual journeys were glorious full-costume parades in which the band of the Sacred Woman had precedence and went first, and when sacred objects were unwrapped from their Medicine-bundles and carried openly. They were led by the principal chiefs and Medicine Pipe owners, the latter holding the Pipes so that their feathered stems pointed ahead and cleared a safe spiritual path for the Sacred Woman who followed closely behind. Her horse and the travois bearing the Natoas Bundle were painted red, and she too wore red face paint and had the same sacred colour rubbed into the surface of her buffalo robe; while warriors with society lances and banners rode in long lines of several abreast, dressed in their finest regalia and carrying their sacred Medicine shields.

With the fourth move they reached a level prairie where one of the warrior societies had placed a ring of boulders to mark the boundaries of the ceremonial circle-camp. Since stone was the symbol of destruction and yet the circle-camp concentrated its creative power at the centre of this ring of stone, there was an obvious opposition between creation and destruction, and it may well be that the structure of the circle-camp was in fact a visual representation of the purpose of the Sun Dance: the integration of conflicting forces resulting in balance, harmony and strength through which the spiritual life of the nation was renewed, since power derived from the unification of opposites.

The visual impact of the circle-camp was tremendous. A solitary tipi's symmetry is already beautiful, but the effect must have been breathtaking when hundreds were pitched in a vast circle around an inner circle of magnificent painted Medicine tipis. Among them were the different Otter Tipis, and those of the Snake, Bear, Yellow Deer, and Thunder's House; together with the Big Stripe and Red Stripe Painted Lodges, the Yellow Buffalo and Black Buffalo, and many others. The tipi of the Sacred Woman would have stood inside the inner circle and to the west of the camp centre, its base surrounded by green cottonwood boughs as a sign that no undue noise was to be made in its vicinity, while close by were the big double-tipis, or ceremonial lodges, of the warrior societies.

Quiet was maintained near the Sacred Woman's tipi to prevent its occupants being disturbed while performing sacred preparatory rites – mostly concerned with the preparation of regalia and the rehearsing of the Natoas Bundle's songs and paints – but for most people the first few days of the Sun Dance were ones of intense social activity: of minor ceremonies, bundle openings and transfers, public dances and so forth.

Walter McClintock's description of a Blackfoot (Piegan) Sun Dance camp at the turn of the nineteenth century – although written shortly after the tribe had been confined on a reserve – clearly expresses this social character and is all the more vivid because he had been adopted into the family of Mad Wolf whose wife, Gives to the Sun, was the Sacred Woman at the time.

When the sun was setting, I walked through the camps of the Lone Eaters and Don't Laugh bands along the shores of the lake. The picturesque lodges, with their painted decorations and blue smoke rising from their tops, were perfectly reflected on the surface of the quiet lake. I crossed a rich meadow, very beautiful in the soft evening light, with its long waving grass and brilliant wild flowers, and climbed to the summit of a neighbouring butte, where I had an excellent view of the entire encampment. On all sides larks, thrushes, and Savannah sparrows were singing. In the surrounding meadows, large herds of horses were quietly feeding, while upon the summit of a ridge was a solitary horseman, who had left the noisy camp for quiet and meditation.

Right: Plains landscapes, with their vast spaces and sudden contrasts, often have a mystical atmosphere. The dramatic sky in this photograph of Saint Mary's Lakes, Montana — at the eastern fringe of a Rocky Mountain glacier — contrasts with the stillness of the water and the looming presence of the mountain peaks. Known to the Blackfoot as the 'In-Lakes' because they extend so far into the mountains, the Saint Mary's Lakes served to illustrate the forces of Earth, Sky and Water with which humans were placed in harmony through the circle-camp ceremonies.

In the deepening twilight the great circle of Indian lodges showed a ghostly white against the darkening hue of the eastern sky. The tipis were lighted by bright inside fires, and the flickering lights of the many outside fires resembled fireflies in the summer's dusk. Young men, with their wives, or sweethearts, were making the rounds of camp on horseback singing Riding songs in unison. I heard the plaintive voice of a young brave singing a Love song near the lodge of his sweetheart. It was probable the girl alone knew for whom the song was intended.

The sound of beating drums came simultaneously from six different lodges, where dances and ceremonials were taking place. In Mad Wolf's sacred tipi a solemn chant, accompanied by heavy and regular beating of rattles on the ground, was being given as a preparatory ceremonial of the Sun-dance. . . . In the clan of the Grease Melters a group of young men and women were singing and dancing round an outside fire. The Brave Dogs were assembled in their big lodge drumming and singing a society song. A group of Crazy Dogs were dancing in front of the lodge of a chief, who was under obligations to their society and from whom they expected a feast.

Beside O-mis-tai-po-kah's tipi, a band of young men were singing a Wolf song together. They stood in a circle, holding a raw hide between them, upon which they beat time with sticks. They sang no words, but gave the wolf howl at regular intervals, the young women, who stood near, joining in the wolf howl. They said this song was very ancient, having been handed down through many generations. It was sung in time of danger when hunting, or upon the war path, in the belief that the wolf would inspire the singer with his cunning. In another part of the camp a large throng was gathered about Sepenama's tipi to see the Sina-paskan [Sioux Dance: either a dance being given by a group of Sioux Indians on a friendly visit, or given by the Blackfoot but learnt from the Sioux on a previous visit].[3]

While it is perhaps impossible to imagine the intensity that the dances and songs had, or to appreciate the rhythmic changes that made a social dance distinct from a ceremonial one or from a war chant without actually hearing them, the first-hand accounts of people like McClintock enable us to gain some impression of the many small, incidental and personal things that let us share part of the atmosphere of the old-time circle-camps. One evening,

Red Fox (Sepenama) and his young wife, riding the same horse, made circuits of the camp, singing a Night song of remarkable beauty. The woman rode in front, wearing a magnificient bonnet of eagle feathers, belonging to her husband, and a buckskin dress heavily beaded across the shoulders. Red Fox wore a band of weasel skin around his head, with an eagle feather erect in his back hair. A beautifully tanned elk-skin robe, decorated with red stripes of porcupine quills, extended in graceful folds from his shoulders backward over the horse's tail. He carried a string of bells, which he used in marking time for their singing. Their song had a very pronounced rhythm, which was in perfect time with the slow trot of their horse. They continued their striking duet at intervals throughout the night, passing my lodge many times and not stopping until day began to break in the northeast.[4]

The subtleties of featherwork and costume detail were so highly individual that no description can ever be complete, yet this passage vividly conveys the visual power of Plains cultures – expressed even in such relatively insignificant ways.

There were, of course, also collective social occasions, of which dances were the most spectacular. A witness wrote, in 1846, of the 'dancers circling round and round the fire, each figure brightly illumined at one moment by the yellow light, and at the next drawn in blackest shadow as it passed between the flame and the spectator. They would imitate with exactness the motions and voice of their [animal-spirit] patron'.[5] From this, and other almost identical descriptions, it is apparent that dances were not only an opportunity for socializing on a scale that was impossible for most of the year, but were also occasion for the participants to restate the connection they had with the natural (animal) and supernatural worlds.

They also gave warriors the chance to wear and carry their symbols of achievement before the whole tribe. From a simple row of porcupine quills wrapped around the scalplock, to full war costumes of hair-fringe shirts and leggings worn with an eagle-feather bonnet and long trailer, they served to link the owner with the source of his power. Their delicacy and fragility, an impression given by the use of insubstantial materials such as a feather or quill, belied the strength and presence the symbols acquired in the dance when they reflected the nature of the Plains themselves where nothing is static and where power derives from movement. They are symbols that 'return art to nature',[6] and as such lie at the very core of Plains Indian thinking.

The dance concentrated warrior power in the circle-camp, where it was given tribal significance by being socially recognized. Some men, having performed exceptionally brave deeds in war, were further honoured by the special forms of particular dances: there was one in which only men who had never turned from battle took part, another for those who had received honourable wounds or who had risked their lives saving a comrade, and perhaps one in which a warrior 'carried the carved wooden figure of a horse to remind people of his bravery and skill in raiding enemy horses'.[7]

Although war deeds were featured because it was through them that a man came to the attention of the tribe, there were other dances including one for generous givers 'who had a reputation for being openhanded and gave freely of their possessions';[8] a particular aspect of the Sun Dance was to promote harmonious relationships. Visiting warriors from other tribes contributed to the atmosphere of friendliness and sociability by giving

Tribal ceremonies allowed full play to the Indian's aesthetic sense for decorative elements in costume.

Left: Armbands like these, decorated with porcupine quillwork and feathers, would have been worn on the upper arm by a Sioux dancer as part of a set of dance-costume accessories.

Right: These Crow forehead pieces, which were always worn as a pair, are made from leather which has been bound in the centre with a brass plate, to form a tube through which a strand of the dancer's hair was threaded. The decoration is completed with white tusk shells (dentalia), traded into the area by coastal tribes, and beads.

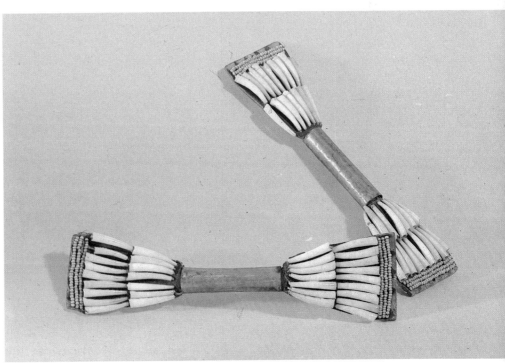

Above: Cross-cultural influences are apparent in ceremonial paraphernalia. The Blackfoot (Blood) ceremonial skewer in this photograph featured in the dances of the Kaispa, or Parted-Hair Society, and although the Blackfoot did not eat dogs they copied it from neighbouring tribes who would plunge similar skewers into kettles of dog meat at ritual feasts.

Right: Many items of dance regalia spread across the Plains from the Woodlands and South-East. The roach headdress, made from deer and porcupine hair or from deer hair and turkey beard, was especially common among the Pawnee and Siouan groups along the eastern edge of the Plains — the one shown here, for example, was made by the Siouan-speaking Osage who lived in Kansas and had tribal peace and war moieties identical to those of the South-East Woodlands tribes — but was also used in exhibition dancing by tribes in the North-West. The single eagle feather represented the owner of the roach and was attached to the elk-horn roach spreader so that the feather pivoted. The headdress was secured by threading the scalplock through a hole behind the feather socket.

exhibitions of dances that were intrinsically difficult to execute. As these were not bound by restrictions that demanded a prior qualification or established right to perform, they were copied over virtually the entire Plains area. Part of their widespread appeal lay in their visual splendour. Dancers wore elaborate crow feather bustles and extensive paint and ornaments which blurred into a stunning pattern of feathers and colour. In some of the dances the drumming and singing increased in pace and then suddenly stopped, and restarted; or the rhythm changed unexpectedly in the middle of a fast beat while the dancers had to keep perfect time.

But of all the collective events, the one that must surely rank as the most spectacular was the Horse Dance. Mounted warriors assembled on a ridge overlooking the camp and then rode in from the four cardinal directions to encircle a group of men and women who represented an enemy camp. Painted ponies, some marked with red hand prints as a sign that they were war ponies that had been taken (captured) on the warpath, their tails tied up for war and a few of them wearing beautifully quilled headstalls or war masks, were raced back and forth by men wearing war paint and carrying weapons, shields and lances: the excited ponies, sounds of war cries and of guns fired in the air, and the spirit and vigour of it all, created a sensational effect.

Here, too, was a chance for the warriors to display their fighting skill as they leapt from their ponies and engaged in sham hand-to-hand combat, a re-enactment of the traditional method of Plains warfare. The Horse Dance might continue with the dismounted riders imitating the prancing motions of their ponies which they halter-led beside them, while the whole community joined in with Wolf songs and shouts of encouragement that urged the warriors to brave acts and victory.

All the 'war' and exhibition dances were restricted to limited groups of active male participants: in fact, men and women rarely danced together and women's dances were either very sedate or were representations of the war exploits of husbands and brothers. But ample opportunities existed in some dance-ceremonies for more direct collective involvement. Community participation was, for example, so vital in the public ritual of the Dance Pipe that it could only be properly performed at the circle-camp. In this, one of the major Medicine Pipe Bundle ceremonies which brought good health and happiness to everyone in the camp, the owner danced carrying the decorated pipe stem, and was followed by a long line of men, women and children that wound its way around and between the tipis, sometimes reaching across the full width of the circle.

As well as social dances the warrior societies held their reunions and the Medicine ceremonies associated with them, while private feasts took place in individual tipis throughout the camp. Power was therefore generated at a number of levels: through individual, society and communal effort. During this time power of an even more intense nature was being 'called into' the circle through the secret rites held in the Sacred Woman's tipi. Many of these were connected with the formal transfer of the Natoas, since a promise to sponsor the Sun Dance was also an agreement to 'purchase' the Natoas Bundle from a former owner (purchase being a literal exchange of material goods – horses, clothing, quillwork and so forth – for an immaterial right to the ceremonial use of the bundle's songs, paints and regalia).

Before transfer could be effected the power of the bundle had to be renewed by opening it and removing the tokens it contained so that they could be purified and their rituals performed. At the same time other ceremonies began the process of unifying the oppositions inherent in the Medicine World and resolving the conflict between sacred and secular forces. The two most important of these were the sweat-lodge ceremonies of the Sacred Woman's husband and his male attendants, and the 'cutting

Above: The Natoas headdress, worn by the Sacred Woman in the Blackfoot Sun Dance, was a visual representation of the Sun Dance myth. It symbolized the power that the woman acquired through ritual participation. The plumes on the head-dress represent the leaves of the sacred turnip, dug up by the girl who married Morningstar: by doing this she made a hole in the sky — to which Morningstar had transported her — through which she returned to Earth and brought the Natoas to the Blackfoot. A pair of raven feathers is fastened to it and mounted on a strip of rawhide cut like a lizard, the symbol of long life. Fixed to the front is a 'doll', a stuffed weasel skin containing tobacco seeds that the first Beaver-man contributed, with a flint arrow point, given by another mythical character, tied to its head.

the tongues' ceremony of the Sacred Woman and her female attendants.

The special form of the Sun Dance sweat-lodge, known as the hundred-willow sweat-lodge from the number of poles in its frame, was believed to encompass the opposing powers of the Sun and Stars, of Day and Night, Sky and Underground, and of Earth, Fire and Water, as well as containing the material power of the Rock and the immaterial vapour of the sweat bath. Four lodges were built, one at each of the camps made on the tribe's formal movements, and these were positioned to follow the path of the Sun – the first was at the east side of the circle, then at south, west, and finally at north – so that they symbolized the Four Directions and completed a Sacred Circle; while unification of the oppositions within this circle was emphasized by the men's songs, which were sung in groups of four making a total of sixteen to symbolize completeness.

'Cutting the tongues' – which involved the ritual skinning and slicing of the consecrated buffalo tongues – generated feminine power as a balance to the male power of the sweat-lodge. Each of the women taking part in this had made a vow in which faithfulness was asserted, and the ceremony acted as a 'test': any mistake cast doubt on their veracity as it disrupted the precision and exactness of the ritual's order, causing an imbalance which was believed to be linked with falsity and untruth.

Although these two ceremonies seem quite different, when the colour symbolism of the two is compared it appears that both incorporated masculine and feminine power and that both were intended to bring the two oppositions together. Thus in the sweat-lodge the north side was painted red, representing the masculine forces, whereas the south was black, or feminine; and the tongues prepared by the Sacred Woman were painted half red and half black, with similar paint applied to the knife used for slicing, the tripod from which the kettle hung when the tongues were boiled, the kettle hook, and two pairs of stirring sticks. The kettle itself was marked with four vertical bands of red and four of black.

The symbolism was, of course, much more complex than this and had a deep significance that used abstract reasoning to link many apparently dissimilar objectives. There was certainly far more to Plains ritualism than was shown on the surface. However, within the framework of the Medicine Lodge the concern was always with opposing forces, with consolidating them and bringing generative power into the circle-camp.

During the preliminary rites power was specifically brought into the Sacred Woman's tipi and it was her task to transfer this to the Medicine Lodge, on the fourth or fifth day of the ceremony. This was an important day for the Sacred Woman as she finally had a right to the Natoas headdress given her. In effect she carried the power of the Natoas (the power of giving life) into the Medicine Lodge itself. This was actually a dance enclosure, exactly in the centre of the circle-camp in which the final four days of the Sun Dance were held, and is the single most characteristic material feature of the whole ceremonial complex: similar structures, with only minor differences in detail, were erected by almost all the tribes. It was built in a circle and consisted of a series of upright perimeter posts connected by rafter beams to a central forked post known as the centre-pole. A space was left at one side to form an entrance, usually facing east as this was the direction of the sun's rising, and hence of renewal, while the other sides were partially covered with woven boughs of green wood and leaves.

The centre-pole had special significance; it was the only one of the posts to be felled with any ceremony. Acting as a war party, everyone in the tribe set out to scout for and bring in the centre-pole, and when the tree was cut down coup was counted on it and branches stripped off and carried away as war trophies. All the tribes practised this in some form, perhaps to indicate past defeat so that a new cycle of growth could begin.

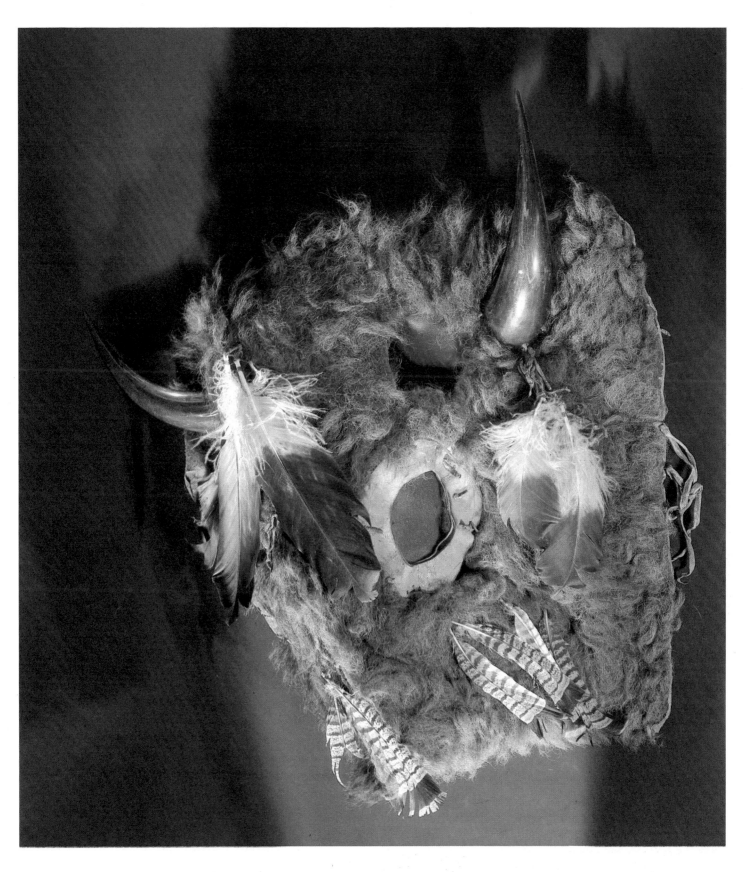

Above: The buffalo-runner, or war and hunting pony, featured strongly in war dance contexts and parades, since the warrior's success was attributed in large part to the assistance of his highly trained horse. During dances the horses sometimes wore elaborate war masks that reflected their importance as symbols of the owner's achievements. Many of these had porcupine quill and feather decoration or, as in this Sioux example, linked the pony with the spiritual power of other animals such as the buffalo.

115

At the time of the Sacred Woman's procession the dance lodge was incomplete; the centre-pole had been brought in but had yet to be raised into position and lay on the ground with its fork pointing to the west. It was painted in red and black bands that represented the whole tribe; a similar purpose is suggested in the distribution of sacred buffalo tongues so that everyone attending the ceremony might receive a piece which they 'ate with the Sun and with the Underground Spirits'[9] (i. e. with both Sky and Earth Powers) and through which they shared in the Sacred Woman's blessing for a long life that was free from sickness.

The means of ensuring growth and health was scattered throughout the circle-camp, but could be symbolically drawn into the Medicine Lodge from the four directions by the warrior societies who approached from the cardinal points while the complete tribe sang the Sun Dance song: an appeal for health and security that was also sung by any large body of Blackfoot entering a strange country for the first time. This took place shortly before sunset on the fourth or fifth day. It was followed by the final act of the day which had to be performed as the sun touched the western horizon behind the fork of the centre-pole. As the sun set it cast a red glow – the colour of fire, and symbol of the Sun's regenerative power – over the sacred ritual of the Medicine Lodge.

At this moment the warrior societies broke through the circle of spectators and quickly raised the centre-pole into position while the Sacred Woman motioned with the edges of her robe as if guiding it into place, thereby ritually transferring her power to the pole and thence to the tribe. The rafter beams were lashed to their supports so the lodge could be completed before the descending sun dropped from view and the Sacred Woman then retired to her tipi, her duties finished and, for many people, the essential part of the Sun Dance having been brought to its conclusion.

Responsibility for the ritual functions of the Medicine Lodge now passed to the Weather Dancers. These men were shamans rather than priests and, as well as being responsible for blessing children who were brought before them, they transferred Sun-power to some of the major Medicine-bundles, which were opened and blessed within the dance enclosure; and it was under their auspices that the 'dancers' fulfilled their pledges.

Although their dance was simple – really little more than a slight raising and lowering of the body caused by flexing the knees – it was arduous since the participants danced almost continuously for the last four days of the ceremony and neither ate nor drank throughout this period. They were believed to draw the strength they needed to sustain themselves from the centre-pole, which was considered to be a repository of power. This benefited them as individuals since they retained the power they had been given, while residual power was thought to overflow for the benefit of the drummers and singers who supported them and thence to the spectators.

The idea that the centre-pole sacrificed power to sustain the dancers, although sincerely believed in, must be taken in an abstract or symbolic sense rather than a literal one. It was rather that the pole represented the tribe whose support and encouragement enabled the dancers to fulfill a sacred duty from which tribal strength was believed to derive. It was a statement of tribal unity, identity and power; and when the circle-camp broke up immediately after the dances, the bands dispersed carrying this conviction and power of new life with them back to their own camps.

Left: Sweat-lodge rituals still take place inside pole frameworks covered with heavy buffalo robes. A pile of robes can be clearly seen in this photograph, taken at Bear Butte Mountain, South Dakota. The circular depressions are fire-pits in which stones are heated before they are passed into the lodge where the men sprinkle them with water to produce a cleansing vapour for spiritual purification.

When this ideal is compared with the similar ceremony of other tribes it becomes clear that they had almost identical functions; in fact the Cheyenne stated that the intention of the Sun Dance was to make the whole world over again. The Blackfoot ceremony was atypical only in that the Sacred Woman's role was basically a Medicine-bundle transfer – which is a highly characteristic Blackfoot trait – and that once this had been accomplished control passed out of her hands to the Weather Dancers. However, if we consider the Blackfoot divisions and associations between feminine and masculine powers, then we find parallels between these in the rituals of other groups as well: they are simply expressed differently.

The Cheyenne, for instance, instead of combining the oppositions within a single ritual, did so in two major tribal ceremonies which, although mutually supportive, are nevertheless quite distinct. This is because the tribe is composed of two originally separate groups – the Cheyenne and the Suhtaio – each of which contributed a ceremony, and this fact is reflected in the form their ancient circle-camp takes: a half-moon shape pitched on the south bank of a river, emphasizing the southerly position of the more dominant group (the Cheyenne), and which had a ritual central division separating the Cheyenne tipis in the southern half of the camp from those of the Suhtaio in the north.

Two closely related myths account for the acquisition of the ceremonies. In both of them a culture hero – Sweet Medicine for the Cheyenne and Erect Horns for the Suhtaio – travels to a distant mountain where he receives a rite (Medicine-bundle) by which he can bring buffalo to a famished tribe.

Sweet Medicine travels alone to the mountain and obtains a bundle in whose rituals women may not participate, as they were not represented at the original gift. This bundle is Mahuts, the Sacred Medicine Arrows, and contains two Man Arrows with power over men and two Buffalo Arrows that give power over animals. The ceremony associated with these brought 'Maheo's [the Great Medicine's] own life for renewing the Cheyenne wholeness as the People',[10] by concentrating power inwards to unite the nation. Sweet Medicine is therefore credited with creating the tribal organization and ensuring its continued existence, and represents the masculine forces.

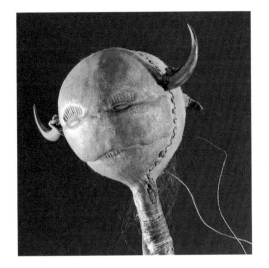

Erect Horns, however, travels with a female companion who is not his wife and she is essential in the ceremony he receives, which is the Sun Dance, since it incorporates woman's procreative power and the ability of renewal. The Sun Dance 'represents the creation [in actual fact the re-creation] of the ancient animal and vegetable worlds, the earth and all that is on it, the water and its creatures, the blue sky, the sun, moon, stars, the clouds, the winds, the thunder, rain, hail and the rainbow',[11] renewing the Cheyenne's world by dispersing power outwards. The forces controlling this are contained in the bundle known as Is'siwun, the Sacred Buffalo Hat.

Either ceremony was a re-enactment of its origin myth and was pledged by a person who would fulfill the role of the culture hero. They could, consequently, only be given in response to a man's vow. That of the Medicine Arrows, more specifically, had to be sponsored by a chief – who was considered to guide his band as Sweet Medicine guided the tribe. This chief (pledger) travelled to the other bands with invitations to form the circle-camp. His travels represented Sweet Medicine's journey, and he was painted red and wore red to symbolize the original costume.

The Sacred Medicine Arrows are not the same as ordinary ones: they have flint points that are covered with downy eagle feathers; whole eagle wing feathers, split through their centres and painted red, are fastened at the blunt ends of their shafts; and figures of the world are painted on them: blue paint for the blue heavens, symbols of the sun, moon, and stars, and red paint for the earth. The shafts also represent the Cheyenne, the downy feathers the spirit world, the points of the flint eternity, and the red fox

Ceremonial songs were accompanied primarily with rattles and/or drums which were often used to represent the characteristic sounds of the animal intermediaries with which the ritual brought the participants in contact. Both the rattles shown here depict buffalo-

wrapper in which the Arrows are kept represents Maheo's own being.[12]

When Sweet Medicine gave these to the Cheyenne, he also warned them that the Arrow shafts would only remain indestructible if the Cheyenne acted responsibly and the bundle's power was not abused; they would be able to renew the shafts four times, but after that the Cheyenne would cease to exist (spiritually) as a tribe.

From the symbolic meaning of the Arrows, it followed that the participation of the complete tribe was a necessary part of the ritual; but since the Arrows renewed the men's powers as warriors and hunters, they were displayed before only the male members of the tribe, and the origin myth actually precluded women being directly involved and a tabu forbade them seeing the bundle's contents. The anomalous situation this created was circumvented by using a symbol – in the form of a peeled willow stick – to represent each family, and placing this inside a double-tipi known as the Renewal Lodge where the bundle was opened and the spiritual life of the Cheyenne symbolically renewed by repairing the Arrows' feathering.

Prominent in Cheyenne ritualism was the use of sacred 'earths': two small patches of cleared turf on opposite sides of the Renewal Lodge marked with a spiral. These symbols were indicative of the respective powers of the Cheyenne and Suhtaio: the Cheyenne-earth was a diminishing spiral drawing power into itself, whereas that of the Suhtaio increased as power was dispersed from its centre. Both were important in the Arrow ceremonies as these were an affirmation of the 'wholeness' of the nation and of the

119

affiliation of the two tribal divisions.

In contrast to the Medicine Arrow ceremony, that of Is'siwun – which is the Sun Dance and follows completion of the Arrow ritual – emphasized feminine power and was a re-enactment of Erect Horns' journey. A solitary tipi, known as the Lone Tipi, represented the Sacred Mountain in which Maheo had concentrated all the elements of the world before granting the power of distributing them to Erect Horns. Inside the tipi the floor space was cleared of all vegetation as the 'barren earth' or 'the time before anything existed', and the ritual progressed through a series of five earths that symbolized growth and new life.

The first of these, called 'the beginning of vegetation', represented the ancient world about which little is known: in the second the world started to grow and the earth was made larger; the third symbolized the 'moving forward of the warriors' or expansion of people. Growth continued with the fourth earth, and by the fifth 'the world had reached its full growth'.[13]

The principle of the Sun Dance was to move symbols of generative power out of the Lone Tipi and into the dance enclosure, called the New Life Lodge by the Cheyenne, from where it 'spiralled outward' and caused the world to be 'reanimated'.

Much of this movement of power centred on a buffalo skull which had been painted to represent all the forces of creation; when the Medicine Woman carried this from the Lone Tipi she carried all the powers symbolized by it and used these to form an 'altar' behind the centre-pole. She also assisted in raising the centre-pole by making four motions with a sacred pipe, which indicated as well her willingness to re-enact the role of Erect Horns' female companion through symbolic or actual union with the priests conducting the ritual (who represented Maheo and the Sacred Persons who gave Is'siwun to the Suhtaio).

Her sacrifice brought the feminine power of procreation into the New Life Lodge, where the dancers – all of whom were members of the pledger's warrior society – received power from her and from the symbols that the lodge contained. This power was channelled along four painted lines or 'trails' – forming part of an unalterable sequence of body paints – that ran from the dancers' wrists and ankles to the sun or morningstar symbols on their chests, and which were said to be 'lines of the body that ran to the heart'.[14] When they left the lodge at the completion of the ceremony they 'represented the people going to their homes, full of life and animation'.[15]

In both the Blackfoot and Cheyenne ceremonies individual power is used for a collective purpose, but in the Sun Dance of the Crow there is an ideological base that is the reverse: here an individual uses a collective ritual to gain a vision that will grant him success against an enemy at whose hands he has suffered a personal loss. It is essentially a war Medicine ritual centred on an individual vision quest. Yet in another important Crow ceremony, the adoption ritual into a Chapter of their Tobacco Society, it is evident that the masculine-feminine opposition expressed by the Blackfoot between the Sacred Woman and the Weather Dancers, and by the Cheyenne between Mahuts and Is'siwun in which power is realized in the resolution between the opposites, is very similar to that expressed by the Crow between Tobacco Society adoptions and the Sun Dance.

The Tobacco Society rituals, while not actually performed at the circle-camp, took place annually at the time when the tobacco seeds were planted.

Right: Tokens of the prayers that were made at sweat-lodge rituals were left fastened to trees. Although formerly in the form of gifts of paint or painted hide, these tokens have been made from trade cloth since the earliest days of European contact. The red cloth represents an offering to the Sun, the green to the Earth, and the blue to the Sky at this sweat-lodge site at Bear Butte Mountain, South Dakota.

They were intended to bring increase and were directed towards assisting fertility – in this case of the sacred tobacco plant, a species distinct from ordinary smoking tobacco and only grown in a ceremonial context. As adoption into the Society was initiated by a vow similar to that made by the Sacred Woman, and the new member then subject to ceremonial restrictions while the plant grew to maturity, its purpose seems to relate closely to that expressed in the ceremonies of the Okan and Is'siwun: the generation of feminine power, that of growth and new life, for collective good. This parallel is more obvious because sacred tobacco was only used in supplicating the Sacred Powers, particularly Thunder, in an attempt to bring benefit to the tribe.

There is also a striking similarity in that participation in the most sacred parts of the ritual was restricted to members of the particular Society Chapter into which adoption was made, and that the rest of the tribe had a supportive role as spectators and indirect beneficiaries, while the initiate had the central role in being the recipient of Medicine-power. By metaphysical power the tobacco plant was made to grow strong and in abundance, and by analogy the Crow tribe would do likewise.

In comparison with this, Crow Sun Dances appear to have little to do with collective purposes: they were pledged by a man who had lost a son or younger brother killed by an enemy, and who sought to overcome his opponents and gain revenge. Their basic characteristics are explained in the myth of Prairie Dog Man who, at a time before the Crow had enemies, took his son with him on a deer hunt and some strangers (the Forest People) killed the boy. When Prairie Dog Man went alone into the hills to mourn the loss of his son, he heard a voice telling him to build a structure for the sun, in which the most important element was a pine tree which had fastened in its top a willow hoop with seven eagle feathers tied to it in the shape of a fan. All this was revealed to him in a dream (vision) and as he looked at the pine tree a screech owl flew to it and transformed into an effigy doll.

The pledger, who was always a mourner, was instructed in the ceremony by the owner of a Sun Dance Bundle that contained a replica of the effigy figure in Prairie Dog Man's vision, and which is a highly distinctive feature of the Crow ritual. Although there were several of these effigies in use, each with its own history and rules, they all followed the same basic pattern. One owned by Two Leggings was:

> . . . painted red and yellow to represent the early morning sky with its varicoloured clouds. The red semicircle on its forehead indicates the rainbow, and the two streaks beneath its eyes, the marking under the eyes of the screech owl, symbolizing the sacred powers of vision. The broad blue stripe down the body indicates the sky, and the smaller horizontal stripes represent, on one side, the wrinkles of old people, insuring for the owner health and long life, and on the other side, eagle plumes, symbolic of fog. The little black spots around the neck of the effigy represent hail and rain, indications of sudden storms. In event that the owner found himself at any time pursued by the enemy, he thus was endowed with the power to call forth a sudden storm between himself and his pursuer.[16]

Extremely complex preliminary rituals, extending over several days, involved both the pledger and his wife as central characters but also included virtually the entire tribe in an attempt to accumulate power that would promote the receipt of a vision. The whole ceremony, however, centres on the effigy doll and, as Crow Sun Dance lodges were built in the shape of a large tipi and did not contain a centre-pole, this was fastened at eye level, suspended inside a willow hoop, on a small forked post set up in the

Above: Sioux Sun dancers stared at rawhide cut-outs like this one whilst undergoing self-torture in the form of incisions through the skin. In this way the dancer hoped to increase his fertility and thus ensure the growth of the tribe.

Left, above: One of the main features of circle-camp dances, with their emphasis on a public display of individual achievement, was the richly decorated 'war' costume of the leading warriors. This shirt is Omaha and, although the right to wear it was granted by the war-leader, the beaded bear paw designs stem from a personal vision of the shirt wearer.

Left, below: The most sacred object to the Crow was the Sun Dance effigy, used in the tribal ceremony to assist the pledger in obtaining a vision that would lead to the defeat of an opponent. There were several bundles containing effigies in use, and although all the dolls were traditionally made from the skin of a white-tailed deer and stuffed with sacred sweetgrass and white pine needles mixed with sheep and deer hair, the paint on each was different and derived from a vision of the doll owner.

centre of the lodge to represent the pine tree in the myth.

Here it became the focus of the pledger's attention, and in many ways symbolized his powers of concentration that were directed towards fulfilling his vow, and his unwavering commitment to continue fasting and dancing to the point where physical exertion culminated in a faint. His belief in the power of the effigy gave him the strength to continue until a vision was received; at which time the ritual reached its conclusion and the warpath opened.

This ceremony obviously exaggerates the power of the individual warrior, but can be seen as a complement to the Tobacco Society adoptions; forming between them an integrated ritual scheme that encompasses both collective and individual purposes, and masculine and feminine forces.

The Sioux were the only tribe to make self-torture a prerequisite for the principal participant who 'had to have a wound that caused the blood to flow',[17] whereas among all other tribes, although self-torture was at times fairly common, it was engaged in only by secondary dancers who were fulfilling vows and was forbidden to the pledger of the ceremony. Also, as the Sioux ceremony was partly conducted in order to achieve shamanic power, its ritual was highly formalized and the significance of the ceremony was described by the shamans in terms that underscore the esoteric reasons for circle-camp rituals in general.

The shamans explained that there were different degrees of dance that might be performed for different purposes; from a desire to fulfill a vow, which could be undertaken by anyone including women and children, to the seeking of supernatural power, by which a person could aspire to the position of a shaman. The higher degrees of dance, involving incisions cut through the skin, were restricted to warriors; thus a man might have his back pierced and buffalo skulls, which he dragged behind him while dancing, tied to pegs inserted in these incisions; or the flesh of the breast would be cut and lines from it attached to posts or the centre-pole. When dancing, the supplicant for power 'gazed at the sun' and threw his weight against the lines by which he was attached in an attempt to tear free. If the power he sought was shamanic he was literally hoisted from his feet and suspended from the centre-pole during part of the ceremony.

By successfully enduring what must have been an extremely painful ordeal, he demonstrated possession of the four great virtues: bravery, generosity, fortitude and integrity. Bravery was shown by not making obvious signs of pain, generosity by the sponsorship of feasts for all members of the tribe who became actively involved, fortitude was in the ability to withstand the rigours of the dance, and integrity because he could only participate by agreeing to the four conditions of the ceremony: that it was undertaken for a proper purpose, that he complied with its essentials, conformed to the customs of the tribe, and accepted the mythology of the nation.[18]

The ideas expressed by the Sioux shamans held equally for all Plains tribes, and although the Sioux ceremony was extreme it was only another method by which the people made direct statements of their beliefs. These beliefs remain undiminished in spite of the encroachment of white settlement that has forced the tribes into confined areas and which has created an environmental imbalance against the natural harmony symbolized by the Sacred Circle. There is no space here to deal adequately with the desperate and heroic stand that the Plains Indians have made since Manifest Destiny[19] – that mid-nineteenth century doctrine invented in Washington to justify white expansion by decreeing that the white man was destined to rule America – in their attempts to retain a traditional way of life against the European ideals of acquisition and compromise. It must be said, however, that in contrast to these ideals those of the Indian encompassed a world-view that committed him to accept responsibility for maintaining the balance of nature through personal sacrifice. In this the circle-camps had the same function – and a similar form – as the ancient Medicine Wheels, since it was from here that power obtained from all the forces, both human and super-human, was passed by individuals to the community and thence distributed in the environment. The beliefs, if not specific rituals, have a history that goes back several thousand years and which extends yet further into the future.

Ceremonies are performed today and, notwithstanding that there have been adaptations because the problems the Indian has to face have changed with time, the People are still charged with the duty to fulfil their obligations to the Sacred Powers, thus ensuring world-renewal and the continuation of the cyclic pattern of natural events. The Sacred Circle, though stretched and shaken by the thoughtless acts of those who do not believe that the Earth and humans are of one mind, remains unbroken: prairie flowers blossom, trees bear fruit, and healing winds drive back those of the north; and al-though buffalo no longer freely roam, they whose senses have not been dimmed can still look across the grasslands and see the positive influences of the world's mysterious forces. Movement – in all its significance – con-tinues in a sacred circular direction that is in harmony with the motion of the world.

The Indian sees this world as a totality, composed of interrelated and interdependent elements; whereas at least one modern anthropologist has defined the 'scientific mind' as one which 'proceeds step by step, trying to give explanations for very limited phenomena ... we are able, through scientific thinking, to achieve mastery over nature (while using) consider-ably less of our sensory perceptions'.[20] 'Mastery over nature' is not and has never been a preoccupation of the Plains Indians, who seek only to cooperate with nature in order eventually to reach understanding. The consequences of their actions are obvious, as their perception is not blinkered by the limited view of the scientific thinker, and it is because of this that they are able to establish a correlation between the spiritual and the material from which they draw the strength for survival and the capacity to retain their cultural identity.

Above: The principal dancers in the Sun Dances of many Plains tribes used eagle bone whistles like this Cheyenne example to help them reach a trance-like state. They were clenched between the teeth so that they emitted their sound each time the dancer exhaled.

Left: This buffalo robe bears a characteristic Black War Bonnet design, which is related to the Sacred Circle as a symbol of harmony, and attests to the maturity of its wearer.

Right: With the completion of its circle-camp ceremonies in autumn, each tribe would separate into bands for a buffalo hunt before moving into the winter villages along river valleys such as this one in north-western Wyoming.

NOTES

CHAPTER 1

1 Grinnell, G. B. *Blackfoot Lodge Tales* (London 1893) pp. 137-8
2 Catlin, G. *Letters and Notes on the Manners, Customs, and Condition of the North American Indians* (Ross & Haines, Minneapolis 1965) Vol. II, p. 18
3 *ibid.*
4 Neihardt, J. G. *Black Elk Speaks* (Sphere Books, London 1974) p. 138
5 McClintock, W. *The Old North Trail* (London 1910) p. 501
6 *ibid.* p. 217
7 Catlin *op. cit.* Vol. I, p. 249
8 *ibid.* p. 72
9 'Caleb' — a Hebrew masculine name literally meaning 'dog' — was applied anecdotally to the grizzly bear by many fur trappers and backwoodsmen.
See Catlin: Vol. I, p. 181
10 Maximilian, 'Travels in the Interior of North America', journal entry for January 30, 1834 quoted in Thomas, D. and Ronnefeldt, K. (Eds) *People of the First Man* (E. P. Dutton, New York 1976) p. 193
11 Chief Joseph quoted in Brown, D. *Bury My Heart at Wounded Knee* (Pan Books, London 1972) p. 249
12 Many archaeologists are still dubious if dates in excess of 25,000 years are suggested for the presence of man in the Americas. However, there are fairly conclusive indications that the Alberta find places these more conservative estimates in serious doubt, since the Taber skeleton is under a glacial pile with a definite date of more that 23,000 years, and other glacial deposits suggest greater antiquity for this same site. Early dating of man in the New World to about 60,000 years would raise the problem of a period as long as 35,000 years, for which there is no evidence anywhere of man's presence. By itself this does not question the earlier dating, which seems quite probable, but it does mean that sites need to be found for the interim period. Possibly we should be looking outside the Plains for these intermediate dates as long drought periods on the Plains may have forced people out of the area; even so, there should be some evidence of their presence somewhere.
(Based on a conversation in July 1979 with Richard Forbis, Dept. of Archaeology, University of Calgary, who has been investigating the Taber site)
13 For a detailed account of the Olsen-Chubbock site and its excavation, see Joe Ben Wheat: *A Paleo-Indian Bison Kill*, Jan 1967, in *Early Man in America —Readings from Scientific American*, W. H. Freeman, San Francisco, 1973
14 Neihardt *op. cit.* p. 67
15 See Simms (1903) cited in Waldo Wedel: *Prehistoric Man on the Great Plains*, University of Oklahoma Press, Norman, 1961. pp. 266-70
16 See John A. Eddy: *Astronomical Alignment of the Big Horn Medicine Wheel* in Science, American Association for the Advancement of Science, Vol. 184, No 4141, June 7, 1974.
John A. Eddy: *Probing the Mystery of the Medicine Wheels* in National Geographic, Vol. 151, No 1, Jan. 1977, pp. 140-146.
Alice Kehoe and Thomas Kehoe: *Solstice Alignment and Boulder Configurations in Saskatchewan*, Canadian Ethnology Service, Paper No 48
17 For a fuller discussion of Plains prehistory, and of the Adena, Hopewell, and Mississippian Cultures, see Ralph Coe: *Sacred Circles*, exhibition catalogue, Arts Council of Great Britain, 1976.
George Hyde: *Indians of the Woodlands from Prehistoric Times to 1725*, University of Oklahoma Press, Norman, 1962.
Robert Silverberg: *The Mound Builders*, Ballantine Books, N.Y., 1974.
Dean Snow and Werner Forman: *The American Indians — Their Archaeology and Prehistory*, Thames and Hudson, London, 1976.
Waldo Wedel: *Environment and Native Subsistence Economies in the Central Great Plains*, Smithsonian Miscellaneous Collections, Vol. 101, No 3, Washington, 1941.
Waldo Wedel: *Prehistoric Man on the Great Plains*, University of Oklahoma Press, Norman, 1961.
Howard D. Winters: *Some Unusual Grave Goods from a Mississippian Burial Mound*, Indian Notes, Museum of the American Indian, N.Y., Spring 1974, Vol. X, No 2
18 But see the counter-argument that ancient Prairie-Plains dwellers had incipient social class in Preston Holder: *The Hoe and the Horse on the Plains*, University of Nebraska Press, Lincoln, 1970
19 See Waldo Wedel: *Prehistoric Man on the Great Plains*, 1961
20 James Mooney: *Origin of the Kiowa-Apache* in *Calendar History of the Kiowa Indians*, Smithsonian Institution, Washington, 1979 (reprint). pp. 246-251

CHAPTER 2

1 Catlin *op. cit.* Vol. I, p. 217
2 Dorsey, G. A. *Traditions of the Arikara* (Carnegie Institution of Washington 1904) p. 17
3 Wildschut, W. *Crow Indian Medicine Bundles* (Contributions from the Museum of the American Indian, Heye Foundation, Ewers, J. C. (Ed) Vol. XVII, New York 1975) p. 115
4 Ewers, J. C. *The Horse in Blackfoot Culture* (Bulletin 159, Bureau of American Ethnology, Smithsonian Institution, Washington 1955) p. 128
5 Catlin *op. cit.* Vol. II, p. 66
6 Catlin *op. cit.* Vol. II, p. 65
7 Neihardt *op. cit.* p. 39
8 North Piegan Indian in conversation with the author
9 Schmitt, M. & Brown, D. *Fighting Indians of the West* (Bonanza Books, New York 1968) p. 63
see also:
Clark Wissler: *Some Protective Designs of the Dakota*, American Museum of Natural History, Anthropological Papers, Vol. I, part 2, N.Y., 1907. pp. 23-31
10 Wildschut *op. cit.* p. 115
11 Catlin *op. cit.* Vol. I, p. 23
12 see Catlin: Vol. I, pp. 192-193 and plate 76
Catlin painted several versions of this warrior and the reader is referred to:
Horst Hartmann: *Die Plains- und Prärieindianer Nordamerikas*, Museum für Völkerkunde, Berlin, 1973. Colour plate II, p. 49.
Harold McCracken: *George Catlin and the Old Frontier*, Bonanza Books, N.Y. 1959. Colour plate opposite p. 93 (where the warrior is referred to as a chief and named 'He Who Outjumps All').
William Wildschut: *Crow Indian Beadwork*, Contributions, Museum of the American Indian, Vol. XVI, N.Y., 1959 (second edition). Frontispiece (where he is named as He Who Jumps Over Everyone).
Further examples of the extraordinary length of Crow men's hair, as depicted by Catlin, can be seen in: Catlin: Vol. I, plates 77 and 78.
William H. Truettner: *The Natural Man Observed*, Smithsonian Press, Washington, 1979. Plate nos. 163 and 164
13 Alfred L. Kroeber: *The Arapaho*, Bulletin, American Museum of Natural History, Vol. XVIII, N.Y., 1902-1907, p. 27.
for visual references to hairstyles see:
Carl Bodmer: in *People of the First Man* (Davis Thomas and Karin Ronnefeldt — eds.), E. P. Dutton, N.Y., 1976.
Catlin: Vols. I and II.
James Horan: *The McKenney-Hall Portrait Gallery of American Indians*, Crown Publishers, N.Y., 1972
14 Kroeber, A. L. *The Arapaho*, Bulletin of the American Museum of Natural History, Vol. XVIII, New York 1902-07, p. 9
15 Dorsey, G. A. *The Cheyenne* (Field Columbian Museum, Anthropological Series, Vol. IX, nos. 1 and 2, Chicago 1905) p. 14
16 Lowie, R. H. *The Northern Shoshone* (Anthropological Papers, American Museum of Natural History, Vol. II, New York 1909) p. 208
17 Lowie, R. H. *Notes on the Social Organisation and Customs of the Mandan, Hidatsa, and Crow Indians* (Anthropological Papers, American Museum of Natural History, Vol. XXI, New York 1924) p. 82
18 Wissler, C. *Social Organisation and Ritualistic Ceremonies of the Blackfoot Indians* (Anthropological Papers, American Museum of Natural History, Vol. VII, New York 1912) p. 23
19 *ibid.* p. 24
20 see Paul Raczka: *Minipokas — Children of Plenty*, American Indian Art Magazine, Vol. 4, No. 3, Scottsdale, Summer 1979
21 Wissler, C. *op. cit.* p. 18
22 Provinse, J. H. 'The Underlying Sanctions of Plains Indian Culture' in Eggan, F. (Ed) *Social Anthropology of North American Tribes* (University of Chicago Press 1972) p. 358
23 Lowie, R. H. *Social Life of the Crow Indians* (Anthropological Papers, American Museum of Natural History, Vol. IX, New York 1912) p. 55
24 This was especially true in cases where the band derived its name from the leading chief, whose name was avoided after his death for fear of bringing bad luck by associating the band with his spirit or by encouraging his ghost to remain near the camps.
See Alvin M. Josephy (ed.): *American Heritage Book of Indians*, Simon and Schuster, 1961 p. 379 and p. 381
25 see Walter McClintock: *The Old North Trail*, University of Nebraska Press, Lincoln, 1977 (reprint) pp. 134-8
26 Laubin, R. and G. *The Indian Tipi* (Ballantine Books, New York 1973) pp. 115-7
27 No white pigment was actually used on these robes. The designs were painted with pigment derived from brown lignite (a soft brownish-black coal), and with a colourless glue size that was made by boiling the tail of a beaver or the scrapings, tendons, bones etc. of buffalo. The design was applied before the hide was pounded to soften it, and as the pounding process dulled the flesh colour of the hide but did not affect the impervious sized areas this revealed the treated portions in a lighter tone. With use, the untreated areas discoloured further and showed the brown and white design with greater clarity. Other colours might be used in addition to brown and white, but these two colours were the basis for many early robes.
For a general comment on pigments and hide painting see Norman Feder: *American Indian Art*, Harry N. Abrams N.Y. 1969. p. 70
28 Peter Powell, *Sweet Medicine*, Vol. II. University of Oklahoma Press, Norman, 1969 p. 495

CHAPTER 3

1 Kroeber *op. cit.* p. 8
2 see Catlin: Vol. I, pp. 42-43
Edwin T. Denig: *Of The Crow Nation*, Anthropological Paper No 33, Bulletin 151, Bureau of American Ethnology, Smithsonian Institution, Washington, 1953 (John Ewers, ed.) p. 71
General W. F. Raynolds: *Report on the Exploration of the Yellowstone River*, Washington, 1868. p. 51
3 *Narrative of David Thompson*, 1787. pp. 330-332
(see John Ewers: *The Blackfeet — Raiders on the Northwestern Plains*, University of Oklahoma Press, Norman, 1958)
4 Culin, S. *Games of the North American Indians* (Dover Publications, New York 1975) p. 32
5 Wissler *op. cit.* p. 60
6 Lesser, A. *The Pawnee Ghost Dance Hand Game: Ghost Dance Revival and Ethnic Identity* (University of Wisconsin Press 1978) p. 144
7 For further information on Plains mythology, see Robert H. Lowie, *Myths and Traditions of the Crow*, Anthropological Papers, American Museum of Natural History, Vol. XXV, N.Y., 1922
8 see Stewart Culin: *Games of the North American Indians*, Dover Publications, N.Y., 1975 (reprint) pp. 420-527
9 Lesser *op. cit.* p. 144
10 Although horse racing was very common between individuals, the inter-society races were not held by all Plains tribes. The description here is based on Blackfoot races and follows John Ewer's account given in *The Horse in Blackfoot Indian Culture*, Smithsonian Institution, Bulletin 159, Washington, 1955. pp. 227-32
11 McClintock *The Old North Trail* p. 463
12 McClintock, W. *Blackfoot Warrior Societies* (Leaflet no. 8, Southwest Museum, Los Angeles 1937) p. 18
13 *ibid.* p. 30
14 Skinner, A. *Ponca Societies and Dances* (Anthropological Papers, American Museum of Natural History, Vol. XI, New York 1916) p. 785
15 see George A. Dorsey: *The Cheyenne*, Field Columbian Museum, Publication 99, Anthropological Series, Vol. IX, Part I, Chicago, 1905. pp. 24-6
16 Wissler *op. cit.* p. 41
17 Lowie, R. H. *The Crow Indians* (Farrar & Rinehart, New York 1935) p. 218
18 Dorsey, G. A. *Traditions of the Skidi Pawnee* (Memoir, American Folk-Lore Society, 1903) pp. 157-63
19 The terms 'red' and 'white', essentially Cheyenne in this context, are used here to indicate the symbolic colour-dualism typical of many Plains tribes. Specific colour associations varied widely, sometimes even within a tribe from one individual to another, and the interpretation of the 'meaning' of any particular colour can only be understood in the context of when it is used and by whom. Certain colour-dualisms, for example red-black, were principally used in combination for ceremonial reasons; however, warriors returning from raids frequently used black to indicate victory, while red might be used to signify war honours through an association with blood or, in Arapaho symbolism, to indicate the earth from which it was obtained when used in combination with blue (indicating the sky).
For a fuller discussion of Arapaho and Sioux colour symbolism see:
Alfred L. Kroeber: *The Arapaho*, Bulletin, American Museum of Natural History, Vol. XVIII, N.Y., 1907.
James Walker: *Lakota Belief and Ritual*, University of Nebraska Press, Lincoln, 1980
20 Catlin *op. cit.* Vol. II, pp. 5-6
21 Grinnell *op. cit.* p. 244
22 Blackfoot Indian in conversation with the author

CHAPTER 4

1 Irving 'The Rocky Mountains, or Adventures in the Far West', quoted in Catlin *op. cit.* Vol. II, p. 252
2 Lowie, R. H. *Myths and Traditions of the Crow Indians* (Anthropological Papers, American Museum of Natural History, Vol. XXV, New York 1922) p. 14
3 McClintock *The Old North Trail* p. 169
4 Wissler, C. & Duvall, D. C. *Mythology of the Blackfoot Indians* (Anthropological Papers, American Museum of Natural History, Vol. II, New York 1908) p. 23
5 For a discussion of Old Man's character see: Lowie, R. H. *Religion of the Crow* Anthropological Papers of the American Museum of Natural History, Vol. XXV, 1922, pp. 315-322.
Wissler and Duvall *Blackfoot Mythology* Anthropological Papers of the American Museum of Natural History, Vol. II, 1908, pp. 5-18
6 Lowie *Myths and Traditions of the Crow Indians* p. 15
7 Jung, C. G. *Man and His Symbols* (Aldus Books, London 1979) p. 185

8 Walker, J. R. *The Sun Dance and Other Ceremonies of the Oglala Division of the Teton Dakota* (Anthropological Papers, American Museum of Natural History, Vol. XVI, New York 1921) pp. 81-8
9 *ibid.* pp. 156-60
10 Wildschut *op. cit.* p. 3
11 For a general background to Cheyenne religious concepts see George A. Dorsey: *The Cheyenne*, Field Columbian Museum, Pub. 99, Anthropological Series, Vol. IX, Parts I and II, Chicago, 1905
Peter Powell: *Sweet Medicine*, 2 vols., University of Oklahoma Press, Norman, 1969
12 Grinnel *op. cit.* pp. 141-2
13 Lowie *The Religion of the Crow Indians* (Anthropological Papers, American Museum of Natural History, Vol. XXV, New York 1922) pp. 330-31
14 Neihardt *op. cit.* pp. 33-4
15 *ibid.* p. 34
16 *ibid.* p. 40
17 For further information about Crow bundles and religious concepts see
Robert H. Lowie: *The Religion of the Crow Indians*, Anthropological Papers, American Museum of Natural History, Vol. XXV, N.Y., 1922
William Wildschut: *Crow Indian Medicine Bundles*, Contributions, Museum of the American Indian, Vol. XVII, N.Y., 1975 (reprint — John C. Ewers, ed.) pages 43-47 are concerned specifically with Hoop Medicines.

18 see William Wildschut: *Crow Indian Medicine Bundles* pp. 77-78, and fig. 36
19 James Walker writes about Iktomi's character in *Oglala Sun Dance*, Anthropological Papers, American Museum of Natural History, Vol. XVI, N.Y., 1917 p. 90 and pp. 192-193
Lakota Belief and Ritual, University of Nebraska Press, Lincoln, 1980. pp. 128-129
20 Wildschut *op. cit.* pp. 119-20
21 Wildschut *op. cit.* p. 52
22 Henry & Thompson, *New Light on the Early History of the Greater Northwest* (Coues, E. (Ed) New York 1897) pp. 727-31
23 Wildschut, *op. cit.* p. 119
24 McClintock *The Old North Trail* p. 270
25 see Clark Wissler: *Ceremonial Bundles of the Blackfoot Indians*, Anthropological Papers, American Museum of Natural History, Vol. VII, Part II, N.Y., 1912 pp. 168-209
26 see George A. Dorsey: *The Cheyenne*, part I.
Peter Powell: *Sweet Medicine*, vol. I.
27 Walker, *Oglala Sun Dance*, p. 81
28 Catlin *Notes* Vol. I, p. 40
29 Jones, D. E. *Sanapia, Comanche Medicine Woman* (Case Studies in Cultural Anthropology, Spindler, G. & L. (Eds) Holt, Rinehart & Winston, New York 1972) p. 23
30 *ibid.* pp. 97-8
31 Lowie *The Religion of the Crow Indians* pp. 349-51
32 Neihardt *op. cit.* p. 148

CHAPTER 5
1 Walker *op. cit.* p. 160
2 McClintock *The Old North Trail* p. 175
3 *ibid.* pp. 240-44
4 *ibid.* pp. 282-83
5 Parkman *The Oregon Trail* (1944) pp. 299-300
6 Coe, R. *Sacred Circles* (Arts Council of Great Britain, London 1976) p. 15
7 McClintock, W. *Dances of the Blackfoot Indians* Southwest Museum Leaflets, No 7, 1937, p. 12
8 *ibid.* p. 11
9 McClintock *The Old North Trail* p. 175
10 Powell, P. *Sweet Medicine* (University of Oklahoma Press, Norman 1969) p. 113
11 Dorsey *The Cheyenne* p. 46
12 *ibid.* p. 2
13 *ibid.* Part II, the Sun Dance *passim*
14 *ibid.* p. 171
15 *ibid.* p. 163
16 Wildschut *op. cit.* p. 28
17 Walker *op. cit.* p. 61
18 *ibid.* pp. 60-62
19 For an Indian impression of the wars with the U.S., 1860-1890, see:
Dee Brown: *Bury My Heart at Wounded Knee*, Pan Books, London, 1971
20 Claude Lévi-Strauss: *Myth and Meaning*, Routledge & Kegan Paul, London 1978

BIBLIOGRAPHY

The following list of books, selected from the full bibliography, is recommended to the general reader interested in finding out more about the Plains Indians. Wherever possible the most recent edition has been given.

Brown, Dee *Bury My Heart at Wounded Knee* Bantam Books Inc., New York and Pan Books, London 1972
Catlin, Geo. *Letters and Notes on the Manners, Customs, and Conditions of The North American Indians* Dover Publications, New York 1973 (first published in 1841)
Culin, Stewart *Games of the North American Indians* Dover Publications, New York 1975 (first published 1902-03)
Dockstader, Frederick *Indian Art in America* New York Graphic Society, Greenwich, Conn. 1966
Ewers, John C. *The Blackfeet: Raiders on the Northwestern Plains* (Civilization of the American Indian Series) University of Oklahoma Press, Norman 1958
Feder, Norman *American Indian Art* Harry N. Abrams Inc., New York 1972
Hartmann, Horst *Die Plains- und Prärieindianer Nordamerikas* Museum für Völkerkunde, Berlin 1973
Holder, Preston *The Hoe and the Horse on the Plains*, University of Nebraska Press, Lincoln, 1970
Jorgensen, Joseph G. *The Sun Dance Religion: Power for the Powerless* University of Chicago Press 1972
Laubin, Reginald & Gladys *The Indian Tipi* Ballantine Books, New York 1973
Lowie, Robert H. *Indians of the Plains*, Anthropological Handbook No. 1, American Museum of Natural History, N.Y., 1954
Lowie, Robert H. *The Crow Indians* Irvington Publishers, New York 1956

McClintock, Walter *The Old North Trail* University of Nebraska Press, Lincoln 1977 (first published 1910)
Neihardt, John G. *Black Elk Speaks* Pocket Books Inc., New York and Sphere Books, London 1974
Powell, Peter *Sweet Medicine* 2 vols. (Civilization of the American Indian Series) University of Oklahoma Press, Norman 1969
Snow, Dean, with photographs by Werner Forman *The American Indians: Their Archaeology and Prehistory* Thames & Hudson, London and Viking Books, New York 1976
Wedel, Waldo R. *Prehistoric Man on the Great Plains* University of Oklahoma Press, Norman 1961
Weltfish, Gene *The Lost Universe: Pawnee Life and Culture* University of Nebraska Press, Lincoln 1977

ACKNOWLEDGMENTS

Werner Forman and the publishers would like to acknowledge the help of the following in permitting the photography shown on the pages listed:-

By courtesy of the Trustees of the British Museum, London: 37 top, 41, 42, 58 bottom, 59, 73, 90.
Field Museum of Natural History, Chicago: 76 top, 82, 106, 107.
Glenbow Museum, Calgary, Alberta: 10 top, 62, 80, 97, 112.
Museum of the American Indian, Heye Foundation, New York: 21, 22, 23, 24, 58 top, 115, 118 bottom.
Museum für Völkerkunde Abteilung Amerikanische Natur-völker, Dahlim-Berlin: 28, 32 bottom, 33, 36, 37 bottom, 40 bottom, 43, 49, 53, 56 top, 63, 69, 70, 71, 81 bottom, 98-99, 102.
Peabody Museum, Salem, Mass. 124 right.
Plains Indian Museum, Buffalo Bill Historical Center, Cody, Wyoming: 13, 14, 16-17, 94, 104. Hope Williams Read Collection: 4, 10-11, 69 top. Royal B. Hassrick Collection: 30, 34. Larry Larom Collection: 35, 81 top, 101 bottom, 122. Chandler Pohrt Collection (lent by Richard A. Pohrt: 40 top, 57, 65, 72, 91, 124 bottom. Robert L. Anderson Collection: 44, 45, 101 top, 113. The Bradford Collection (Gift of the W. R. Coe Foundation): 47. The Harold Guy Arnold Collection: 54-55. Adolf Spohr Collection: 92, 93, 100, 123. Adele K. Willoughby and Loretta Howard Collection: 95.
Robinson Museum, Pierre, South Dakota: 46, 51, 77.
Smithsonian Institution, Washington: 32 top, 118 bottom.

Werner Forman would also like to thank the following for their assistance: Bob Edgar, Robert Elder, Rosemary Ellison, Roland W. Force, Gary Galante, Julia D. Harrison, David Hartley, Horst Hartmann, Peter H. Hassrick, Georg Hors-captor, Jonathan King, Malcolm Macleod, Tom Martin, Leo A. Platteter, Phyllis Rabineau, John E. Rychtarik, Carol Sheehan, James G. E. Smith, James E. Vanstone, Ronald L. Weber.

Norman Bancroft-Hunt is grateful to his wife Sylvia for all her help and for access to her invaluable research work.

INDEX

Figures in italics refer to
illustrations

CONTENTS

A Mirror publication
Marketing Manager: Fergus McKenna
Mirrorpix: David Scripps and Alex Waters
020 7293 3858

Produced by Trinity Mirror Sport Media,
PO BOX 48, Liverpool L69 3EB
0151 227 2000

Executive Editor: Ken Rogers
Senior Editor: Steve Hanrahan
Senior Art Editor: Rick Cooke
Editor: Paul Dove
Compiled and written by: Alan Jewell, James Cleary
Designer: Glen Hind

Part of the Mirror Collection
© Published by Trinity Mirror
Images: Mirrorpix, PA Photos
Printed by PCP

DAILY MIRROR, Wednesday, June 5, 1940.

Daily Mirror

JUNE 5

No. 11,385   ONE PENNY

Registered at the G.P.O. as a Newspaper.

WE NEVER SURRENDER

DUNKIRK —LAST MEN GO

UNDER the bullets of German machine-guns, the last of the Allied forces defending Dunkirk were embarked yesterday, it was officially announced last night.

Admiral Abrial, the French commander of the forces who have been defending Dunkirk while the embarkation operations were proceeding, was the last to leave the town, said the French radio commentator.

The evacuation ended at seven o'clock yesterday morning, it was stated.

And already some of the soldiers rescued from Flanders have taken their place in the defence line, stretching from the Somme to the Rhine, against which the next great German offensive is almost immediately expected.

The last two Britons to reach England from Dunkirk landed yesterday with a crowd of French troops—Corporal C. Huntington, of Shirebrook, Nottingham, and Private J. Cowlam, of Hull, both of the East Yorks regiment. They were picked up by a French fishing boat.

Last night's French official communique stated:—

"The embarkation from Dunkirk was completed today in conformity with the prearranged plan.

"Until the last moment, first in the suburbs and then in the town itself from house to house, the rearguard put up a heroic resistance.

Port Now Useless

"The enemy, constantly reinforced, ceaselessly continued his assaults and was ceaselessly counter-attacked. The last embarkation took place under the fire of German machine-guns.

"This implacable defence and the success of this difficult and vast operations under the orders of Admiral Abrial and General Falgade have had a definite influence on the development of the struggle.

"Admiral Abrial declares that the work accomplished by the British was magnificent."

An earlier French communique had stated that the port of Dunkirk had been made useless.

The French Navy, it was added, had lost in the Dunkirk operations seven destroyers—Jaguar, Chacal, Adroit, Bourrasque, Foudroyante, Ouragan and Sirocco—and the supply ship Niger.

"Most of the crews of our lost naval vessels were saved."

NEW CHARGE—SPREAD HAW-HAW RUMOUR

A charge of being responsible for a rumour that he had heard from a German broadcast by Lord Haw-Haw that the Nazis were going to attack a Mansfield school is being brought today against a man at Mansfield.

This was stated yesterday by Mr. J. L. Nicol, Regional Information Officer, at the inaugural meeting at Nottingham of the North Midland Regional Advisory Committee, which will function under the jurisdiction of the Ministry of Information.

This will be the first case of its kind under the new regulations.

"**E**VEN if large tracts of Europe fall into the grip of the Gestapo and all the odious apparatus of Nazi rule, we shall not flag or fail. We shall go on to the end, and shall fight in France, on the oceans and in the air. We shall defend our island, whatever the cost, and shall fight on the beaches and landing grounds, in the fields and streets. We shall never surrender.

"Even if—which I do not for a moment believe—this island or a large part of it were subjugated, our Empire abroad, armed and guarded by the British Fleet, would carry on the struggle until, in God's good time, the New World, with all its force and men, set forth to the liberation and rescue of the old world."

IRONSIDES FOR HOME DEFENCE

SMALL bodies of highly mobile and strongly-armed troops—to be called "Ironsides"—are being organised for home defence by General Sir Edmund Ironside, Commander-in-Chief, Home Forces. There will be many hundreds of these formed from the Regular Army.

The War Office, announcing this last night, says that Sir Edmund has sent to each "Ironside" a copy of the following saying by Oliver Cromwell:—

"Your danger is as you have seen; and truly I am sorry it is so great. But I wish it to cause no despondency, as truly I think it will not: for we are British. It's no longer disputing but out instantly all you can."

The name Ironside, first given to Cromwell himself by Prince Rupert after the battle of Marston Moor in 1644, was later given to the troopers of his cavalry — those "God-fearing men," raised and trained by him in an iron discipline.

It traditionally implies great bravery, strength and endurance.

400,000 Local

Defence Volunteers

Lord Croft, Under-Secretary for War, stated in the House of Lords last night that 400,000 had volunteered for the L.D.V.

"It is no mere outlet of patriotic emotion that we are endeavouring to recruit," he said, "but a fighting force which may be at grips with the enemy next week or even tomorrow.

"That is the attitude the War Office takes towards these forces. The response has been absolutely magnificent. I doubt whether it has been equalled in any part of the world."

Lord Strabolgi said that besides making open spaces unusable for the landing of invading planes we should do the same with large spaces of water.

Lord Breadalbane suggested that each local area should have a lorry, armoured against splinters and bullets and armed with a couple of guns.

254 DEAD IN PARIS RAID

Death-roll in Monday's Paris air raid was 254, of whom 195 were civilians and fifty-nine soldiers, says the Paris War Ministry. It adds: 652 were wounded—545 civilians, 107 soldiers.

Twenty - five of the German bombers which took part in the raid were brought down.

MILITARY objectives in Munich, Frankfort-on-Main and the Ruhr were bombed by Allied warplanes as a reprisal for Monday's raid on Paris, the official Havas Agency announced last night.

A Berlin report yesterday stated that a "suburb of Munich" was bombed by an Allied plane, and eight people were killed. One bomb, it was stated hit a factory, causing much damage.

R.A.F. fighters maintained offensive patrols throughout Monday and early yesterday in the Dunkirk area.

In Germany refineries, oil tanks, supply depots and marshalling yards in the Ruhr Valley, Rhenish Prussia and in the neighbourhood of Frankfort were among the important military objectives attacked.

Factories which were hit included one of the most important motor works in Germany. Many fires and explosions were caused.

At Monheim several attacks were made on a munitions works. Hundreds of incendiary bombs were released.

Paris Bombs Picture—page 3.

THAT proclamation of the unbreakable Allied will to fight on for freedom was made by Mr. Winston Churchill in his speech to the House of Commons yesterday — the greatest speech ever made by a Prime Minister of Britain.

Standing as the staunch embodiment of that will to fight, he declared:

"I have myself full confidence that if all do their duty, and if nothing is neglected, and the best arrangements made—as they are being made—we shall prove ourselves once again able to defend our island home.

"We shall ride out the storms of war and outlive the menace of tyranny, if necessary for years."

A roar of cheers answered his superb, stark confidence.

"The British Empire and the French Republic, linked together in their cause and in their need, will defend to the death their native soil, aiding each other like good comrades to the utmost of their strength," said Mr. Churchill.

✦   ✦   ✦

These were other vital points in the Prime Minister's speech (the full report of which starts on page 3):

WE MUST EXPECT ANOTHER BLOW ALMOST IMMEDIATELY —EITHER AT FRANCE OR OURSELVES.

We shall not be content with a defensive war. We shall build up the B.E.F. once again.

Meantime we must bring Britain's defences to the height of efficiency.

✦   ✦   ✦

From Flanders 335,000 British and French soldiers were evacuated. Our casualties were 30,000 dead, wounded and missing. The enemy's casualties were far heavier.

✦   ✦   ✦

But thankfulness at the escape of the B.E.F. must not blind us to the fact that what happened in North France and Belgium was a colossal military disaster.

We lost 1,000 guns, and all the transport and armoured vehicles.

✦   ✦   ✦

Yet in the record-breaking arms effort now on that loss should be made up in months.

The Noble Story of Calais

Given an hour to surrender, 4,000 British and French troops, ordered to hold Calais to the end, spurned the demand to give in and kept the German hordes at bay for four days.

Then silence fell on the port. Thirty unwounded survivors were taken off by the Navy.

This noble story of the heroic defence of Calais is told on page 3.

Pictures of the Evacuation: Pages 8 & 9

CHURCHILL'S RALLY CRY

IN APRIL AND MAY 1940 THE NAZIS ANNEXED MAINLAND EUROPE AND ALLIED FORCES HAD TO MAKE A MIRACLE RETREAT FROM DUNKIRK. BRITAIN WAS NOW IN ADOLF HITLER'S SIGHTS BUT PRIME MINISTER WINSTON CHURCHILL ROARED DEFIANCE AS HE RALLIED THE NATION

"The Battle of France is over. I expect that the Battle of Britain is about to begin."

With these words, spoken on June 18, 1940, Prime Minister Winston Churchill prepared the nation for what was to visit its shores over the coming months.

Nine months after the outbreak of the Second World War, Great Britain was about to come under attack.

Britain declared war on Germany in September 1939 after the Nazis invaded Poland. From that point a phoney war existed as political discussions continued and land, sea and air forces assembled.

The peace was shattered in April 1940 when Germany invaded Denmark and Norway. A month later Belgium, Holland, Luxembourg and France were attacked and, over differing timescales, all were conquered.

The German advance pushed the Allied armies to a northern French port, Dunkirk. Despite being isolated, 350,000 members of the British Expeditionary Force were evacuated as 800 sea-worthy vessels, large and small, made their way across the Channel to mount a desperate rescue in late May and early June. The RAF managed to keep the majority of German bombers and fighters away while the evacuation was in process, shooting down 150 aircraft, although they lost 100 of their own fighters and 80 pilots.

A Daily Mirror correspondent was among the last to leave the port on a warship and he reported: "Our men came home in former cross-Channel steamers, luxury yachts, liners, cargo boats and trawlers. Before them they had a 24-hour voyage, with the threat of enemy bombing."

Although over a million Allied prisoners had been taken by the Germans over a three-week period, the successful evacuation, described as a "miracle of deliverance" by Churchill, provided a huge boost to British morale. Although a military defeat, Dunkirk became a symbolic victory and it ensured the Allies could fight on.

On June 12, the French commander, General Maxime Weygand, told his Prime Minister, Paul Reynaud, that the battle for France had been lost, a month after the invasion. Ten days later a Franco-German armistice was signed, dividing France into two zones. The northern region was occupied by Germany, while a new French government, led by Marshal Philippe Petain, controlled the south-east.

The Nazis, now in situ across the Channel and with a huge base from which they could attack Britain, expected Churchill ►

A soldier relaxes and reads the Daily Mirror after being evacuated from Dunkirk. Above, Prime Minister Winston Churchill appears ready for the Germans while, opposite, the front page of the Mirror on June 5, 1940 – the day after his "We shall fight on the beaches" speech

DAILY MIRROR, Wednesday, June 19, 1940.

Daily Mirror

JUNE 19

No. 11,397   ONE PENNY
Registered at the G.P.O. as a Newspaper.

The Premier leaving Downing-street for the House.

LEADERSHIP, GIVE US LEADERSHIP

1,750,000 MEN FOR DEFENCE

Strength of the defence forces now in Britain, Mr. Churchill stated, are:

1,250,000 Regular soldiers.
500,000 Local Defence Volunteers.
The Dominion Armies.

Report of Mr. Churchill's speech begins on page 2.

" **T**HE battle of France is over. I expect that the battle of Britain is about to begin."

Thus, Mr. Churchill in the House of Commons yesterday, and now there can be no illusions in anybody's mind about the ordeal before us.

Mr. Churchill spared the feelings neither of the politicians who have failed us, nor of the public who must face the dangers to come.

" Hitler," he said, " knows he will have to break us in this island or lose the war."

He explained that the Navy makes a mass invasion impossible, but that " the Navy have never pretended to be able to prevent raids by 5,000 or 10,000 men thrown ashore at several points on some dark night.

He went on to "the great question of invasion from the air, and the impending struggle between the British and German Air Force."

Our Air Force could deal with any air invasion " until our Air Force has been definitely overpowered."

We must expect enemy bombers now. There may be raids by parachute troops and attempted descents by air-borne soldiers They would get a warm welcome

" But," he went on, " the great question is—Can we break Hitler's air weapon ? "

He paused, and there was a deep regret for the past in his voice as he added, " It is a very great pity we have not got an Air Force at least equal to that of the most powerful enemy." In his broadcast speech last night he added a further comment on this " We were promised five years ago" he said

R.A.F. Hope of Improvement

His next words were a tribute to the gallantry of the R.A.F. who at Dunkirk undoubtedly beat the German Air Force, inflicting a loss of three or four to one.

" We hope," he said amid cheers, " to improve on that rate."

In his other glance at the past Mr. Churchill said:—" There are many who wish to hold an inquest on the conduct of the Governments and of the Parliaments during the years that led up to this catastrophe

"They seek to indict those who are responsible for the guidance of our affairs. This also would be a foolish and pernicious process There are too many in it"

" There are too many in it." That makes tragic reading, Mr. Churchill. It tells a tale of deception and cowardice.

But you ask us to forget the past, and we respect you.

Therefore. until the future becomes the past, we leave it at that.

Having dealt with the politicians of the past. Mr. Churchill turned to the people of the present.

He did not underrate the ordeal before us, but believed that our countrymen and women would prove capable of standing up to it.

" Much will depend on themselves. Every man and woman will have the chance to show the finest qualities of our race, and render the highest service to the cause, and all will be helped to remember 'He nothing common did or mean upon that memorable scene.' "

You need not worry about the men and women of Britain, Mr. Churchill.

The common people of the land have the courage.

Give them arms and give them leadership and they will not fail as they have been failed.

BUT ABOVE ALL GIVE THEM—

LEADERSHIP

DICTATORS FIX TERMS

HITLER and Mussolini, in a four-hour meeting at Munich last night, decided their terms for an armistice with France. The terms, which were not disclosed, were sent to Bordeaux.

It was reported in Rome tha the Dictators ordered their armies to take positions for a final attack on France if their terms should be refused Earlier. Berlin declared the terms would be unconditional surrender—or "destruction of the French system."

For two and a half hours the Dictators conferred alone. Then they called in Von Ribbentrop and Ciano, their Foreign Ministers, and their Chiefs of Staff. Both Hitler and Mussolini left Munich when the talks ended.

The French made a peace approach to Italy yesterday through the Papal Nuncio

FIGHT ON—PETAIN

MARSHAL PETAIN last night ordered all French and Allied combatants on land. sea and air to keep on fighting

He said armistice negotiations had not even begun, and warned the Allied soldiers that German forces were using the white flag to take important points without fighting.

The French military spokesman said the Germans now had full possession of all France north of the Loire, except part of Brittany.

Four French armies were still fighting a desperate retreat, and inflicting severe losses on the enemy.

The First French Army along the Seine had withdrawn to a line running east from the Gulf of St Malo on the north-west coast

Tunnel Blown Up

The French communique (see page 2) admitted that enemy advance guards were in Cherbourg.

The German thrust toward the Swiss frontier threatens the left flank of the French Army of the Alps.

And there were indications that the French were regrouping their forces on a new line with an east wing based on the Jura Mountains —which cover the southern end of the Maginot Line.

French troops blew up the four-mile railway tunnel under Cold Mountain, in the Jura, through which famous expresses travelled in peacetime. The eastern mouth of the tunnel lies on the Swiss side of the mountain

Refugees Barred

Petain's Government took action against the refugee problem which as hampered resistance.

Civilians in the war zone were told to stay at home and leave the roads clear for the army.

All French towns of over 20,000 inhabitants were declared open owns. to provide shelter from battle ad bombardment.

The commander of the powerful nch forces in Syria. General Mittauser has issued a proclamation ; the fight continues on land sea air

U.S. TO GO CONSCRIPT

PRESIDENT Roosevelt announced in Washington yesterday that some form of compulsory Government service for men and women of all classes would be proposed soon

The proposal, he said was being studied and might be sent to Congress by him within the next three to six weeks.

Compulsory service would be military only in its broadest terms. It would probably represent about one year's training for all young Americans, women as well as men.

Technical Training

Training would include combat duties, as well as duties behind the lines, such as communications, technical, a' aft and mechanical work.

He envisaged technical training for work of industrial production necessary to support a fighting army.

The President emphasised that compulsory training did not necessarily mean boys were to be trained solely to be infantrymen. pilots and other fighting personnel. but training in all skilled technical jobs.

Mr. Oliver Simmonds, M.P for Duddeston, Birmingham, who has returned to London after having flown to New York and back in three weeks —his visit was concerned with aircraft production—said yesterday that of many Americans whose views he valued, not one believed America could stay out of the war.

Prevailing opinion appeared to be that the United States would not declare war earlier than one month or later than six months hence

BOMBS ON THAMES TOWNS

ENEMY aircraft over the Thames Estuary last night dropped high explosive and incendiary bombs. They also fired machine-guns.

Air-raid warnings were sounded in six counties, and in East Anglia villagers cheered as they saw a Nazi bomber shot down in flames.

A British fighter engaged the bomber, which was caught in the beam of a searchlight, and shot it down.

An explosion. obviously caused by a bomb. shook one town on the Thames Estuary.

A plane was heard overhead, and searchlights tried to locate it. People ran to air-raid shelters. Several explosions were heard. Half an hour later people returned to their homes. but three more explosions occurred

Heavy Fire

At another point near the Thames Estuary air-raid sirens were sounded, and the sky was streaked with searchlight beams. There was intense A.A. fire. No bombs were dropped.

Enemy planes flying at a great height were seen to be firing their guns.

The raid on the Thames Estuary was seen by many people travelling on late trains from London to East Kent towns.

They could see searchlights playing in the skyline, and had a dis-

Continued on Back Page

Wednesday, June 19, 1940

Daily Mirror

Geraldine House, Fetter-lane, E.C.4. Holborn 4321.
42-48, Hardman-street, Deansgate, Manchester, 3.
Blackfriars 2185-6-7-8-9.

THE BATTLE OF BRITAIN

THE Battle of France is over. The Battle of Britain is about to begin.

So the Prime Minister summarised the situation yesterday.

After repeated blows of nearly catastrophic violence we remain steady. But we needed Mr. Churchill's rallying call.

It is a call, first, of encouragement based on facts, not upon illusions.

So far—for much of our part in it—this war may be described as a " war of rescue."

Dunkirk was a magnificent example of that. And now, again, large forces from the lost—or seemingly lost—Battle of France are saved for us—saved to fight on at home.

Once rescued, as the majority have been, they add enormously to the strength of our home defences. Already they are the " veterans " of battle. They have seen and they know.

They have seen desolation scattered over France by an enemy without mercy. In their hearts they will resolve that their own homes and fields and familiar places shall be defended with all the strength that their bitterness inspires in brave men.

With these we gather the best of our airmen, both for defence and for the carrying of his own terror into the enemy's country. For we **must** attack. The defensive-victory delusion is dead.

We gather also (this is a weak point) all our able-bodied men and women for the auxiliary work of local defence. We must increase that part of our resistance to the utmost of our powers. It is a main part of the needed speed-up. All can help in it.

Lastly we gather our resolution and fortitude and patience for the bitter struggle. The civilian is in this war. He knows it at last. It is his privilege to be in it—to bear his part, as the men in the air, the men at sea, the soldiers armed for battle, are ready to bear theirs.

To hearten them they have this thought—there is no other way. For the peace of Hitler would be, for all of us, an agony much worse than the pain of wounds or death.

Meanwhile, out there in Munich, the two blood-drunken Dictators, little lion and podgy jackal, were busy lapping up Europe and bits of Africa according to their premature pleasures of gluttonous anticipation. Another peace is devised, like those of death, already imposed by Hitler on his earlier victims.

When the unfortunate Petain, in antique soldierly language, speaks of " honour," he forgets that the word has no meaning for insatiable brigands. As a veteran of the last war, he may remember the peace of Brest-Litovsk between victorious Germany and fallen Russia. That treaty somehow never came off. We commend the good omen, with all devoted sympathy, to wounded but immortal France.   W. M.

Opposite page and left: How the Daily Mirror reported Winston Churchill's speech of June 18 when he coined the phrase 'Battle of Britain' while warning the nation of the ordeal ahead. Above, a group of children practise wearing gas masks at Bedworth's air-raid precautions training event

▶ to come to terms with Germany. They were wrong to do so. The Prime Minister remained defiant and declared: "[Adolf] Hitler knows he will have to break us in this island or lose the war."

On June 18 the Government published a pamphlet containing seven rules to follow if Britain was invaded. They were:

● Stay where you are.
● Don't believe rumours or spread them.
● Keep watch – tell the police or military quickly and accurately if you see anything suspicious.
● Never give Germans anything.
● Be ready to work blocking roads.
● Help to organise a defence system to resist sudden attack at work.
● Always think of Britain before yourself.

The German Chancellor's attempts to force the nation to submit began in earnest on July 10, generally accepted to be the first day of the Battle of Britain.

Six days later Hitler announced that an invasion force would be ready to sail by August 15. The operation, codenamed 'Sealion', was hastily assembled.

Meanwhile, battle had been joined in the air as the RAF's Submarine Spitfires and Hawker Hurricanes met the Luftwaffe's Messerschmitts, Dorniers, Junkers and Heinkels.

At the beginning of July, RAF Fighter Command, led by Sir Hugh Dowding, had 640 fighters but the Luftwaffe had 2,600 bombers and fighters.

The Germans initially targeted the Channel ports, military airfields and shipping. They knew they needed to establish air superiority to attempt an amphibious invasion.

In Britain, anti-invasion defences had been set in motion from late May. The Local Defence Volunteers (LDV) was one example, comprising men too old or infirm to join the services and those in protected trades who were exempt from conscription. They became known as the 'Home Guard' when Churchill coined the phrase during a BBC broadcast. By the end of that month, over a million-and-a-half men had volunteered.

The air fighting continued and gradually moved inland. The Luftwaffe had greater resources but operated close to their fuel limit and lacked a coherent strategy. The Junkers Ju 87 'Stuka' dive-bomber was very accurate but they proved vulnerable to attack – the Hurricanes and Spitfires found ▶

them easy prey. Because of their heavy losses, they were withdrawn from the battle in mid-August.

An obvious advantage of fighting over these shores was that downed British pilots could, if they weren't seriously injured, rejoin the fray. A German who fell to earth was heading towards inevitable capture.

The defence force also benefited from the new radar early warning system, developed by Robert Watson-Watt, which gave Fighter Command enough time to mobilise its planes and target incoming German raiders.

At this stage of the battle, the Luftwaffe was effectively probing British defences, searching for weaknesses before launching a major assault.

After a month's fighting, their leader, Reichsmarschall Hermann Goering, decided to intensify the bombing. A major assault began on August 13, aimed at the airfields of 11 Group in Kent and Sussex. This was strategically important as their role was to defend London and the south-east.

The situation for 11 Group became serious as maintenance and supply became dangerously stretched and ground crews, working in the open, suffered heavy casualties. Despite their difficulties, crews worked magnificently to keep aircraft combat-ready and the group continued providing fast response.

After Churchill visited 11 Group's operations room at RAF Uxbridge, he was moved to remark: "Never in the field of human conflict was so much owed by so many to so few."

Because of the strength of opposition the Luftwaffe encountered, the planned invasion of August 15 did not materialise. The Germans had lost significantly more aircraft than the RAF but Fighter Command remained under enormous strain.

On August 24 civilian areas of London were bombed in error – Hitler had prohibited such attacks as he was hoping Britain would accept the situation was hopeless and sue for a negotiated peace. The RAF retaliated by striking at Berlin the following evening.

On September 5 Hitler moved the battle into a new phase by issuing

Above: Air Chief Marshal Sir Hugh Dowding, the leader of RAF Fighter Command, photographed in 1940. Right: Robert Watson-Watt, the man who invented radar. The RAF's ability to detect incoming German aircraft gave them a crucial advantage

A squadron of Hawker Hurricanes rehearse for Empire Flying Day over Kent in 1938. Two years later the same aircraft would be defending Britain against German bombing

a directive to begin "disruptive attacks on the population and air defences of major British cities, including London, by day and night." Two days later 'The Blitz' began as nearly 1,000 aircraft attacked the capital city, which experienced the first of 57 consecutive nights of bombing.

Although the Nazi raids devastated London, the Luftwaffe was now operating at the limit of their range and the switch to city bombing allowed 11 Group a chance to repair airfields and radar stations. By moving further north, the Germans were also in the range of 12 Group, who provided air defence for the Midlands, Norfolk, Lincolnshire and North Wales.

Knowing London and industrial centres to be the target, Fighter Command was able to assemble large numbers of fighters and break up the German formations. The Luftwaffe's change of tactics was a mistake and they were shocked by the numbers of Hurricanes and Spitfires confronting them.

There was huge damage inflicted on the ground with significant loss of life but the bombing only served to harden resolve amongst the public.

Civilian organisations worked heroically to look after the injured and deal with damaged buildings.

When Buckingham Palace was hit, Queen Elizabeth (who later became the Queen Mother) memorably declared: "I'm glad we've been bombed. It makes me feel I can look the East End in the face." Royal visits to this area became a symbol of the nation standing together.

While the attacks continued, Luftwaffe losses mounted. Goering launched another major attempt to destroy Fighter Command on September 15 but 176 enemy aircraft were destroyed on that day, compared to 25 defence planes. Two days later Operation Sealion was postponed indefinitely as Hitler turned his attention towards the USSR (which he went on to invade in June 1941).

The Nazis began to accept that the RAF could not be defeated in 1940. Although 'The Blitz' continued for another six months, the fighting became less fierce and the Battle of Britain ended on October 31. The RAF had seen off the threat of an invasion and achieved a crucial victory.

THE BATTLE BEGINS

AFTER THE WARNINGS AND THE PREPARATION, JULY 10 MARKED THE START OF MAJOR
HOSTILITIES AS THE NAZIS ATTEMPTED TO ESTABLISH AIR SUPERIORITY OVER BRITAIN.
THEY BEGAN BY TARGETING SHIPPING CONVOYS, RADAR STATIONS AND THE CHANNEL
PORTS. HOWEVER, THE PILOTS OF THE RAF WERE READY TO FIGHT FIRE WITH FIRE

Two Hawker Hurricanes take off from RAF Hawkinge in Kent to intercept German aircraft

RAF's battle score – 37

Thursday, July 11, 1940

The biggest enemy air challenge over our coasts was fought off by the RAF yesterday. In furious combats our fighters shot down 14 German machines and so seriously damaged 23 others that they were unlikely to reach home, the Air Ministry announced early this morning. Two British machines were lost, but the pilot of one is safe.

One hundred and fifty RAF and enemy planes fought the battles as German bombers, escorted by fighters, attacked shipping and our Channel coast.

The Air Ministry said the enemy losses represented the greatest damage on the German Air Force since bombing raids on this country began.

A convoy was attacked by 38 Dorniers with an escort of 25 Messerschmitts. Waves of Spitfires and Hurricanes went into action. The raiders lost three bombers in three minutes.

The captain of a ship in the convoy said: "The sky was black with planes. I saw enemy machines falling in flames, and before two of them hit the water, their tails, chopped by machine-gun bullets from our fighters, dropped off."

A fisherman told the Daily Mirror: "The first Spitfires to arrive did a wonderful bit of work. They got round to the back of the Germans and kept them from getting away.

"Then the other RAF lads taught them a bit about encirclement, and drove them back towards the English coast."

Below: Observer corps at work, watching the skies and reporting the movements of all planes, whether friendly or enemy. Left, an Air-Raid Protection (ARP) warden by the road-side and a notice for motorists

THE PRICE HITLER IS PAYING

Sun.	— — 7
Mon.	— — 8
Tues.	— — 9
Wed.	— 37
Thurs.	23
Fri.	— — 11

KEEP IT UP, BOYS

Hermann's Getting Rings Under His Eyes!

Left and above: The Daily Mirror provides a tally of the German planes shot out of the sky in the first week, while this cartoon (from July 15) mocks Hermann Goering, the commander in chief of the Luftwaffe

Greatest hero of them all

Monday, July 15, 1940

Blasting enemy planes out of the sky is the one passion of 30-year-old Douglas R S Bader, Britain's most amazing RAF fighter command pilot.

The Daily Mirror understands that Bader is the legless pilot who, in his Hurricane, shot down a Dornier 17 into the sea at the weekend.

But to ex-aerobatic RAF ace Bader, who lost his legs in a flying accident nine years ago, this remarkable feat is "just a swell start".

"Nothing can stop him continuing his career in the RAF," his mother-in-law, who lives in Bagshot, told the Daily Mirror yesterday.

"The more fights he can get himself into, the better he is pleased, despite his great physical handicap. He intends adding many more 'downed' planes to his credit before the war is over."

When Bader crashed and lost his legs, rescuers who dragged him unconscious from his plane feared that he would die. But, in the words of a friend, he just refused to die.

He was fitted up with metal legs and invalided out of the RAF but he kept on flying – besides playing strenuous games.

When the war started he determined to get back into the RAF. He argued his way to a medical board and argued the board into giving him a flying test. He came through it first class and is now leading a squadron of Canadians.

He had a minor crash recently and bent both his legs…he sent them to an artificer to be straightened, and within half-an-hour was in the air again.

Below: Douglas Bader lifts one of his artificial legs into the cockpit prior to a thanksgiving flight over London in September 1945. Group Captain Bader was known as "tin-legs" by his comrades

Right: A pilot catches
up on his sleep
between missions

Heavy flame-throwers were stationed
at English Channel ports to repel the
Nazis, if an invasion materialised

A Messerschmitt Bf 109 and MK II
Spitfire engage in a dogfight over
the outer harbour of Dover at the
height of the Battle of Britain

A direct hit on this pub doesn't stop the locals from enjoying a pint of beer and a game of darts

A downed Messerschmitt is examined by the RAF technical team on July 30

A Heinkel He 111 bomber shot down in southern England. Although it was capable of inflicting significant damage, the Heinkel was exposed in this battle because of its poor manoeuvrability, relatively low speed and weak defence

Hitler says submit

Saturday, July 20, 1940

Adolf Hitler gave Britain an ultimatum last night: "Talk peace or I destroy you." As he piled threat on threat, he called it his final appeal to reason.

He made not a single concrete proposal. He spoke to Britain in the way he had spoken to every country he planned to make a Nazi vassal – as a reasonable man of peace.

Despite the war aims announced by his press and other Nazi leaders, he declared he had never desired the destruction of the British Empire. He said he was still sad that he had not reached an agreement with Britain.

"There are no grounds for the prolongation of the war," he said. Then he proceeded to threaten.

"British statesmen probably have no real conception of what it will mean once the German offensive begins in earnest against the British Isles.

"What is coming will visit the British people, not Churchill, who will probably go to Canada. He may think the outcome will be the annihilation of Germany, but it will be the destruction of a great world Empire."

Preparing the way for a threat of air attack, he used the claim, repeatedly refuted, that the RAF was bombing German civilians.

"Thus far," he said. "I have hardly answered this bombardment, but when my answer comes, it will be terrible for millions of people.

"In this hour I consider it my duty to relieve my conscience and to direct my last appeal to England. This time, I think, I shall be believed, as I am not the defeated who is begging.

"Churchill could, of course, cry to the world that I am afraid. Anyway, I have relieved my conscience towards the things which are to come.

"This war can only end with the destruction of England or Germany. I know it will be England."

Clear your loft today

Tuesday, July 23, 1940

You must clear your loft of everything today as a precaution against incendiary bombs. Local authorities are empowered to enter your home and see that it is done.

An order to this effect has just been issued by the Ministry of Home Security.

Clearing the loft will not only minimise air-raid fire risks. The junk will make good salvage and help the war effort.

The order applies to lofts and attics in dwelling houses in urban areas.

Nurses and patients watch the fighting between the RAF and the Luftwaffe in the skies above them. Perhaps the man taking aim from his bed is an injured pilot

The wreckage of a parade of shops after a daylight air raid on Dover. A man can be seen emerging from the rubble as he attempts to salvage some possessions

Queen Elizabeth (later
the Queen Mother) talks
to 86-year-old Lydia
Grange, from Hull, who
escaped unhurt after a
Nazi raid destroyed her
home at the end of July.
The residents were inside
an Anderson shelter
when the bomb fell. The
Queen's visits to bombed
inner-city areas became
a feature of the war

Sea blitz new Nazi attack

Saturday, July 27, 1940

The Germans have launched a new form of sea attack.

Dive-bombers are being sent into action against convoys in the English Channel to prepare the way for surface raids by motor torpedo boats.

The 'spearhead assault' tactics developed in Flanders and France – with dive-bombers blasting the way for tank attacks – is being adapted for a 'blitz' (lightning) war at sea.

Exactly the same aeroplanes are being used, the Stuka dive-bombers.

The new sea tactics, it was revealed last night, were introduced in Thursday's raid on a British convoy in the Channel.

Stuka bombers raided the ships, then nine motor torpedo boats sped to the attack.

The enemy were routed but not before some loss to us. The dive-bombers sank five small coasters.

Then the RAF went into action and the majority of the 28 enemy planes shot down on Thursday were machines which took part in the convoy raid.

As the enemy motor torpedo boats came in to attack the convoy, they were sighted by two British destroyers. Immediately the raiding craft turned away, put out a smokescreen and fled.

The destroyers, with two of our own motor torpedo boats racing alongside as 'escort', steamed through the smoke, their guns firing toward the enemy craft.

Then 20 Stuka bombers dived out of low clouds to attack the destroyers.

The warships manoeuvred rapidly away from each other to dodge a hail of bombs and threw out thick smokescreens. Their anti-aircraft guns drove off the aeroplanes.

They again sped in pursuit of the enemy torpedo boats – and were once more attacked by German bombers.

Water spouted hundreds of feet high beside the destroyers. Time and again watchers on the shore saw the ships' bows appear from behind a huge screen of spray. Both destroyers steamed on.

Then Spitfires swept up to fight off the enemy planes.

Below: Winston Churchill chairs a war meeting in 1940. On the far right is Clement Atlee, part of the national government and the man who succeeded Churchill as Prime Minister in 1945

Bottom: The wreckage of a bungalow and adjoining villa on which a Heinkel 111 fell after being shot down by anti-aircraft guns. The bomber's crew baled out and were captured (as were the German airmen pictured immediately below). To the right, downed Nazi aircraft is piled in heaps before the material is salvaged

She sold them to help Red Cross!

Saturday, August 3, 1940

Hitler has found a new weapon – the leaflet. His airmen dropped thousands of them on Thursday night in south-east and south-west England and in Wales.

And what a leaflet. A typically German production.

It has four pages, is the size of a small newspaper, and there are, roughly, 13,000 words.

It contains in its dreary fullness Hitler's recent speech in Berlin and is headed: "A Last Appeal to Reason, by Adolf Hitler."

In it there is a suggestion that the British public know nothing of the speech.

Actually it was given wide publicity in the press, on the BBC and in parliament.

Nobody was impressed.

So the dropping of the leaflets is a wasted effort – from Hitler's point of view.

In this country it has a farce value, as people are asking: "Why leaflets?" They are amused or scornful.

Some of the leaflets are being sold in aid of the British Red Cross.

One of the people who did this said: "A farmer down here has been charging sixpence each to sightseers who wanted to look at bomb craters in his field.

"He has given the money to the Red Cross and I thought I might do the same sort of thing.

"I picked up a lot of the leaflets and people have been only too glad to have one of them from me and make a contribution to the Red Cross. I have collected over £2 already.

"No one is taking them seriously for one moment."

Below: Leaflets dropped by the Luftwaffe are the source of much mirth among these British people. The leaflets were sold as souvenirs to raise funds for the Red Cross

Why Hitler has waited so long

Tuesday, August 6, 1940

Hitler has delayed mass air raids on Britain in order to pile up the resources of his air force and train hundreds of extra air crews for an attempt at a knockout blow.

Probably the Germans are not quite ready. But when their air blitzkrieg comes, we may expect not 50 or 100 machines in an attack, but hundreds.

To set against this is the fact that British air production is now running neck and neck with that of the Nazis. Although it must be remembered that we have a big leeway to make up, our production rate has by no means reached its peak. This authoritative view was given last night.

Hermann Goering spoke quite fairly when he said that his airmen have done little more as yet than conduct reconnaissances over England.

These operations make small demands on his bomber strength. Goering is using them to train more 'front-line' crews.

But the airmen he is using at present are not mere youths. Their average age is 26. Nor is their morale poor. Those captured are tough, truculent and worthy representatives of their service.

When they dodge away in day raids it is probably under orders – to conserve machines.

This is our air defence situation: We have many more fighters. We have more reserves and more experienced pilots than ever before.

Hitler's bombers will meet a tremendous RAF opposition. And our pilots have been much better at keeping the enemy from his objectives than he has been against our own attacks.

But this must be remembered: Neither the Germans nor ourselves have yet solved successfully the problem of intercepting bombers at night. In any raid, a number of planes are sure to get through the defences.

In the intensified raiding which must be expected, our fighters cannot cover the whole of the sky. They operate over specified defence zones.

It is now seven weeks since Hitler started fairly extensive night bombing over this country, using anything from 50 to 100 machines for widespread objectives. In those seven weeks the confirmed German air losses totalled 307 machines. We do not know how many others did not get back home. Our own losses were 172.

Evacuee children help the farmer bring in the harvest

Children from a Yorkshire village aim a toy revolver at Winston Churchill from behind a farm cart during the Prime Minister's tour of the north-east in August

16 warplanes gift by MP

Saturday, August 10, 1940

A millionaire MP, father of eight children, has given Britain 16 Hurricanes and Spitfires (cost £100,000) to replace the losses sustained in Thursday's rout of the Nazis over the English Channel.

The MP, Mr William Garfield Weston, a 41-year-old biscuit manufacturer who sits for Macclesfield, Cheshire, hit upon the idea of his gift while he was reading the heroic story of the RAF's Channel victory, in which 60 German planes were brought down and Britain lost 16 machines.

Yesterday he telephoned the Ministry of Aircraft Production and said a cheque for £100,000 was on its way round "to buy 16 Hurricanes or Spitfires we lost in yesterday's battle".

Last night, in the oak-panelled lounge of his house at Marlow, Buckinghamshire, Mr Weston told the Daily Mirror: "I've only one regret; all the money in the world can't buy back the lives of those RAF pilots.

"What fellows. While England has men like them to guard her from the air, there's no need for any worry about this war.

"I hope people won't get me wrong. I'm a wealthy man and I've given this money as a private expression of gratitude and of admiration of a set of heroes.

"I know no money could mitigate the sorrow of relatives of those pilots who willingly sacrificed their lives. I'd gladly give every penny to restore those boys to their folk. I can't. The next best thing is to replace their machines."

BRITAIN STANDS TOGETHER

A MONTH INTO THE BATTLE, THE NAZIS ASSEMBLED INVASION FORCES ON THE FRENCH COAST AND RAIDS INTENSIFIED. CITIES AND CIVILIAN AREAS SUFFERED HEAVY BOMBING AS THE BLITZ BEGAN. ALTHOUGH MANY AREAS WERE DEVASTATED, MORALE WAS NOT BROKEN. INDEED, THE LUFTWAFFE'S LOSSES SOON BECAME UNSUSTAINABLE

Above: A fireman's hose sends water on to the smouldering remains of shops in the centre of Portsmouth. The city was a primary target for the Luftwaffe because of the naval dockyards

Nazi raid Naval port, 39 down

Tuesday, August 13, 1940

Goering again launched all-day air attacks over the Channel yesterday. It was estimated that at one time nearly 500 enemy aircraft were in action in mass raids – the greatest total since war began.

The fiercest raid was on Portsmouth and the dockyard. Bombs landed on several RAF aerodromes.

But again Goering's squadrons were slashed by RAF fighters and anti-aircraft guns. Man after man baled out from wrecked German machines.

And last night the Air Ministry announced: "In today's air engagements round our coasts, the total of enemy aircraft so far known to have been destroyed is 39. Nine of our aircraft are missing."

Spitfire and Hurricane pilots got 32 of the Nazi bombers and fighters already confirmed.

And anti-aircraft gunners had their best day since the south coast raids began – they shot down seven bombers.

Children play on a makeshift swing amidst rubble and overlooked by the shell of what were people's homes

144 down out of 1,000

Friday, August 16, 1940

One hundred and forty-four enemy raiders were brought down up to midnight yesterday.

That was Britain's answer at the end of the day of the greatest air attacks, in which the German 'blitz' swept the length of Britain.

Twenty-seven RAF fighters were lost in the mighty defence battles, but eight of the pilots are safe.

For hour after hour through the day and into the night, our fighters swept against the huge raiding squadrons.

The German Air Force used more than a thousand bombers and fighters in the attacks.

Croydon Aerodrome, London's airport before the war, was raided last night. Sirens were sounded in a wide area of Greater London.

Many towns were attacked during the day and a number of people killed. RAF aerodromes in the south-east and north-east were bombed.

Heavy attacks on south-east areas went on into the evening hours. All the time German machines were being shot out of the sky.

Over one coast district RAF fighters and the guns smashed up a three-hour attack by 250 raiders. Once again there was a spell in which German planes were dropping out of the sky at the rate of one a minute.

It was the most gruelling day for the RAF fighters. And their greatest.

Fourteen dive-bombers, protected by fighters, attacked Croydon Aerodrome. High explosive screamers and incendiary bombs were dropped. Some people were killed and a number injured.

The raiders were first seen when they started to dive about three miles from the aerodrome. People in the streets saw them come to a few hundred feet before the bombs were released.

Within a few seconds anti-aircraft guns put up a fierce barrage. RAF fighters swept up to the attack. Three of the raiders are believed to have been smashed. One bomb narrowly missed a gasworks but houses in an adjoining road were hit. The main casualties of the raid were caused by a bomb which wrecked a building where men worked. Hours afterwards workers were still digging in the debris for bodies of the victims.

Above: A Daily Mirror cartoon glories in the repeated delays to Hitler's planned invasion of Britain, which was code-named 'Operation Sealion'. To the right, a man leans outside a house that has taken a direct hit

Children and adults inspect the scene on a wrecked street in Malden, south-west London

Raiders bomb London suburbs and gun streets

Saturday, August 17, 1940

Goering's blitz raiders struck for the first time at London last night. They dropped bombs in south-western suburbs.

Several points on the Thames Estuary were also attacked, including Tilbury and Northfleet.

As the German press and radio screamed that daring Nazi squadrons were wrecking military objectives round Britain's capital, the raiders' bombs were in fact falling on civilian property and one railway station.

The day's raids cost Goering's air force at least 70 machines. Seventeen British fighters were lost, but ten of the pilots were saved.

The bombers swooped to machine-gun the streets in hit and run attacks. Bombs caused damage in several areas, but casualties were relatively small.

Waves of bombers dived from the clouds and rained bombs on residential districts in the south-west suburbs of London.

One of the bombs fell on the booking office of a railway station and killed a number of people, some of whom had gone to seek shelter. Others were injured. Rows of houses, shops, a club, two stores and a garage were either wrecked or badly damaged. A church was smashed

and a mission hall cut in two. Some trolleybus lines were destroyed.

In one suburb more than 30 bombs were dropped. There were miraculous escapes. Crowded trains were running when bombs dropped close to the Southern Railway line.

"I threw myself flat on the floor as a bomber dived," said a signalman. "The train was just passing the box as the raider came down within a few feet and released a bomb. The back coaches of the train were riddled with shrapnel. It was a deliberate attempt to bomb the train. The windows of my cabin fell in on me, but I escaped without a scratch."

The windows of nearly every shop in one street were shattered and scores of people sustained minor injuries from flying glass.

"It was a murderous thing," one woman said. "I saw only one bomber and he dived right along the street. He released his bombs and then, not satisfied, he tried to machine-gun ARP men at their post."

"I saw a black mass in the sky as the Germans swooped from the clouds," said one man. "I had got my wife and two kiddies in a club-room when the shrapnel started to fly. It got so hot that I pushed them under the billiard table."

140-16: RAF's biggest victory

Monday, August 19, 1940

The German Air Force, renewing mass raids on south and south-east England after Saturday's lull, lost at least 140 machines. Only 16 RAF fighters were lost – eight pilots were safe.

Declared the Air Ministry early today: "Having regard to the numbers employed, this represents the heaviest defeat the enemy has yet suffered at the hands of our fighters and ground defence."

The grand total of enemy planes shot down since they began attacking Britain and our shipping has now soared to at least 1,033.

More than 600 machines were used in the mass raids yesterday. The RAF's work reached new heights of brilliance.

Twice the Germans were beaten off as they tried to penetrate London's defences. During the second raid in the evening, there were terrific combats over the Thames.

For the first time, Londoners heard their anti-aircraft guns open fire. Seventy German bombers paid our AA gunners the biggest compliment in their power – they turned back.

Driven off from the city, German planes dived to bomb and machine-gun towns on the southern outskirts of London, and attacked areas in Kent and other parts of the south and south-east.

This was another attempt at terror raiding on civilians. More delayed action bombs were dropped. Attacks on several RAF aerodromes killed and injured some service personnel.

The first attacks came just after 1pm, when raiders crossed the Kent coast. A squadron of Spitfires tackled bombers which were about to attack their aerodrome in Surrey, and in a few minutes destroyed 11.

At the same time a Hurricane squadron was shooting down eight over Hampshire. Another squadron of Hurricanes, on patrol, sighted five Messerschmitt fighter-bombers at 21,000ft.

Over Kent a crack Spitfire squadron, which is approaching its century of successes, attacked 80 enemy planes flying "in a huge rectangle".

Above: A Mirror cartoon from August 20 depicts the Luftwaffe's planes flying into a ferocious reception. Below, firemen rescue a woman who was trapped in a building on City Road, London. To the right, wardens and rescue workers search the rubble of an office block. All that remains intact is a coat rack and two jackets, which stand exposed on the side of the building

Enemy bring scrap

Thursday, August 22, 1940

German planes brought down by the RAF are contributing valuable scrap to Great Britain's salvage campaign.

Already many tons of iron, brass and aluminium have been recovered from the raiders that have fallen to our anti-aircraft guns and fighters.

These metals have reached the factories and will soon be used against the enemy in the form of new aeroplanes, bombs, tanks and guns.

Every plane brought down in this country is examined by officers of the maintenance command of the RAF. They examine the angles of bullet holes because this gives valuable information to our fighter pilots. They test the oil and petrol and look for new instruments or constructional features.

Then the planes are handed over to salvage experts for transformation into war material.

On a 20-acre site somewhere in England, nearly 200 men are hard at work every day, breaking up a constant stream of German bombers and fighters.

Here in a mountainous pile lie the grey-green and black bodies of machines that have paid the penalty for daring to attack our shores. Shattered and broken, these hundreds of planes are being tackled by men who sort out the different metals with sledgehammer and blowpipe.

Above: Wardens clear up the remains of a crashed German bomber in Merton Park, Surrey

German guns shell Kent coast

Friday, August 23, 1940

Hitler's long-range guns on France's Channel coast opened their first big bombardment of the English coast at dark last night. Shells landed in the Dover area.

The bombardment was still going on in the early hours of today. Shells fell at roughly half-hour intervals.

A church was hit and wrecked. Damage was fairly widespread, but there were remarkably few casualties for so heavy a bombardment.

As the batteries were firing, RAF machines roared down in fierce bombing attacks in an attempt to locate and destroy them.

Earlier, the German batteries had shelled a British convoy without scoring a hit – an attack which showed that the guns were planted along a 24-mile stretch from Boulogne to Calais.

A salvo of three shells opened last night's bombardment of the Kent coast. Gunflashes were seen stabbing the darkness over the Channel. Shells were heard tearing through the sky. Then big explosions shook places on the coast.

A convoy is bombed in the straits of Dover as the Luftwaffe continued aerial attacks on shipping. Hermann Goering wanted to lure British planes into dogfights over the Channel as he felt that if a fighter was shot down in this area, there was more chance of the pilot being killed

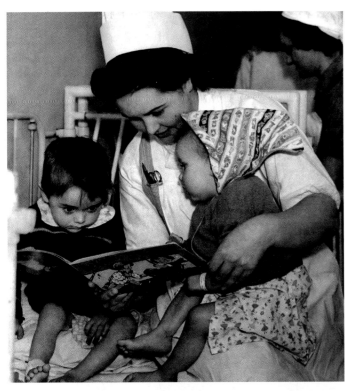

Left: A nurse reads to children during an air-raid alarm while, below, another nurse holds a baby as they look through the smashed window of a bomb-damaged maternity unit

The view of a raid on Germany through a bomb-aimers' window

Bombers over Berlin, London

Monday, August 26, 1940

While Hitler's bombers were making another raid on the London area early today, RAF bombs shook Berlin.

Berliners hurrying to their shelters soon after midnight heard heavy explosions as bombs burst to the north-west. Ten explosions were clearly heard in the first 10 minutes and the centre of Berlin shook.

In the famous Unter den Linden boulevard, the silence between the bomb blasts was broken by the noise of official cars tearing along at full speed with their hooters screeching.

The hum of plane engines was heard faintly in the centre of Berlin. It was estimated that bombs were falling 20 miles away.

London had two air-raid warnings within two-and-a-half hours last night and early today.

The first one lasted about an hour and no bombs were dropped near London, but there was anti-aircraft fire. Bombs were dropped in the second raid.

When the sirens sounded earlier, the drone of planes could be heard in the outskirts. Searchlights swept the sky and people in the streets heard the sound of gunfire.

Many went to Underground railway stations and were asked by officials if they were travelling. Those who were not were told to go to the nearest public shelter.

German raiders who bombed the London area early yesterday during widespread raids over Britain failed to do any damage which could affect the capital's war effort.

Bombers six hours over London

Tuesday, August 27, 1940

For six hours last night and early this morning, German bombers circled over London. It was London's longest raid of the war and the second to take place yesterday.

Occasionally bombs were dropped and anti-aircraft guns roared in reply. Buildings are reported damaged in the outskirts.

A well of light encircled the capital for hours as the searchlight crews sought the raiders.

A salvo of bombs was dropped in one area and flash followed flash for some minutes before the raider sped away, only to return at a different point some minutes later.

Thudding of bombs could be clearly heard among the sharper cracks of AA guns, firing quickly.

At a West London theatre, Ivor Novello entertained the audience after the performance of 'I Lived With You' by playing the piano, including his last-war song 'Keep The Home Fires Burning.'

Members of the audience, both professional and amateur, contributed to an impromptu concert.

At the Duke of York Theatre, the manager stopped the show, 'High Temperature', and offered the audience the chance of going to shelter.

Nobody left: the show went on to the end. Then the audience took over the stage, the band struck up popular numbers and audience and cast danced.

Top and above: An overturned car rests at an unusual angle in Kingston, London, while a car showroom is ruined in the same town

Above: Prime Minister Winston Churchill visits Dover and Ramsgate on August 30 to inspect air-raid damage and meet local ARP wardens. There was an almost continuous air-raid warning during his visit and as he was about to enter a shelter, the local Mayor had to tell Churchill: "No smoking down here, sir." The Prime Minister also witnessed an air battle and saw two machines shot down into the sea. Right, an injured German pilot who parachuted to the ground is the focus of much attention

Swansea at dawn after a
three-night 'blitz' attack

Their home may have
suffered bomb damage but
nothing is going to stop this
family's Sunday lunch

Second night in battle of London

Monday, September 9, 1940

The battle for London was on again last night, when Hitler once more launched his bombers at the city. Bombs crashed in the London area.

All day long London had been coolly patching up the damaged spots left after the heavy and prolonged attacks made on Saturday – the first day of the battle.

Immediately after last night's warning – it was London's second of the day – a fierce anti-aircraft bombardment opened up. It started in one outer district, shaking doors and windows, but in a few seconds the central London guns were in action.

It was evident that the German airmen had used the smouldering fires of Saturday's raids to guide them, for the attacks were directed at the same area – London's dockland.

The first hour of the attack was considerably less formidable than Saturday's raid – fewer enemy planes were penetrating the intense defensive barrage from the coast to London. At the end of the hour there was a hushed lull.

Ten minutes passed then all hell broke loose – the whole of London's defensive barrage roared and crashed into action, heralding the return of the raiders.

Dull menacing crunches, whining and quivering reverberations were heard. Livid flashes leapt across the darkened sky as the planes dropped their bombs.

Below: The remains of a tram that is missing its top half. At the bottom of the page, ARP workers and the police search a house wrecked by a German bomb

King goes to his bombed people

Tuesday, September 10, 1940

While ARP workers were still hard at work and firemen were still fighting fires caused by Nazi raiders, the King yesterday undertook a three-hour tour of the bombed areas in east and south-east London.

He talked to people who had been injured in the raids, with others who had lost their homes and with the ARP wardens. He was given a tremendous ovation.

"It is wonderful – really wonderful – to see how brave everyone has been," the King said.

The King's tour was a surprise to the people of London. Mrs Mary Price was busy clearing away debris caused by a bomb that had dropped yards from her house when the King walked by.

Mrs Price said: "If it's not the King – and me so untidy." She waved to him and the King smiled back.

The King shook hands and chatted with policemen, noticing the little Union Jacks among the piles of fallen masonry.

On one street he stood upon the edge of a bomb crater that would have held three or four omnibuses.

On the other side of the crater a line of houses stood backless, showing furniture damaged and scattered, and pictures hung awry upon broken walls.

At the King's feet was a crashed photograph of a wedding party, the bride holding a horseshoe for good luck.

As he walked in the south-east, his Majesty saw many homeless people walking the streets with bundles of their belongings carried over their shoulders.

He met the unknown warriors of our home front – the ARP workers who have been on the job night and day; the ambulance drivers, first aid and demolition squads – the people who yesterday wore grubby uniforms and old overalls, and whose eyes were tired.

Two ARP workers, young Sergeant W J Clark and Corporal A W Williams, were especially congratulated. Going against orders, they entered a house where a delayed action bomb had been dropped and saved the lives of two people.

Miss Kathleen Goff, an ambulance driver, was also praised by the King. At great danger to herself, she rescued some people from a wrecked ambulance shelter.

People gathered in most of the streets to cheer the King.

A woman broke through the crowd in one street to grasp the King's hand and say: "God bless and save you sir, and the Queen and the Princesses."

The King, obviously touched, shook the women's hand and thanked her.

Below: King George VI tours the East End of London following an air raid

A double-decker London bus at 45 degrees after being caught by the blast of a bomb. The driver and passengers had managed to take cover in a shelter when the raid began

Hövis

Not Just 'Brown'

Good Taste Demands

Young boys play as air-raid wardens amongst some rubble, apparently unconcerned by what's happening around them

Above: City workers carry on with their daily routines, close to the Bank of England

Hitler plan to invade is ready

Thursday, September 12, 1940

The Prime Minister told the nation last night that the Germans are thoroughly planning a full-scale invasion which may be launched at any time in England, Scotland or Ireland – or all three.

Hundreds of barges and dozens of merchant ships are massed in French, Dutch, Belgian and Norwegian harbours. Troops are waiting.

An invasion attempt could not be long delayed. "Therefore we must regard the next week or so as a very important week, even in our history," said Mr Churchill. "It ranks with the days of the Armada.

"Every man and woman will therefore prepare himself to do his duty, whatever it may be, with special pride and care."

But he also declared that the German effort to secure daylight mastery of the air over England had so far "failed conspicuously". And our air, naval and military strength was greater than ever.

Said Mr Churchill: "When I said in the Commons the other day that I thought it improbable that the enemy's attacks in September could be more than three times as great as in August, I was not, of course, referring to the barbarous attacks on the civilian population, but to the great air battles which had been fought out between our fighters and the German Air Force.

"You will understand that whenever the weather is favourable, German bombers, protected by fighters, often 300 or 400 at a time, surge over this island, especially Kent, in the hopes of attacking military and other objectives by daylight.

"However, they are met by our fighter squadrons, and nearly always broken up, and their losses average three to one in machines, and six to one in pilots.

"This effort of the Germans to secure daylight mastery of the air over England is, of course, the crux of the whole war. So far it has failed conspicuously. It has cost them very dear and we have felt stronger, and are actually and relatively a good deal stronger, than when the hard fighting began in July.

"There is no doubt that Hitler is upping his fighter force at a very high rate, and that if he goes on for many more weeks, he will wear down and ruin this vital part of his air force. That will give us a very great advantage.

"On the other hand, for him to try to invade this country without having secured mastery in the air would be a very hazardous undertaking.

"Nevertheless, all his preparations for invasion on a great scale are steadily going forward."

My home, too, was bombed

Thursday, September 12, 1940

When the Queen visited the bombed homes of women in the south-east of London yesterday, she went with a realisation of their own feelings.

Because her own home at Buckingham Palace had been bombed the night before, and had been damaged.

As the Queen saw the bombed little houses, and the wreckage of years of toil, she became a woman and mother, and broke down in tears.

"We are proud of you all," the Queen yesterday told an elderly woman, whose daughter and grandson were killed in south-east London.

"And we are proud of you and the King," the woman replied.

The King and Queen were touring bomb-damaged areas.

When an alarm was sounded, they went into a shelter and were offered a cup of tea. Before it was made, the 'all-clear' sounded but they stayed to have their tea.

Continually, the Queen expressed sympathy with women who had lost dear ones. One woman told the Queen: "We are not afraid. We can face it all right."

Another woman said to the King and Queen: "Hitler has to have a bodyguard wherever he goes, but you come down here just like this. God bless and keep you."

As they came from a crater marking the spot where a bomb had fallen in the middle of a block of workers' flats, men and women pressed about them cheering, and began to sing: "They'll always be an England."

They climbed over great heaps of rubbish that had once been twelve small houses. Dust gathered thick upon the Queen's shoes and stockings.

Just before the King and Queen began their tour with Sir John Anderson, Home Secretary, sirens caught them in a street. They went into a shelter beneath a police station.

In the starkly-lit room there was one of the strangest assortments of humans that the sirens have thrown together.

In the centre sat the King and Queen on wooden chairs – the King in the service dress of a Field Marshall and the Queen in a two-tone suit of almond beige.

On the floors around the walls sat policemen in uniform and plain clothes, court officials, ARP workers and white-smocked women from the police canteen.

When the King and Queen walked into the canteen, the 30 people already in there stared in astonishment and clapped.

Then they all stood up but the King told them to sit down. Their Majesties sat down and chatted with the men and women members of the canteen staff.

The King leaned back in his chair, crossed his legs comfortably and lit a cigarette. The Queen sat composedly and smiling with a fox fur across her knees. One of the canteen women bustled about to make some tea, but it was not quite ready when the sirens sounded.

The King, who was the first to hear them, remarked: "That is the all-clear but I am going to wait for some of this tea."

In a few moments the King and Queen were drinking tea from thick china cups with the mark of the police canteen upon them.

Members of the Auxiliary Fire Service at work at St Marks, Surbiton

DAILY MIRROR, Saturday, Sept. 14, 1940.

Daily Mirror

SEPT 14

No. 11,472 ✦ ✦ ✦ ✦ ONE PENNY
Registered at the G.P.O. as a Newspaper.

KING AND QUEEN IN PALACE, BOMBED

DAYLIGHT RAIDER DIVED THROUGH CLOUDS YESTERDAY AND DROPPED FIVE BOMBS ON BUCKINGHAM PALACE, ALREADY SLIGHTLY DAMAGED BY A TIME-BOMB. THE KING AND QUEEN, WHO WERE IN THE PALACE, ARE UNHARMED.

After the "All clear" sounded, quite unshaken by their experience, they left on a tour of other bombed areas.

The Palace chapel, where the Princesses were christened, was damaged. Nearly all the windows on the south side of the inner quadrangle were broken. Bomb fragments pitted the walls. Three of the Palace staff were injured.

Incendiary bombs fell in Downing-street, but did no damage.

News of the Palace bombing was released by the Ministry of Information yesterday towards the end of London's longest day raid warning yet.

After a night of limited air activity in which the Nazis were repelled by a mighty A.A. barrage—a barrage which met enemy planes in the provinces also—London had several day warnings.

The first, just over an hour and half after the all clear following the eight and a half hours' night raid, was short, but soon after a further warning was given which lasted over four hours.

Deliberate Attack

During these day raids enemy planes—dodging in between clouds—were seen from all parts of London.

A.A. fire broke out from time to time and a number of bombs, the majority incendiaries, were dropped.

There are reports of a number of enemy planes being shot down, and at some points observers saw enemy airmen baling out from their crippled craft.

The Air Ministry and Ministry of Home Security issued this communique:

"Following last night's ineffective attacks in which bombs were dropped in London at random through heavy clouds, a small number of enemy aircraft have today deliberately bombed a number of conspicuous buildings in various parts of London irrespective of their nature.

In Downing-st.

"It is feared that the enemy has succeeded in killing and injuring a number of civilians.

"Buckingham Palace was attacked, several bombs falling within the precincts, one of which damaged the palace chapel.

"Their Majesties were in residence but fortunately escaped injuries. Three members of the staff of the Palace were injured.

"Incendiary bombs also fell in Downing-street, but did no damage."

Continued on Back Page

The altar in the private chapel at Buckingham Palace. Generations of British Kings and Queens have worshipped in this chapel; the sons of Kings have been married in it under The Cross. The cross of Nazi-ism has wrecked it in moments.

WATCH FOR FIRES: THEY HELP RAIDERS

THE danger arising from outbreaks of fire in unattended buildings is stressed in an urgent warning issued by the Ministry of Home Security.

It is pointed out that if an outbreak occurs in such a building, the fire may not only involve a serious call on the local fire services through not having been detected at an early stage, but may also serve as a beacon to raiding aircraft.

A single person in the building could at least summon the fire brigade at once, even if he could not extinguish the fire before it got a hold.

The main classes of premises to be considered are factory and warehouse buildings and timber yards. Occupiers of all such premises are strongly urged to arrange that at least one person is always on the premises for the purpose of giving an alarm in case of fire, and also to provide simple fire-fighting equipment for use until the brigade arrives.

R.A.F. "Leaves" Made Him Shiver

The new British "incendiary leaf" was shown to the Berlin correspondents of Spanish newspapers at the Nazi Ministry of Propaganda.

The correspondents were told that the leaf is composed of a paste of celluloid, cotton and phosphorus and the slightest contact is sufficient to turn them into "perilous tongues of fire."

The correspondent of the newspaper "Ya" states that thousands of these leaves have been dropped in Berlin and Hamburg. "I give you my word that these leaves make me shiver," he adds.—Reuter.

AMBULANCES FROM N.U.R.

The National Union of Railwaymen are to provide four ambulances for the British Red Cross Society and a mobile canteen for the Forces.

FIRE BOMBS ON ULSTER

INCENDIARY bombs were dropped on a Northern Ireland coastal town yesterday and houses and shops set on fire, according to an official statement issued in Belfast.

The announcement stated:—

"A single enemy aircraft made an unsuccessful attack on shipping off the coast of Northern Ireland. Subsequently a small number of incendiary bombs were dropped on a coastal town.

"A few fires were caused which were soon brought under control by the local fire brigade and A.F.S. The damage was slight and there were no casualties."

Opposite: The front page of the
Daily Mirror on September 14, the
day after Buckingham Palace was
bombed with King George and Queen
Elizabeth inside. Workmen can be
seen clearing up rubble outside
the Palace in the picture above.
The Queen famously remarked
afterwards: "I'm glad we've been
bombed. It makes me feel I can look
the East End in the face." To the left,
a family eat dinner in the bombed
remains of their cellar

Left: Members of the Home
Guard inspect the wreckage of
a downed Luftwaffe Dornier 17
pencil bomber, which crashed
on to the rooftops of a parade of
shops in a London suburb

Right: Postmen sift through the wreckage of their sorting office, while, below, the aftermath of an evening raid in Hull

A RAF Bristol Beaufighter flies over the burning hulk of a German tanker. The 'Beau' saw extensive action during the Battle of Britain

Plan for sleeping in Tubes

Tuesday, September 17, 1940

The Ministry of Home Security is examining the question of using the London Underground as a raid shelter and a fresh effort is to be made in the House of Commons to persuade Sir John Anderson of the need for building deep shelters.

Mr James Hall, MP for Whitechapel, will raise the matter of deep shelters in the House and a deputation from the ARP co-ordinating committee is seeking to see Sir John.

The practice adopted by some Londoners of buying a ticket and using the tubes as sleeping quarters is being examined by the Ministry of Home Security, the London Passenger Transport Board and the police. An authoritative announcement will be made almost immediately.

It is essential, in the view of the Government, that the use of the tubes for transport purposes should not be interfered with, and the problem now being considered is to find some use of the tube system for sheltering those who have no alternative cover.

The continued use of shelters as dormitories is causing concern to the authorities. There is a tendency for people to go to large underground shelters – in some cases quite distant from their homes – in order to spend the night, while smaller shelters in the immediate vicinity are almost deserted.

Some shelters, therefore, become grossly overcrowded, while others are hardly used. It is the official view that the country cannot afford this wasteful use of shelters.

Sir John Anderson said yesterday: "Our view is that all types of shelter are standing up better than expected to all types of bombing.

"The degree of protection given by surface shelters is quite equal to the protection given to the normal type of strutted basement or covered trench shelter."

A committee is now investigating the public health aspect of the shelter problem.

Right: On September 17, 19 women began work at London Underground stations, taking the place of porters called up for service. It was a feature of the war that women undertook jobs that had previously been a male preserve. Below, families take cover in a disused London Underground railway tunnel

Left: A mother tends to her young son in an underground shelter during an air raid. Her daughter settles into a bed made from a wooden fruit box. Below, the Mirror cartoon from September 20 suggests the sands of time are running out for Adolf Hitler

"Need Some More Sand, Adolf?"

INVASION HOUR GLASS

Candlelight in an air-raid shelter

Queen Elizabeth
hands over a
picture of her two
daughters, Elizabeth
and Margaret, which
she found amongst
debris during a tour
of the East End.
Her husband, King
George, looks on
from behind her

The Queen finds sadness and smiles

Friday, September 20, 1940

The King and Queen visited, again, the bombed areas of London yesterday. They saw little homes blasted out of occupation.

And once, while the King was being told how damage had been caused, the Queen wandered a few steps alone…to a spot where another woman and mother once had a home.

The King and Queen, standing amid a scene of devastation, near wrecked houses which had received a direct hit from a bomb, yesterday talked to men and women who had astonishing escapes from death.

This occurred during a tour of three districts of London which have received bad bomb damage.

Looking round at the destruction, in the middle of which were two unharmed Anderson shelters, the King remarked: "These Anderson shelters are wonderful, wonderful."

He and the Queen listened with interest while survivors who had been in the shelters told their Majesties of their escapes.

Mrs Eales, 66, was in one shelter with a woman friend, aged 74. "Neither of us had a scratch," she told the Queen. "Wasn't it wonderful, your Majesty?"

The Queen agreed and asked Mrs Eales: "But you must have been badly shaken?"

"Oh, yes, but I'm quite all right now," this dauntless Londoner replied.

Mr Walter Warner, who was in the next shelter with four women, told the King and Queen that they had gone into the shelter only a few moments before the bomb dropped.

"We thought for a moment that the shelter was going to be blown away," he said, "but nothing happened and we were all right."

"You are very fortunate indeed," said the King.

"The worst thing was waiting for about six hours before we could get out of the shelter because of the wreckage," said Mr Warner.

At Chelsea three ARP workers, Mr George Pitman, Mr Wally Capon and Mr George Woodward, were presented to the King and Queen.

They told the royal visitors the story of how they had received Miss Castillo, the daughter of a doctor, after she had been buried for four days beneath 10 tons of wreckage.

The three men had to form living struts at the end of their tunnelling operations, eventually taking seven-and-a-half hours to rescue the young woman.

"You have done absolutely grand work," the King said.

Capon told the Queen: "I am 54. This shows that there is still a job for old men to do and not leave everything for the young men."

Left: The King is surrounded by his people when he visits a bomb-damaged street in London. Below, a Mirror editorial hails the spirit of Londoners

Saturday, September 21, 1940

Daily Mirror

Geraldine House, Fetter-lane, E.C.4. Holborn 4321.
62-68, Hardman - street, Deansgate, Manchester 3.
Blackfriars 2185-6-7-8-9.

GREATEST WEEK

THIS has been a week of suffering for many thousands in London. A week of intense anxiety for all those outside London who have friends here.

It has been a week during which the eyes of the world beyond—particularly of America—have been turned towards London; towards that multitudinous "heart" that the Nazi terrorists counted upon breaking with bombs.

But we do not indulge in the usual wartime heroics of bragging confidence and complacency when we say that this has been a week, too, of "our greatest hour." Our greatest week! Perhaps the greatest in the history of London. Never to be forgotten.

And the witness of that greatness lies in the splendid constancy shown by millions whose very hard duty it has been to stand and wait; patiently to bear the long hours of danger in darkness; uncomplainingly to endure; to submit to the inevitable and to the blind strokes of cruel Chance.

Even harder (you may think) to wait and expect than to labour and save! For difficult and dangerous work can at least turn the minds of men and women from all but the task in hand.

Yet what praise or thanks could adequately describe or reward those in the front line who have, in this greatest week, ceaselessly toiled to bind up the wounds and efface the scars of London?

Who will find words of praise for our A.R.P. workers, our firemen, our police, our workers in vital services who have faced death hour after hour, or simply carried on under the shadow of death? Who can praise these workers who have thus laboured for our common salvation?

Some day the learned and eloquent will add this chapter to the long history of London. They will tell the story and write the distant, detached estimate of things endured and done.

Today the world can only salute the heroism of London under fire.　W. M.

They may have lost their homes but they still have a song in their hearts. All around them is a scene of devastation but the piano plays on for these spirited cockneys in Bow

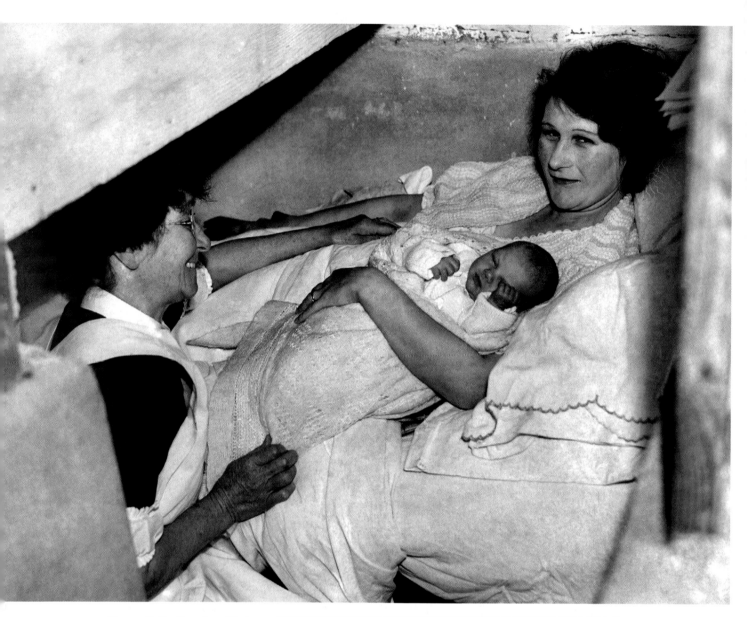

Above: Betty Ceaplen, 29, has just given birth to a baby girl in an air raid shelter in Brighton. Nurse Ryman cares for the pair of them. Mrs Ceaplan's husband had built the shelter under the garden shed in their back yard. So comfortable was Betty, she planned to stay there for a fortnight

Right: Presumably this was a very clever dog

A bomb is removed
from Brixton Hill,
south London

20

L155858

DAILY MIRROR, Thursday, Oct. 17, 1940

Daily Mirror

OCT 17

No. 11,500   ONE PENNY
Registered at the G.P.O. as a Newspaper.

I WON'T LET THEM HURT YOU

The Story of a Great Picture

BY A SPECIAL CORRESPONDENT

MRS. MARY COUCHMAN, twenty-four-year-old warden in a small Kentish village, sat smoking a cigarette in the wardens' post. She was resting between warnings.

★

Suddenly the sirens sounded again.

She saw her little boy, with two friends, playing some distance away.

The cigarette still in her hand, Mrs. Couchman ran out of the post. Bombs began to fall as she ran.

The children, Johnnie Lusher, aged four, Gladys Ashsmith, aged seven, and her four-year-old son Brian, stood i_ the street, frightened by the scream and thud of the bombs.

Gathering them in her arms, she huddled over them, protecting them with her own body.

Bombs were still thudding down only a short distance away.

There she crouched, to save the children from flying shrapnel and debris.

★

A "Daily Mirror" photographer was on the spot when the incident occurred.

He took this picture.

Afterwards, when the planes had passed over, he told Mrs. Couchman, "You are a brave woman."

"Oh, it was nothing. Somebody had to look after the children," was her reply.

★

THE NAVY WIPES OUT A CONVOY, AND BLASTS DUNKIRK

—See Page Three

Opposite page: A stunning Daily Mirror front page from October 17 shows Mary Couchman, 24, protecting children in Kent as bombs fall around them. To the left, life goes on as normal as Belgian pilot Charles Molleman strums the banjo during a party in underground tunnels in Marble Arch. Below, the Women's Voluntary Service serve tea and sandwiches in a shelter

RAF's 100-a-minute bombing

Monday, October 21, 1940

Land and air bombardments of German positions over the Channel rose to a terrific climax last night as the RAF launched a bomb avalanche at the estimated rate of 100-a-minute.

Earlier the Kent coast had rocked while British and German batteries fought a two-hour duel in which the British guns subjected the Nazi-occupied coast to the heaviest shelling of the war.

The RAF struck just as the German batteries attempted to re-open their bombardment.

An unbroken rumble of terrific bomb explosions sounded like thunder. Doors and windows in the Kent coast towns rattled. Inside the houses, ornaments tumbled to the floor.

Even people who thought they were used to the noise of the RAF's Channel attacks ran out to see an almost non-stop succession of vivid bomb flashes lighting the French coastline.

Clusters of parachute flares, dropped by the British planes, burned brightly above a wall of dense grey mist covering the sea.

Streams of anti-aircraft shells poured into the sky. Searchlights played confusedly as they tried to pick out the bombers.

The enemy shelling killed one man, Mr Frank Victor Ashby, a 57-year-old Dover licensee, who was walking along a street when a shell struck an empty hall nearby. Two other men were seriously injured, but no other casualties were reported. One shell dropped into the middle of a bomb crater in the Dover area. The two craters fitted exactly.

A hotel was hit and another shell wrecked a church. ARP squads went to work after the first salvo and stuck to their task while shells were falling around them.

As the British and German land guns were roaring, waves of Nazi raiders were repeatedly trying to penetrate inland over the Kent coast.

Above: Farmers continue to milk cattle despite the damage and debris at Allington, near Chippenham, Wiltshire. To the right, Hawker Hurricanes in formation

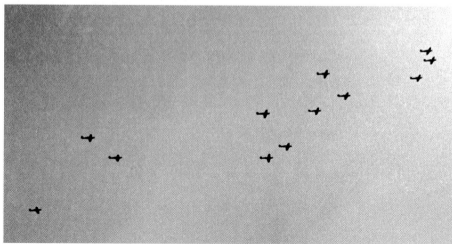

The date of this wedding had been
fixed for October 20. A few bombs
weren't going to stop the ceremony

A shipping convoy in October 1940. While the Battle of Britain was fought in the air, British seamen were also under attack from the Nazis, who attempted to prevent supplies reaching our shores

Big U-boat blitz on our ships

Tuesday, October 22, 1940

Hitler has started an intensified U-boat war in the hope of starving Britain into subjection by blockade, now that his air attack and invasion plans have been rebuffed.

Prowling in the wastes of the Atlantic, U-boats are hunting shipping and attacking on a scale greater than ever before.

Scantily armed cargo boats, carrying food, raw material and munitions, are their prey.

More U-boats have been ordered into the Atlantic than at any time since the outbreak of war.

In remote shipyards in Norway and the Baltic, work has intensified to repair the losses inflicted on the German underwater fleet in the early stages of the war by the Royal Navy and the RAF.

The new vessels have been dispatched direct from their trials with the instructions: "Britain must be blockaded at all costs. Merchant ships must be intercepted and sunk."

But Britain's food chiefs give the lie to Hitler's starvation threat.

"It will be averted," said Lord Woolton, minister of food, last week. "By the grace of God and the vigilance of the Royal Navy, the courage of the Mercantile Marine, the devotion of the dock labourers and transport workers and of food traders, and the patient efforts of the farmers."

Members of the Royal Navy rescued following an attack by German U-boats

Above: Rescuers help a man out of the rubble after an air raid in Brixton

Above: A bomb crater
beside a garden shelter

Above: An RAF pilot with his
girl, backstage at the Windmill
Theatre in Westminster, London

Soldiers from the Auxiliary Military Corps enjoy a bath after labouring on air-raid wreckage, shifting debris and salvaging household goods

Don't think air war is over

Friday, November 1, 1940

After the quietest day London has had since the 'blitz' began, the alert which sounded last evening ended at the earliest hour since September.

But don't assume because of this, and the fact that raids on the London area have been much less severe over the last few days, that the air war is over for the winter.

The all-clear signal sounded so early last night that people in shelters looked at each other almost in disbelief. Some went home, but the wise stayed where they were.

For already too many people are beginning to "chance their luck" in the streets at night and an increasing number are not bothering to take cover during a raid.

Well-informed circles in London believe that the raids have slacked off because more Italians are coming over and getting their bearings before they begin anything like intensive bombing.

But heavy bombing can be expected to start again at any time.

It is known also that many experienced Nazi pilots have been sent east, and that their places are being filled by men who have had little or no experience of flying over London.

Last night the raiders appeared disconcerted by the fierceness of the barrage and fled hastily, after dropping what seemed to be in most cases a single bomb.

Top right: Caroline Roberts, 65, feeds stray cats made homeless by Nazi bombing. Mrs Roberts refused to move to a safe area and looked after hundreds of moggies. She explained: "After a good supper of cat's meat, bread and milk, they curl up in front of my sitting room fire and doze. When the bombs fall particularly close, I go under the stairs and the cats follow me. All the bombs in the world won't shift me." To the right, the RSPCA collect strays while, above, this dog is ready to donate his bone so it can be melted down for glue

Smoky salutes: This cat was rescued after an air raid in 1940. Ann Twynam of Paddington took him home and taught Smoky to salute whenever service personnel visited

WE SHALL NEVER FORGET

THE BATTLE OF BRITAIN WAS ONE OF THE DEFINING CONFLICTS WITHIN
THE SECOND WORLD WAR. THE NATION IS ETERNALLY THANKFUL
TO THE PEOPLE AND THE PLANES RESPONSIBLE FOR
DEFENDING OUR ISLANDS FROM THE NAZIS

PL983

Seventy years on...

The Battle of Britain is firmly established as one of the most significant events in the nation's history.

The first important campaign to be fought entirely by air forces, it was the Nazis' first major defeat of the Second World War and proved to be a turning point in the overall struggle.

If the Luftwaffe had established aerial superiority over Britain, the course of the war would have been very different.

The RAF's Spitfire aeroplanes and the pilots who flew them have become a symbol of a defiant, brave and heroic Britain.

They are commemorated annually on September 15, which is 'Battle of Britain Day' in the United Kingdom. This is the anniversary of one of the fiercest struggles in the conflict when Fighter Command fought off the Luftwaffe's final major push to wipe them out.

Although the RAF won the battle, there was significant upheaval within the organisation immediately afterwards as Fighter Command's leader, Sir Hugh Dowding, was removed from his post in November 1940. He was criticised for not resolving a tactical dispute between 11 Group (led by New Zealander Sir Keith Park) and 12 Group (commanded by Trafford Leigh-Mallory).

Leigh-Mallory, supported by Group Captain Douglas Bader, had devised a massed fighter formation consisting of at least three squadrons known as 'Big Wing', which they used to hunt German bombers. Park preferred to dispatch individual squadrons to intercept raids. After the battle Park was also moved and Leigh-Mallory became leader of 11 Group

(the failure to limit damage on the ground during the Blitz is also said to have been a factor in the sackings). Despite this, Dowding and Park are generally credited as being the architects of the victory.

A total of 2,936 airmen were awarded the Battle of Britain clasp for having flown at least one authorised sortie with an accredited unit of RAF Fighter Command between July 10 and October 31 1940.

It's important to note that not all of them were British (2,341 came from these shores). Poland, which was occupied by the Nazis at the time, provided 145 pilots, New Zealand 127, Canada 112 and Czechoslovakia (also Nazi-controlled) 88.

The others nations represented were: Australia (32), Belgium (28), South Africa (25), France (13), Ireland (10), USA (9), Rhodesia (3), plus Barbados, Jamaica and Newfoundland (1 apiece).

During the battle, 544 lost their lives and a further 795 were to die before the end of the war. The names of all the pilots are listed on the Battle of Britain Monument, which was unveiled in 2005 and is situated close to the Houses of Parliament in central London.

The National Memorial is situated at Capel-le-Ferne, above the white cliffs near Folkestone in Kent (see page 82). It takes the form of a large, three-bladed propeller carved into the ground, topped by the statue of a lone airman sitting on the propeller boss and looking out to sea. The names of the 2,936 airmen are listed on a memorial wall nearby.

We shall never forget the contribution of the men immortalised as "The Few" by Winston Churchill.

Douglas Bader poses in front of a Hawker Hurricane after officially opening the Swansea Air Show in May 1976

A double demonstration by Spitfires. The top plane is a MK 19 at the Battle of Britain Memorial Flight in September 1966. The bottom image shows a MK IIa P7350 at Biggin Hill for the Memorial Flight of 1980. This one was built at the Castle Bromwich factory in Birmingham and served with 266 squadron and 603 (City of Edinburgh) AuxAF squadron. It entered service in August 1940 and is the oldest airworthy Spitfire

Below and right: The premiere of the 'Battle of Britain' film in September 1969. Sir Hugh Dowding, commander in chief of RAF Fighter Command during 1940, chats to Susannah York and Sir Laurence Olivier, who played him in the movie

Robert Stanford Tuck, a fighter pilot who claimed a series of victories during the Battle of Britain, poses alongside a row of Spitfires and Hurricanes used in the film of the same name in April 1968

Above: Susannah York and Kenneth
More sitting on a Spitfire, supported
by technical advisors, at RAF
Duxford, during a break in filming

A Spitfire and a Hurricane going
through their display routine
above Biggin Hill in May 1978

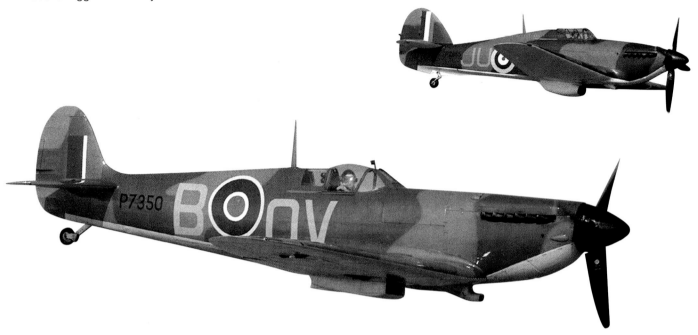

A Bristol Blenheim in 1990.
These light bombers were used
extensively in the early part of
the Second World War, including
during the Battle of Britain

A Spitfire and a Hurricane
at the Memorial Flight at the
Sunderland Air Show in 1996

Above: Henry Allingham, a veteran of the First World War, celebrates his 112th birthday by watching the Battle of
Britain Memorial Flight of 2008, at RAF Cranwell, Lincolnshire. Henry died in 2009, by which time he was 113

A Messerschmitt Bf 109 in
the foreground with a Spitfire
behind it. These planes duelled
throughout the Battle of Britain

The Battle of Britain Memorial looks out over the cliff tops of Capel-le-Ferne, near Folkstone, to a sky that was once filled with RAF aircraft, as they defended these shores from the Luftwaffe